ISIS and the Pornography of Violence

ISIS and the Pornography of Violence

Simon Cottee

ANTHEM PRESS

Anthem Press
An imprint of Wimbledon Publishing Company
www.anthempress.com

This edition first published in UK and USA 2019
by ANTHEM PRESS
75–76 Blackfriars Road, London SE1 8HA, UK
or PO Box 9779, London SW19 7ZG, UK
and
244 Madison Ave #116, New York, NY 10016, USA

British Library Cataloguing-in-Publication Data
A catalogue record for this book is available from the British Library.

ISBN-13: 978-1-78308-965-9 (Hbk)
ISBN-10: 1-78308-965-2 (Hbk)
ISBN-13: 978-1-78308-968-0 (Pbk)
ISBN-10: 1-78308-968-7 (Pbk)

This title is also available as an e-book.

To Keith Hayward

CONTENTS

PREFACE

This book is a collection of essays, polemics and reportage on ISIS, spanning the four year period from its spectacular ascendancy in late 2014 to its no less spectacular demise in early 2018. Although the pieces are unmistakably grounded in my own judgments and opinions, they are informed by a broader scholarly knowledge about deviance, defection, terrorism and violence.

In my day-job I work as a senior lecturer in criminology at the University of Kent. While it's a huge privilege to be paid to teach and do research on a subject that is richly dark, human and endlessly fascinating, one of the downsides is that I have to produce peer-reviewed articles for academic journals that few people read. These articles not only take months or even years to research and write; they also take months or even years to see the light of day, given the rigmarole of the peer-review process. Patience may well be a virtue, but it's not one that I possess. This is why I find ideas-based journalism so appealing: not just because many more people are likely to read it than an academic journal article, but because it's so wonderfully instantaneous. You write your piece and within a few days or weeks it's out there—to be read, praised, tweeted or, more often, trashed, or still more likely, half-read, misunderstood or just ignored.

No doubt some academics, especially those who are instinctively skeptical of any public discourse that is not rooted in hard data, will turn their noses up at the pieces collected in this volume. But that's fine with me. These pieces are aimed at a wider, and not so prickly, audience.

The essays are organized into three thematic sections and vary in length and purpose: some take the form of 1000-word op-eds, whereas others are longer and more ruminative in tone and scope. A few are pieces of reportage. Some were commissioned, but most were not and were written out of an unshakeable urge to correct some misapprehension or myth, as I saw it at the time, or to amplify a point or argument that I needed to make. I don't know where this urge comes from. Obviously it's not very endearing: the desire to correct, the urge to be heard. And obviously I need to get out more. But it seems necessary for the business of banging it out and starting an argument.

All of the pieces were posted online and contained hyper-links to sources—typically news reports and scholarly articles and texts. I have restored these as footnotes. I have also used footnotes here and there to add clarity and context where necessary. I have made only a few revisions, so as to avoid repetitions of certain phrases.

Looking back through the pieces the underlying argumentative threads and purposes are relatively easy to discern and summarize. My aim has been to write about ISIS as, first and foremost, a revolutionary political movement with a theological vision that drives (or at least constrains) much of what it says and does. I have sought to understand the process by which someone (of whatever gender) comes to embrace that vision as an active search for meaning, purpose and existential fulfilment. At the same time I have resisted efforts, deep within our culture, to infantilize those who undergo this process as passive victims who's "vulnerability" makes them susceptible to a type of mind-control performed by sinister outsiders. I have sought to expose some of the limitations of structuralist explanations of terrorism by bringing into focus the low base rate of involvement in terrorist organizations and by emphasizing how crucial social and kinship ties are to this, while also subjecting to the severest criticism any attempts to pathologize terrorism. I have sought to document in ISIS the emergence of a new kind of "liquid jihad" in the West, where involvement, in many cases, reflects more a process of drift than any full ideological conversion, and where commitment is sustained by social networks. I have tried to draw attention to the subterranean aspects of the ISIS phenomenon, arguing that by embracing violence, honor, retribution and machismo ISIS represents not an outright rejection of Western culture but a perverted exaggeration of some of its underlying values. I am aware that this is not a popular line of thought. But I am convinced that it is a necessary condition for understanding the root of ISIS's appeal in the West. And I have repeatedly emphasized just how little we know, and indeed can ever know, about the motives of those who embrace violence and do acts of terrorism.

All the pieces were written in England and America during the end of the Obama administration and the beginning of the Trump presidency. Which is to say they were written in a time of great social upheaval and political division. And much of that division can be seen in our current discourse on terrorism, where putatively objective reflection on its causes all too often degenerates into barely concealed moralizing and political posturing. Some of the essays document this politicization, but it is my hope that, for all their polemical zeal, they do not evince it.

It is probably too early to assess which pieces continue to hold up and which ones don't. One thing that makes me wince is just how impressed I was with the aesthetic quality of ISIS propaganda videos. I wasn't alone in this of course.

Indeed, from mid-2014 onwards, it was hard to find an article on ISIS which *didn't* summon the word "slick" to describe the group's propaganda material. I now think that this was a mistake, and not just for ethical reasons to do with using aesthetic categories to evaluate spectacles of murderous depravity. Some ISIS videos, undeniably, were well put together, such as the soulful *Eid Greetings from the Land of Khilafah* and the not so soulful *Although the Disbelievers Dislike it*. But many were just third-rate and hardly merited the accolades that were showered on them by countless Western commentators. Consider, for example, ISIS's first English language video *There is No Life Without Jihad*, released on June 19, 2014. The former U.S. Ambassador Alberto Fernandez described the video as "a strong, sustained, and emotional appeal to Western Muslims to join ISIS immediately."[1] *Vice* called it "slick".[2] But was it?

Not much really happens in the video. Indeed the action, if it can be called that, focuses on a group of quite odd looking British and Australian men, sitting together with their legs crossed, reading a pre-prepared script from an auto-cue. They are trying to explain, in their thick regional accents, why they left their lives in the West for ISIS's jihad in Syria and Iraq. A man identified as Abu Bara' al-Hindi says: "Are you willing to sacrifice the fat job you have got, the big car you have got, the family you have? Are you willing to sacrifice this for the sake of Allah?"[3] He is wearing what appears to be an Emporio Armani t-shirt, which I don't think is a strong look for a jihadi warrior, especially one at war with Western imperialism. The man sitting to his immediate right has a lazy eye. And Abu Dujana al Hindi (real name Reyaad Khan) sits silently for long periods of time with his mouth ajar. Needless to say, these are not particularly rousing audio-visual tropes. Nor are the production values of the video particularly high. And yet many global media outlets ran a story on the video, praising its "slickness," and giving it worldwide attention.

Another thing that I am no longer so certain about is just how central "sacred values" are to understanding the ISIS phenomenon. I am explicitly referring to Scott Atran's prolific and highly influential work on jihadism, the ruling insight of which is that jihadists, far from being motivated by self-interest or material considerations, are in fact "devoted actors" dedicated to the pursuit of "sacred values," so much so that they are willing to lay down their lives in defense of them. Ever since ISIS started unraveling at the end of 2017, with thousands of its fighters surrendering to Iraqi and Kurdish forces and proclaiming their innocence as lowly cooks and farm-hands,[4] I have started to have doubts about this core insight.

In a 2016 paper, titled "The Devoted Actor," Atran contends that contemporary wars, revolutions and global terrorism are driven by "devoted actors," who fight and risk their lives not because they have to or because it is prudent to do so, but out of a profound moral commitment to a value they hold to be sacred or unassailable. "Our research," he writes, "indicates that when people act as 'devoted actors' they are deontic (i.e., duty-based) agents who mobilize for collective action to protect cherished values in ways that are dissociated from likely risks or rewards."[5] Atran further stipulates that when sacred values become indissociably bound up with or "fused" to a group, such that the group embodies the sacred values in question, people's willingness to make costly sacrifices becomes even greater. "Case studies of suicide terrorism and related forms of violent extremism," he observes, citing his earlier work, "suggest that 'people almost never kill and die [just] for the Cause, but for each other: for their group, whose cause makes their imagined family of genetic strangers—their brotherhood, fatherland, motherland, homeland.'"[6]

This framework, based on painstaking and dangerous fieldwork, clearly has a lot of explanatory promise. It tells us something fundamentally important about jihadists, how they see themselves and why they do what they do. It alerts us to the crucial role of moral sentiments in violent human behavior, and helps us understand why people do seemingly insane or irrational things in defense of the things they love and care deeply about.

Yet, for all its promise, it seems ill-equipped to account for the darker currents of the jihadist subculture, particularly its cultish embrace of death, violent pornography and narcissistic preoccupation with the self. If ISIS fighters felt duty bound to defend Islam (as they understood it) and their fellow brothers-in-arms, why did they go far beyond the call of duty, not only fighting their enemies but subjecting them to pornographic rituals of degradation and bestiality? What sense of sacred devotion prompted that? Perhaps devotion had nothing to do with it; perhaps it was pleasure: the power-high associated with inflicting suffering on other human beings (The historian Joanna Bourke documents many cases in which soldiers enjoyed killing in war.)

And then there is the curious matter of the towering narcissism of many Western jihadists that the sociologist Kevin McDonald, in his new book on radicalization,[7] writes so well about: the swaggering and self-absorbed jihadi selfies of Europeans in Syria and Iraq, posing with their weapons and the odd severed head; the British-born Iftehkar Jaman live-streaming a video about how to wear a turban and how to apply kohl eyeliner; and the final video testament of Florida-born Moner Mohammad Abu Salha, in which he fittingly declared: "My concern is me." Given that these jihadists grew up in an individualistic culture of self-improvement, it's not surprising that the core scared value in the Western jihadist subculture turns out to be the scared value of "me."

More crucially, if ISIS fighters were so doggedly devoted to cause and comrades why did so many try and save their own skins when it came to the crunch, instead of selflessly going out in a blaze of glory as martyrs to the faith? The obvious answer is that they were more self-interested than

Atran would care to admit. No doubt many who surrendered were not ISIS diehards and were never fully down with the creed, but quite a few, like the British ISIS jihadists Alexanda Kotey and El Shafee Elsheikh, were and chose not to fight to the death. And even among the many foreign fighters who did seek and find "martyrdom" it is hard to know what the more urgent imperative was: their self-interest in saving their souls on the Day of Judgment or their altruistic commitment to saving the *ummah*? Perhaps both imperatives were at work, but Atran doesn't give much credence to the former, and this is a problem.

Finally, and as some of the pieces collected in this volume testify, I continue to have mixed feelings about Hannah Arendt's thesis on the banality of evil. On the one hand, I believe, rather conventionally, that ISIS, morally speaking, is monstrous. Yet I also believe, in Arendtian style, that many of those who carried out its monstrous actions were not themselves monsters. Yet I'm not so sure about the banality of their motives. From an Arendtian perspective, these motives are more shabby than demonic, and are to do with pleasing superiors, preserving privilege, wanting to be liked etc. And while many ISIS recruits were likely activated by these concerns, it seems hard to deny that they were also motivated by grander, more despotic kinds of emotions, to do with power and cruelty, particularly the desire to control, humiliate and degrade.

The self-declared caliphate of ISIS has been a moral calamity. But if it had to happen then I am not sorry that it happened in my lifetime. Its rise and fall has been spectacularly absorbing. What I do regret is watching all those ISIS execution- videos, which did at one point poison my sleep—or at least violently interrupt it. And I do worry about the enduring spiritual impact of ISIS atrocity porn and all the horrible iconography that goes with it on the millions of people who have exposed themselves, or been exposed, to it.

It is hard to know if ISIS represents a new shift in the history of terrorism. My sense is that it does, and that what it represents is a new style of violence that is not only mass-mediated but massively transgressive, where the point is not just to intimidate and provoke for strategic purposes, but also to horrify and scandalize for non-strategic punitive ends. ISIS, of course, is not the first terrorist group to engage in monstrous violence, but its willingness, indeed keenness, to break and theatrically trash every civilized prohibition as far as violence is concerned is one of the group's defining features, as is its embracement of the aesthetics of the violent spectacle. The rise of ISIS, arguably, also reflects a deeper change in the motivational structure of terrorism, in the sense that the motives of those from the West who joined it (as far as we can glean) seem ever more diffuse and weaker in what Zygmunt Bauman calls our contemporary "liquid" age. This book explores these possible changes.

I am extremely grateful to all the journalists who commissioned, edited, fact-checked and improved the essays collected here: Uri Friedman, Kathy Gilsinan and Sigal Samuel at *The Atlantic*; Susan Brenneman at *The Los Angeles Times*; Alicia Wittmeyer (formerly at *Foreign Policy*) and Max Strasser at *The New York Times*; David Kenner and Cameron Abedi at *Foreign Policy*; Jamie Clifton at *Vice*; and Josh Greenman at *The New York Daily News*.

For much of 2017, I was a Senior Fellow at Wellesley College and I am greatly indebted to Thomas Cushman for facilitating and funding this precious opportunity. Thanks are also due to the Airey Neave Trust for funding my research on ISIS videos.

I have incurred many other debts over the past few years, and should like to warmly big up the following: Mikro, Alberto Fernandez, Mark Hamm, Bruce Hoffman, Mia Bloom, Paul Kaplan, Stuart Henry, David Wells, John Horgan, Phil Gurski, Tom Wyke, Seamus Hughes, Amarnath Amarasingam, Alex Meleagrou-Hitchens, Mustafa Akyol, Amandla Thomas-Johnson, Candace Rondeaux, Inela Selimovic, Frank Furedi, Jack Cunliffe and Jules Forder.

I owe a special debt of gratitude to my friends and colleagues in Trinidad: Derek Chadee, Kevin Peters, Maia Hibben, Caroline Alcock, Ken Roodal, Finbar, Umar Abdullah, Mark Bassant, Gail Alexander and Simon Alexis. To my *hoss* Azard Ali I am especially thankful.

I also owe a special debt to Aaron Zelin, not only for his consistently solid and absorbing work on global jihadism over the years, but for assiduously documenting the propaganda of the world's biggest jihadist groups on his website Jihadology.net. At the time of writing there are calls, led by the British government, to kill the site, or at least make it difficult to access it. But were it not for Jihadology.net the pieces in this book would have been far more difficult to research and write.

I should particularly like to express my thanks to Andy Anthony for his advice, encouragement and wit—and for setting the gold standard for what intellectually robust journalism can look like.

Finally, I owe a special thanks to Keith Hayward, whose support, humor and guidance has kept me going for many years now. This volume is dedicated to him.

Simon Cottee
Canterbury, December 2018

Chapter 1

ISIS AND THE THEATRE OF HORROR

The Pornography of Jihadism

In his 2008 book *Blood and Rage: A Cultural History of Terrorism*, the historian Michael Burleigh observes in passing that jihadist martyrdom videos have a similar structure to porn movies. He doesn't dwell on the point, although he does allude to the climactic "money shot": in the jihadist case, the moment when the bomber detonates his explosives.[1]

In light of the many ISIS propaganda videos that have circulated this summer [2014], Burleigh's point deserves further analysis and refinement. One of the most striking aspects of the more violent among these videos—especially the beheading videos of journalists James Foley and Steven Sotloff—is their pornographic quality. They are primal and obscene and gratuitous. And, like most modern porn videos, they are instantly accessible at the click of a mouse. Indeed, ISIS videos have attracted such a large audience online that the U.S. State Department recently launched its own YouTube channel to counter their appeal, superimposing words of mocking condemnation over graphic images of ISIS's brutality, entirely missing the point that ISIS appeals to potential recruits in part *because* of its exorbitant violence.

Jihadists proclaim a fierce opposition to Western modernity, condemning it as soulless, corrupt, materialistic and depraved. But this has not prevented them from exploiting modern technological advances in fields from weaponry to communications. Nor, evidently, has it stopped them from watching porn. The stash of X-rated material recovered from Osama bin Laden's compound in Abbottabad after his killing by U.S. commandos in May 2011[2] may have raised eyebrows among some Western journalists, but it was scarcely news in counterterrorism circles. C. Christine Fair, an assistant professor at Georgetown University, wrote on her Facebook page at the time that the U.S. government "has recovered terabytes of the stuff from terrorist computers."[3]

In any case, the conventions of jihadists' hardcore film productions unmistakably resemble those of porn. And just as porn has evolved over time, so too has the jihadist propaganda video.

In a 2001 essay on the American porn industry, the British novelist Martin Amis makes a distinction between two types of mainstream American pornography: features and gonzo. "Features," Amis explains, "are sex films with some sort of claim to the ordinary narrative: characterisation, storyline."[4] Or, as a porn industry executive explained to Amis regarding features: "We don't just show you people fucking ... We show you why they're fucking." Gonzo, by contrast, doesn't: "It shows you people fucking," Amis writes, "without concerning itself with why they're fucking." He concludes: "Gonzo porno is gonzo: way out there. The new element is violence."

Violent jihadist propaganda videos can similarly be classified in terms of features and gonzo, with narrative-rich depictions of typically goal-oriented violence in the former category, and narrative-light displays of ostentatious destruction and killing in the latter.

The origins of jihadist features can be traced to the wave of martyrdom videos that came out of Palestine in the mid-1990s. These productions tended to be long—some running to more than an hour—and obeyed a narrative of revenge in which the weak and righteous ultimately triumph over the powerful and unjust. Invariably, the movie featured a bomber whose family had been killed by the Israelis and who plays the role of avenger and martyr. You knew where he was headed and how it would end, but you also knew why, because the bomber himself would tell you: He would look into the camera and read his scripted testimony.

These videos are commemorative and celebratory, focusing on the life and sacrifice of the martyr, who is lionized for his courage and honor. In *The Road to Martyrs' Square*, Anne Marie Oliver and Paul F. Steinberg's rich ethnography of Palestinian suicide bombing, the authors write, "You will never understand anything about the lure of martyrdom, the centerpiece of intifada cosmology, until you realize that someone who has decided to take that path as his own sees himself not only as an avenging Ninja, but also as something of a movie star, maybe even a sex symbol—a romantic figure at the very least, larger than life."[5] Martyrdom videos, which command huge audiences in Palestine, are instrumental in promoting and sustaining this whole illusion.

Gonzo productions are of a more recent vintage and appear to have their origins in Iraq just after the American-led invasion in 2003. These videos are short—some lasting no more than 12 seconds—and low-budget, making use of a single camera and only the most rudimentary editing skills, mirroring the rank amateurishness that is a hallmark of gonzo porn. They typically depict improvised explosive device (IED) attacks on American or Iraqi government forces, but they don't overly concern themselves with why those attacks are happening. Rather, the emphasis is on the spectacle of destruction itself, often replayed over and over, mirroring a technique utilized for the "money shot" in gonzo porn. Reviewing a random sample of videos produced by 10 insurgent groups in Iraq between 2004 and 2006, Arab Salem of the University of

Arizona's Artificial Intelligence Lab and his co-authors reported in 2008 that a large proportion showed IED or rocket attacks. These videos, they wrote, were "often filmed in real-time"—showing attacks as they happened—"instructive [taking the viewer inside the planning and attack execution process] … and low budget."[6] Nine of the 10 groups they examined produced these kinds of videos.

Like Palestinian martyrdom videos, gonzo "shorts" are in a sense celebratory, but the object of celebration isn't a human life and its passage into paradise; it is a human death or several human deaths. There is an overtly sadistic element to these videos, a glorifying of destruction for its own sake. In some, you can hear the enraptured voice of the faceless cameraman,[7] much like in point-of-view gonzo porn movies before and after the finale. These videos are designed to inspire both jihadist foot-soldiers and potential recruits. Much like porn, they also appear tailored to a mass audience with a limited attention span.

ISIS's visual propaganda crosses, and in some cases combines, the categories of features and gonzo. There are features like the technically sophisticated *Eid Greetings from the Land of Khilafah*, where the emphasis is on brotherly solidarity, faith and Islamic justice. The message in this and similar features centers firmly on the goal rather than the means of jihadist violence, yet all the while the promise of menace—many of the foreign fighters interviewed are brandishing machine guns—is never far from the surface.

In another video [*Clanging of the Swords, Part 4*], which blurs the feature-gonzo boundary, there is some stunning aerial footage of the city of Fallujah and embedded reportage of ISIS's recent road to power in northern Iraq.[8] But there are also some truly jaw-dropping montages of executions filmed with the most basic hand-held cameras. This hour-long video fuses the high production values of jihadist features with the raw and anarchic spirit of gonzo.[9]

And then there are ISIS's out-and-out gonzo productions. These are short, low-budget and decidedly thin on narrative. The Sotloff video released in September [2014] is the latest example of this shocking genre. In both this and the Foley video, the executioner gives a brief explanation for what he is about to do—"I'm back, Obama, and I'm back because of your arrogant foreign policy towards the Islamic State, because of your insistence on continuing your bombings"[10]—but the focus is less on the rationale than on the grisly act itself. It is no accident that the killer in each video beheaded his victim with a short blade and deployed the sawing motion favored by Abu Musab al-Zarqawi, the Jordanian leader of al-Qaeda in Iraq who was killed in a U.S. airstrike in 2006: demonstrations of raw fanaticism, power and unrestrained brutality. It is a paradigmatic example of what Mark Juergensmeyer has described, in his book *Terror in the Mind of God: The Global Rise of Religious*

Violence, as "performance violence": a public, theatrical, "symbolic statement aimed at providing a sense of empowerment," and not at achieving any strategic goal.[11]

In recent months, there has also been a proliferation of amateur violent propaganda from ISIS and its supporters, ranging from photographs of bodily mutilation to grainy videos of executions filmed on cell phones. This visual and sickeningly macabre material is made and distributed by ISIS fighters themselves and represents a purer kind of gonzo. A few weeks ago, for example, Abdel Majed Abdel Bary, a 23-year-old from Britain, uploaded to Twitter a picture of himself holding up a severed head. The caption read: "Chillin' with my homie or what's left of him."[12] Other jihadists have similarly made use of social media to publicize their atrocities.

Zarqawi was a pioneer of this particular brand of gonzo. His network, originally known as Tawhid and Jihad, publicly released more than 10 beheading videos between September 20 and October 7, 2004, in addition to the video, circulated in May of that same year, believed to show Zarqawi himself beheading the American businessman Nicholas Berg.[13] Given ISIS's promise to behead more Western civilians, these kinds of videos may yet become the group's signature production.

Like gonzo porn, ISIS's beheading videos are way out there. But the new element isn't violence. The new element is degradation. Walter Laqueur, the esteemed historian and luminary of terrorism studies, writes of the "barbarization of terrorism," where the enemy "not only has to be destroyed, he (or she) also has to suffer torment."[14] ISIS represents the apotheosis of this development, completing the degradation of the enemy by filming the whole process. But the group's propaganda also signifies a new phase in how terrorist acts are communicated and disseminated to the wider world. Forty years ago, the international terrorism expert Brian M. Jenkins remarked that "terrorism is theatre."[15] What Jenkins could not have envisaged at the time was the speed and ease with which images of terror can now be produced and distributed. Nor could he have imagined just how prevalent and grotesquely pornographic terrorist theater has become, and how radically gonzo the groups are who stage it.

The Atlantic, September 12, 2014

Islamic State's Willing Executioners

We knew it was coming, because the masked killer in the David Haines beheading video, released three weeks ago by Islamic State, warned us that it would be.[16] But it is still profoundly shocking. We know the purported rationale. "We take this opportunity to warn those governments that enter this evil alliance of America against the Islamic State to back off and leave our people alone," declared the killer in the Steven Sotloff video.[17] But a rationale doesn't kill. A human being does, often in concert with other human beings.

The conventional wisdom in liberal-dovish circles is that violence is "socially determined," a product of deeper historical, economic or cultural forces over and above the individual.

A second conventional liberal wisdom is that human beings are fundamentally violence-averse and are by nature naturally predisposed to cooperation rather than conflict. When or if violence occurs, it is the corrupting nature of society to which we must look for blame, not our human nature.

The emergence of ISIS and its intensifying barbarism over recent months—the televised beheadings, the mass executions and the brutalization of children—invites us to reconsider these twin liberal pieties and to confront some unpalatable truths: namely, that not only are we hard-wired for killing, but are intoxicated by the killing spectacle and the God-like power it radiates.

The idea that violence is shaped by the broader social context in which it occurs is by no means false and can tell us much about rates of violence in any given place and time. Yet it is ill-equipped to explain the specific tenor and nature of ISIS's murderous violence. Certainly, there is an instrumental logic to it: awesome violence has worked for ISIS, terrifying Iraqi government forces into abandoning their posts in the north of the country and propelling it to the front pages of international newspapers and prime-time television. But there is also a richly expressive quality to ISIS's violence which resists reduction to a means-ends logic. ISIS has killed not just with savagery, but with a demonic creativity, energy and exuberance. This is vividly in evidence in its execution videos and the recent photos uploaded to twitter of ISIS fighters posing with severed heads.[18]

In *Ordinary Men*, a classic study of Reserve Police Battalion 101's role in the open-air slaughter of countless helpless Jewish civilians, of both sexes and all ages, in occupied Poland between 1941 and 1942, Christopher Browning found that 80–90 percent of the Battalion's 500 conscripts—men from all walks of life and many middle-aged—participated in the killing.[19] According to Browning, the men were anti-Semitic, but they were not fanatics. Far more important than ideology, he contends, was conformity to the group or peer pressure and the desire for praise, prestige and career advancement. Equally important, too, was the fear of social ridicule, of being seen to be weak or cowardly for not killing.

In *Hitler's Willing Executioners,* Daniel Goldhagen rebukes Browning's study for failing to explain the initiative, zeal and cruelty of those who participated in the killings.[20] It is a strong critique.

Primo Levi writes of "useless violence," violence "with the sole purpose of creating pain" and "always disproportionate to the purpose itself."[21] Levi recognizes what today's liberal doves don't want to see: that killing can be a drug which doesn't just inflict death and terror, but intoxicates the people who do it. As Professor Joanna Bourke has argued, killing can be a divine delight.[22] ISIS alerts us once again to this demonic secret.

The social psychologist Albert Bandura, a professor emeritus at Stanford University, argues that "it requires conducive social conditions rather than monstrous people to produce heinous deeds. Given appropriate social conditions, decent, ordinary people can be led to do extraordinarily cruel things."[23] Really? Everything we know about the Western recruits to ISIS suggests otherwise: they were not coerced or indoctrinated into joining, but actively signed up on their own initiative. As Shiraz Maher, a Senior Research Fellow at the International Center for the Study of Radicalization, has pointed out, many are "self-starters" or "self-radicalizers."[24] They are there because the want to be there.

Abdel Majed Abdel Bary, a 23-year-old from London, whom British Intelligence officials believe[25] may be the masked killer in the beheading videos of James Foley, Steven Sotloff, David Haines and, most recently, Alan Henning[26] was not "led" into Syria and ISIS. And he was not "led" to saw off the heads of three innocent civilians, as is now suspected. None of this was forced on him. He willed it. And he must have worked very hard for it, catapulting himself to the elite status of ISIS's beheader-in-chief.

There is no reason to doubt the sincerity of Abdel Bary's conviction that doing jihad and killing infidels is right. But there is also no doubting just how empowering all this must be for a former non-entity from Britain. He was once a minor aspiring rapper. Now he is a holy warrior who has made it to the big time.

"I'm back, Obama," the masked killer said in the Sotloff beheading video. Just how much must he have loved uttering those words.

"Nothing happened to me, Officer Starling. *I* happened. You can't reduce me to a set of influences," proclaims Hannibal Lecter in Thomas Harris's *The Silence of the Lambs*:[27] a sentiment Abdel Bary would no doubt share—and would probably love to say, too.

And we can be certain that there are many more like Abdel Bary, waiting in the wings, desperate to prove their worth and become the new rocks stars of global jihad.

We need to stop talking about indoctrination and start talking about intoxication and how spectacular violence, and the power and prestige and notoriety it confers on those who can master it, is its own cause.

"We leave a stain, we leave a trail, we leave our imprint," says one of the protagonists of Philip Roth's novel *The Human Stain*, adding that this is "inherent ... defining."[28] Among the innumerable casualties of ISIS's violence is the wishful idea that this isn't so and that the fury comes from outside.

The Jerusalem Post, October 6, 2014

ISIS and the Intimate Kill

It isn't all shock and gore. Sometimes, it's mock and bore. Consider the video that ISIS released a few weeks ago [October 27, 2014] of the British hostage John Cantlie "reporting" from the besieged town of Kobani on the Syrian-Turkish border.[29] The video's theme is the unreliability of Western media coverage of the conflict in Syria and Iraq, expressed in a tone of mocking contempt. The larger theme is the invincibility of ISIS and the duplicity and weakness of the West. The video opens with some striking aerial footage of war-ravaged Kobani, filmed from a drone. But it's a big yawn thereafter.

On Sunday [November 16, 2014], however, ISIS released what is arguably its most horrifying beheading video [*Although the Disbelievers Dislike it*] to date,[30] reverting to the shock-and-gore doctrine that has come to define it. The viewer doesn't see the actual beheading of American aid worker Peter Kassig, but is shown his severed head, lying at the feet of the suspected British terrorist known as "Jihadi John." The scene is preceded by the mass beheadings of 22 men whom ISIS claims are members of Syrian President Bashar al-Assad's armed forces. The victims are paraded about by knife-wielding jihadists and the camera lingers on the hostages' faces as they kneel, stricken with terror. The pounding of heartbeats commences, just one of the video's many special effects. Then the cutting starts, all at once. Unlike in ISIS's previous beheading videos, there is no merciful cutaway. The viewer sees everything.

It is worth pausing to consider the logic behind this staged mass beheading and how it differs from the notorious doctrine that defined the opening stages of the 2003 war in Iraq: "shock and awe."[31] Comparing the two tells us something important about ISIS and its reverence of the intimate kill—and ours, too.

Face-to-face killing isn't the same as killing at a distance. It is sensually different. And it is harder.

When the navigator of the Enola Gay, the first plane to drop an atomic bomb, returned from that historic mission, he recalled that he "had a bite and a few beers and hit the sack."[32] The death and destruction that his mission visited on the Japanese city of Hiroshima was staggering, resulting in around 135,000 casualties.[33] Yet Theodore Van Kirk claimed to have lost not a single night's sleep over his actions.[34] Whereas when William Manchester, a U.S. Marine and veteran of World War II, killed a Japanese soldier at close range, he vomited over himself and was convulsed by feelings of remorse and shame.[35]

Many scholars agree that violence is difficult, and that killing is especially so. In *Violence: A Micro-Sociological Theory* Randall Collins, a sociology professor at the University of Pennsylvania, writes that "everyone thinks violence is easy to perform, whether one brags about it, fears it, or hopes to eliminate it."[36] But the reality, Collins argues, is very different: "It is hard ... and most people are not good at it, including those who are doing the bragging and swaggering."[37] This is because violence goes against people's "physiological hard-wiring." Killing at close range, he says, is especially challenging: "There appears to be a special difficulty in confronting another person face to face and sticking him with a knife-edged blade."[38]

The idea that violence is difficult was first developed by S. L. A. Marshall, a U.S. Army historian during World War II. Marshall found, through research that remains controversial,[39] that typically only 15 percent of frontline troops fired their guns in combat, reaching 25 percent in the most effective units. Collins, who draws on Marshall, argues that the main barrier to killing is what he calls "confrontational tension," and that what soldiers most fear in combat situations is not the prospect of dying but of killing. "It is easier to put up with injury and death than it is to inflict it," he writes.[40]

Lt. Col. Dave Grossman, author of *On Killing: The Psychological Cost of Learning to Kill in War and Society*, agrees: "There is within most men an intense resistance to killing their fellow man."[41] According to Grossman, distance is the crucial variable in killing: the nearer the "kill target," the harder it is to do, whereas "from a distance, I can deny your humanity; and from a distance, I cannot hear your screams."[42]

Or as the eminent Polish sociologist Zygmunt Bauman puts it in his classic study *Modernity and the Holocaust*, "It is difficult to harm a person we touch. It is somewhat easier to afflict pain upon a person we only see at a distance. It is still easier in the case of a person we only hear. It is quite easy to be cruel towards a person we neither see nor hear."[43]

In recent months, ISIS fighters have seemingly turned this scholarly consensus on its head. They have made killing look easy. And they have mastered the art of the intimate kill. The staged beheadings of James Foley, Steven Sotloff, David Haines, Alan Henning, and, now, Peter Kassig are shocking examples of this. But they are only the tip of a colossal iceberg of depravity and sadism.

From the outside, the group's actions look insane. But they aren't. There appears to be a point to the brutality. It is meant to be polarizing. It is meant to force people to take sides. It is meant to provoke a wider war—a war that ISIS is convinced it will win.[44]

"We must make this battle very violent," wrote the Islamist strategist Abu Bakr Naji in his 2004 book *The Management of Savagery*. Naji—whose thinking paralleled that of Abu Musab al-Zarqawi, the deceased leader of al-Qaeda in Iraq, which has since morphed into ISIS—argued that merciless violence was necessary for the creation of a "pure" Sunni caliphate. Softness, he warned, spelled failure, citing the example of the Companions of the Prophet, who "burned [people] with fire, even though it is odious, because they knew the effect of rough violence in times of need."[45]

The conventional wisdom holds that ISIS's savagery will be its undoing—that it will alienate ordinary Muslims, and that without their support the group cannot succeed. But what this view overlooks is that ISIS's jihad, as its progenitor Zarqawi well understood, isn't about winning hearts and minds. It is about *breaking* hearts and minds. ISIS doesn't want to convince its detractors and enemies. It wants to command them, if not destroy them altogether. And its strategy for achieving this goal seems to be based on destroying their will through intimate killing. This, in part, is what the group's staged beheadings are about: they subliminally communicate ISIS's proficiency in the art of the intimate kill. And this terrifies many people, because they sense just how hard it is to do.

The beheadings also serve as a dramatic counterpoint to al-Qaeda's use of remote IEDs in attacks, and to Western shock-and-awe-style military campaigns. The subtext of the videos appears to be: *You—America and your allies—kill with drones and missiles. We—the true Muslims—kill with our bare hands. You hide behind your military hardware and lack the courage to fight. We stand here tall, holding aloft our swords and the Quran. We will conquer you because our will is greater than yours, because there is nothing we will not do in defense of our just and holy cause.*

One could argue that there is precedent in Islamic theology and history for this kind of ruthlessness.[46] But one must also acknowledge that there is precedent for it also in the "civilized" West. Consider the logic behind the Allied shock-and-awe "area bombings" of German cities during World War II, where thousands of innocent civilians were murdered for the purpose of ending the war and stopping the advance of fascism in Europe.[47] Or the logic behind the bombing of Hiroshima and Nagasaki. "The policy of attacking the civilian population in order to induce an enemy to surrender or to damage his morale," wrote the American philosopher Thomas Nagel, "seems to have been widely accepted in the civilized world."[48]

ISIS has transmuted the shock of intimate killing into a mythical aura. A Kurdish man fleeing ISIS and the Syrian town of Kobani, for instance, recently told a British newspaper, "IS are animals. They're not human. They have a bloodlust the like of which I've never seen—it's as if they enjoy killing. They revel in cutting heads off—it's like their trademark."[49]

ISIS is terrible and terrifying. Despite its recent setbacks on the battlefield,[50] this is now the dominant media narrative about the group both within and outside the Muslim world. It's exactly the narrative ISIS wants to promote.

The Atlantic, November 17, 2014

ISIS and the War on Children

So this is the new face of jihadist terror: an angelic-looking boy, with a tiny frame and delicate features, no more than 10 years old. In the video [released on January 13, 2015[51]], in some ways arguably ISIS's most shocking yet, we see him, shadowed by a bearded jihadist, walk toward two men—and shoot them in the back of the head. The men, who identify themselves in the video as Jambulat Mamayev and Sergey Ashimov and whom ISIS accuses of spying for Russia's Federal Security Service (FSB), are at least three times the age of their assassin. The video, which is entitled "Uncovering an enemy within" and has yet to be independently verified, ends with the young executioner raising his hand up in triumph before trampling over the corpses and walking away.

It is the same boy who featured in an earlier ISIS video showing the training of child soldiers in Kazakhstan. In that video, he introduces himself, in Kazakh, as "Abdullah" and says, "I will be the one who slaughters you, O kuffar [non-believer]. I will be a mujahid, inshallah."[52]

Barely a week goes by now without some terrible jihadist-sponsored slaughter. Last month [December 2014], it was the massacre of 148 people, including 132 children, at the Army School in Peshawar. The killers, sent by the Tehreek-e-Taliban Pakistan (TTP), systematically gunned down the children before "martyring" their own squalid lives.[53] Jihadists have murdered children before, but rarely on this scale.[54] The attacks provoked an outpouring of grief and anger in Pakistan, as well as strident international condemnation.

This month [January 2015], just over half way through, has brought more terrible news: the killings in France last week at the offices of *Charlie Hebdo* and in a kosher supermarket and, at the same time, Boko Haram's deadliest attack to date, in which more than 2,000 Nigerians are reported to have been killed.[55]

It has also brought horrifying news of what may yet become an emergent trend in jihadist circles: the weaponization of children. In addition to the release of ISIS's video with the Kazakh boy, on January 10, a girl believed to be around 10 approached the entrance to a crowded market in Maiduguri, a city in Nigeria's Borno State, and detonated the explosives attached to her body, killing herself and at least 19 others.[56]

We have known for some time that ISIS, in addition to kidnapping and sexually abusing women and girls from Iraqi minorities, has been brutalizing young children in its bases in Syria and Iraq. According to a United Nations report published in November, children in Raqqa, ISIS's stronghold in Syria, have been forced to watch screenings of execution videos and to participate in public stonings.[57] It is also widely known that ISIS has created a large and sophisticated apparatus for recruiting and indoctrinating children, deploying boys as young as 14 to fight in battles and to carry out suicide missions.[58] However, it is deeply shocking to see the harvest of this brutalization so soon and in High Definition.

The brutalization of children in war is not new, of course. The Taliban, for example, was well-versed in the fundamentals of it, forcing children to watch public beheadings, just as ISIS has done. Nor is the jihadification of children exactly novel. In Palestinian society, for example, it is perfectly common to see children in propaganda material brandishing weapons that literally dwarf them.

But the Taliban, however depraved, didn't use children as executioners, much less film them carrying out executions. Although Palestinian insurgent groups have recruited teenagers as young as 16 for suicide missions, they have never sought to enlist children as young as 10. And in stark counterpoint to ISIS, Palestinian insurgents have been very keen to deny any such accusations.

The deployment of pre-pubescent children in suicide missions is an innovation. And so is the casting of a young child as executioner in a jihadist snuff movie. It is yet another taboo broken, yet another boundary crossed.

Classical Islam is clear and emphatic on the point: Killing innocents is an absolute moral wrong. The Quran (5:32) holds, "We decreed to the Children of Israel that if anyone kills a person—unless in retribution for murder or spreading corruption in the land—it is as if he kills all mankind, while if any saves a life it is as if he saves the lives of all mankind." According to one accredited hadith, the Prophet Mohammed is reported to have said, "Set out for jihad in the name of Allah and for the sake of Allah. Do not lay hands on the old verging on death, on women, children and babes. Do not steal anything from the booty and collect together all that falls to your lot in the battlefield and do good, for Allah loves the virtuous and the pious."

Over the past decade and a half, jihadists have effectively rendered the prohibition against killing innocents all but meaningless, widening the scope of "combatant" to include anyone who offers the remotest support to their enemies. Al-Qaeda, for example, included within the category "combatant" not only all military personnel and their staff but also all voting-age Americans. Even so, it never defined children as a legitimate target for attack.

Al-Qaeda pushed the boundaries by taking its jihad to the global stage and justifying the murder of civilians in distant "infidel regimes." The new generation of jihadists has pushed the envelope even further, not only by justifying the murder of children, but also by turning them into murderers. Their jihad is a punk jihad, where anything goes and where the only real currency is spectacular and graphic violence.

The killings last month in Peshawar represent a dramatic ratcheting up of jihadist permissiveness, sending the terrifying message that children are now legitimate targets for attack. This month's carnage in Nigeria and the release of the ISIS video featuring a child as chief executioner introduces yet another layer to the miasma of jihadist permissiveness that is menacing both Muslim and non-Muslim societies.

Children are now on the front line as never before, both as victims and as perpetrators of jihadist horror. It is hard—and disquieting—to imagine what the next horrifying innovation will be. But you can bet ISIS and their co-thinkers are working on it right now.

National Post, January 20, 2015

ISIS and the Logic of Shock

On Tuesday [February 3, 2015], ISIS released another snuff movie: the ritualized burning to death of a captured Jordanian pilot.[59] It is arguably the most shocking ISIS video to date. But then *every* major video ISIS puts out is *arguably the most shocking ISIS video to date*. The film of the mass beheading of some 22 Syrians last year, which ended with the display of the severed head of an American aid worker, was, at the time it was released, arguably the most shocking ISIS video to date. And so was the video, released last month, featuring a child as chief executioner in the slaughter of two men confessing at gunpoint to be Russian spies.

This is the demonic nature of the Islamic State's terrorism: Each act of atrocity must eclipse the previous one. The group's brand of terrorism is like a drug: You need to keep ramping up the dose to sustain the pleasure high. For ISIS and organizations like it, that high is global publicity.

In a classic paper on terrorism and religion published in 1984, David C. Rapoport wrote that terrorism is "a crime for the sake of publicity. When a bomb explodes, people take notice; the event attracts more attention than a thousand speeches or pictures."[60] In an *Atlantic* article two years later, Conor Cruise O'Brien similarly remarked that:

> The combating of terrorism is not helped by bombastic speeches at high levels, stressing what a monstrous evil terrorism is and that its elimination is to be given the highest priority. I'm afraid that the most likely terrorist reaction to such a speech, whether it comes from a President, a Secretary of State, or other important official, is: "You see, they *have* to pay attention to us now. We are hurting them. Let's give them more of the same." And it all helps with recruitment. A movement that is denounced by a President is in the big time. And some kind of big time is what is most wanted by the aggressive and frustrated, who constitute the pool on which terrorist movements can draw.[61]

ISIS has been repeatedly denounced by President Obama, as well as roundly condemned by many other world leaders, including, most recently, King Abdullah of Jordan, who castigated it as a "deviant criminal group" and vowed to take revenge for the murder of the pilot Muath al-Kaseasbeh.[62] ISIS has thus made it to the big time, and continues to draw large numbers of recruits from a wide spectrum of countries.

Rapoport's point that terrorism is "a crime for the sake of publicity" remains as true today as it was two decades ago. But it is not guaranteed that "[w]hen a bomb explodes"—or a shooting occurs—people take notice." For one thing, it depends on the identity of the victims. The *Charlie Hebdo* attacks in France last month, claimed by al-Qaeda in the Arabian Peninsula, captured headlines all over the world. In marked contrast, Boko Haram's reported slaughter of hundreds of civilians in Nigeria days before didn't generate nearly the same level of global media attention.[63] This dynamic helps explain why ISIS has invested so much effort in staging carefully choreographed and slickly produced execution videos of Western hostages—and those, like Muath al-Kaseasbeh, participating in the U.S.-led coalition against the Islamic State—and why, conversely, it has expended so little effort in creating its many grainy and chaotic video montages showing the execution of Iraqi Shiites.

The film of Kaseasbeh's execution has global shock value, but one also senses that it was an intimately personal project for ISIS. In recent months, coalition forces have been bombing the Islamic State in its strongholds. This is starting to hurt. And for much of the video, the dominant narrative is of humanitarian suffering caused by coalition bombing raids, graphically symbolized in footage of charred babies and children. The message, to the world as well as the people in the Islamic State's dominion, seems to be: *We will take revenge for the hellish inferno unleashed on us by unleashing it on our tormentors in turn.*

Frantz Fanon theorized in *The Wretched of the Earth* that violent action can be viewed as a form of catharsis for the perpetrator, particularly when the perpetrator feels he has suffered grave abuses or been condemned to live under tyrannical oppression. "At the level of individuals, violence is a cleansing force," he wrote. "It frees the native from his inferiority complex and from his despair and inaction, it makes him fearless and restores his self-respect."[64] This offers insight into ISIS's reported decision to publicly screen its latest video in Raqqa,[65] an Islamic State stronghold in Syria and a target of coalition aerial firepower—where one presumes catharsis is urgently needed.

Another qualification to Rapoport's point is in order: When a bomb explodes, people are apt to take notice, *but not for long.* Since Rapoport published his article, the rise of the Internet has meant that there is simply too much information out there vying for attention. The web has undoubtedly been a boon to terrorist groups, helping them disseminate their messages to an ever-wider audience. But it has also hindered them in that they must now compete with the world's cacophony of other voices. And this, unfortunately, has served to reinforce the demonic logic of ISIS's brand of terrorism, which requires not only surpassing previous atrocities, but trumping other global news events.

O'Brien remarked in his *Atlantic* article that "one surefire way of attracting instantaneous worldwide attention through television is to slaughter a considerable number of human beings, in a spectacular fashion, in the name of a cause." This, too, needs updating: Today, to borrow from O'Brien, one surefire way of attracting instantaneous worldwide attention through the global media is to slaughter a considerable number of *children* in the name of a cause. The Pakistani Taliban, which deliberately targeted an Army School in Peshawar last December [2014], has apparently embraced this new axiom. Another alternative is to deploy kids as terrorist assassins—to use them as suicide bombers or executioners in propaganda movies, as ISIS has done. Another boundary crossed, another headline guaranteed.

This, as the last point suggests, isn't just a quantity issue in terms of people killed. It is also a quality issue relating to the *how* of killing. It is killing with sadistic and extravagant creativity, in High Definition. This is perhaps the main thrust of the inexorable logic of today's terrorist organizations. And no group appears to understand this better than ISIS's leaders, who first shocked the world by staging the beheadings of Western hostages, using not swords, as is customary in the Islamic tradition, but six-inch knives—so as to prolong the agony of their victims; who kept the momentum going by evolving to the horror show of staged mass beheadings; who pushed the envelope yet further by creating a video in which a child is used as executioner. And now the group has produced the theatrical spectacle of burning alive a Jordanian pilot. The film is arguably the most shocking ISIS video to date—until the next one.

The Atlantic, February 6, 2015

Why It's So Hard to Stop ISIS Propaganda

"We are in a battle, and more than half of this battle is taking place in the battlefield of the media," Ayman al-Zawahiri, then al-Qaeda's second-in-command, purportedly wrote in a 2005 letter to Abu Musab al-Zarqawi, the Jordanian who led al-Qaeda in Iraq at the time.[66] The previous year, Zarqawi's network, originally known as Tawhid and Jihad, had publicly released more than 10 beheading videos, including a video believed to show Zarqawi himself beheading the American businessman Nicholas Berg. This was bad publicity Zawahiri cautioned his hot-headed field commander, and risked alienating Muslims.

Zarqawi was killed in a U.S. airstrike in 2006, but the hyper-violent form of sectarian jihad he pioneered emphatically lives on in the form of ISIS, the direct descendent of al-Qaeda in Iraq. While the group hasn't exactly followed Zawahiri's counsel about winning hearts and minds, it has proven fantastically adept at exploiting new social media to disseminate its message. Indeed, it is no exaggeration—although it may now be clichéd—to say that as well as being one of the most savage terrorist groups in the world today, ISIS also has the slickest propaganda. Its media arm al-Ḥayat has produced hundreds of films, ranging from three-minute beheading videos to hour-long features improbably combining elements of travelogue, historical documentary and atrocity porn. Many are high-quality productions involving Hollywood-style techniques and special effects. One video, titled *Clanging of the Swords, Part 4*, drew particular praise from the late *New York Times* media critic David Carr, who wrote, "Anybody who doubts the technical ability of ISIS might want to watch a documentary of Fallujah that includes some remarkable drone camera work."[67]

"Media is more than half the battle" also happens to be the motto of the U.S. State Department's Center for Strategic Counterterrorism Communications (CSCC), founded in 2010 as the world's first government-sponsored enterprise not run by an intelligence agency to counter online jihadist propaganda.[68] The phrase is emblazoned across the opening PowerPoint slide in all CSCC presentations, according to the CSCC's coordinator Alberto Fernandez. Alongside this quote is a second one, taken from the purported memoir of the American jihadist Omar Hammami, who until his death in 2013 was a leader in the Somali Islamist militant group al-Shabab: "The war of narratives has become even more important than the war of navies, napalm, and knives." Then-Secretary of State Hillary Clinton sounded a similar theme in describing the office's mission a year after it was founded; it was vital, she said, to diminish the appeal of terrorism, and the CSCC was focused on "undermining terrorist propaganda and dissuading potential recruits."

"It's not about Louis Armstrong and isn't jazz great and America loves Muslims," Fernandez told me over a coffee recently, describing what he saw as the general tenor of previous public-relations efforts at the State Department after 9/11. "It's not about quoting the secretary of state, because that's boring, that's lame. Our focus is not on the positive message. What we do is counter-messaging. We're the guys in the political campaign that [do] negative advertising. We're in people's faces."

Despite joining the fray relatively late, the CSCC is now at the forefront of what Hammami and Fernandez have both called "the war of narratives," and has produced well over 50,000 online "engagements" in four languages—Arabic, Urdu, Somali and English. An engagement in the State Department's terminology can be anything from one of the hundreds of "mash-up" videos the team assembles out of pre-existing footage—in many cases from ISIS's own videos—to tweets or graphics highlighting the depredations and hypocrisies of the jihadists.

In addition to this, the CSCC's so-called digital outreach team (DOT) crashes various online forums to troll ISIS sympathizers and regularly jumps onto pro-ISIS Twitter hashtags. For example, in April last year, an ISIS supporter created an Arabic hashtag translating to "#accomplishmentsofISIS." Almost immediately the Arabic DOT used the same hashtag to post a series of sarcastic references to ISIS's "accomplishments" at, variously, "starving people of #Aleppo," "destroying mosques in #Raqqah," "crucifixion of young men," and "squatting, looting and damaging homes." All of these messages linked to incriminating YouTube videos detailing ISIS atrocities in Syria. The CSCC has even entered into dialogue, if it can be called that, with actual jihadists, including Hammami, with whom Fernandez said it "exchanged barbs" in Arabic over Twitter. "He was clearly troubled," Fernandez recalled. "I felt sorry for him. He was killed by al-Shabab, not the Americans. We actually referred to his death in one of our videos—'see what happens if you join these guys.'"

But unlike their counterparts at the hard military end of the battle against ISIS, the American foot soldiers in the war of narratives are at a considerable disadvantage relative to their jihadist adversary.

ISIS has beheading videos. The CSCC doesn't. Beheading videos are shocking and repugnant. But they are also weirdly fascinating—and they go viral for this reason. The CSCC's videos, by and large, are not shocking or repugnant, still less fascinating—and don't go viral for this reason. ISIS's métier is shock and gore, whereas the CSCC's, to put it unkindly, is more mock and bore, more Fred Flintstone than Freddy Krueger. Shock and gore, needless to say, is where the action is—and hence where the Internet traffic tends to go. "You're never going to be able to match the power of their outrageousness," Fernandez said, conceding this disadvantage.

ISIS has a vast network of "fanboys," as its virtual supporters are widely and derisively known, who disseminate the group's online propaganda.[69] (ISIS ennobles them with the title "knights of the uploading.") They are dedicated, self-sufficient, and even, Fernandez said, occasionally funny. And they are everywhere on Twitter, despite the social-media network's efforts to ban them. Fernandez described the group's embrace of social media as "a stroke of genius on their part." The CSCC doesn't have fanboys.

More crucially, ISIS has a narrative. This is often described by the group's opponents as superficial or bankrupt. Only it isn't. It is immensely rich. The International Centre for the Study of Radicalisation estimates that of the

20,000 or more foreign jihadists believed to have gone to fight in Syria and Iraq, around 100 are from the United States.[70] These fighters may be naive or stupid, but they didn't sacrifice everything for nothing. John Horgan, a prominent scholar of terrorism, told me that people who join groups like ISIS "are trying to find a path, to answer a call to something, to right some perceived wrong, to do something truly meaningful with their lives."

The CSCC doesn't have a narrative—not one, at any rate, remotely comparable in emotional affect and resonance to that of ISIS. No one is more sharply aware of this than Fernandez himself. "ISIS's message," he said, "is that Muslims are being killed and that they're the solution … There is an appeal to violence, obviously, but there is also an appeal to the best in people, to people's aspirations, hopes and dreams, to their deepest yearnings for identity, faith and self-actualization. We don't have a counter-narrative that speaks to that. What we have is half a message: 'Don't do this.' But we lack the 'do this instead.' That's not very exciting. The positive narrative is always more powerful, especially if it involves dressing in black like a ninja, having a cool flag, being on television, and fighting for your people."

In his biography of the philosopher Ludwig Wittgenstein Ray Monk discussed Wittgenstein's decision to enlist in the Austro-Hungarian army during World War I. It wasn't really about patriotism, Monk suggested. Rather, Wittgenstein "felt that the experience of facing death would, in some way or other, improve him … What Wittgenstein wanted from the war was a transformation of his whole personality, a 'variety of religious experience' that would change his life irrevocably."[71] One of the greatest challenges in counterterrorism today is working out how to create a narrative that directly speaks to a similar kind of longing among potential terrorists—and channels that longing in a nonviolent direction. As Scott Atran argues in *Talking to the Enemy*, "In the long run, perhaps the most important counterterrorism measure of all is to provide alternative heroes and hopes that are more enticing and empowering than any moderating lessons or material offerings."[72]

The more immediate, but no less intractable, challenge is to change the reality on the ground in Syria and Iraq, so that ISIS's narrative of Sunni Muslim persecution at the hands of the Assad regime and Iranian-backed Shiite militias commands less resonance among Sunnis. One problem in countering that narrative is that some of it happens to be true: Sunni Muslims *are* being persecuted in Syria and Iraq. This blunt empirical fact, just as much as ISIS's success on the battlefield,[73] and the rhetorical amplification and global dissemination of that success via ISIS propaganda, helps explain why ISIS has been so effective in recruiting so many foreign fighters to its cause.

Zawahiri was right: Half the battle is media. But the other half—the reality on the ground—is the more important part of the equation. And as long as that reality supports ISIS's narrative, its message will continue to appeal to disaffected Sunnis both within and outside the Muslim world. This is not lost on Fernandez, either: "Saying ISIS is bad is not good enough. There has to be change on the ground. Messaging can shape and shade, but it can't turn black into white."

The Atlantic, March 2, 2015

The Cyber Activists Who Want to Shut Down ISIS

In August 2014, a Twitter account affiliated with Anonymous, the hacker-crusader collective, declared "full-scale cyber war" against ISIS: "Welcome to Operation Ice #ISIS, where #Anonymous will do it's [sic] part in combating #ISIS's influence in social media and shut them down."[74]

In July [2015] I traveled to a gloomy European capital city to meet one of the "cyber warriors" behind this operation. Online, he goes by the pseudonym Mikro. He is vigilant, bordering on paranoid, about hiding his actual identity, on account of all the death threats he has received. But a few months after I initiated a relationship with him on Twitter, Mikro allowed me to visit him in the apartment he shares with his girlfriend and two Rottweilers. He works alone from his chaotic living room, using an old, battered computer—not the state-of-the-art setup I had envisaged. On an average day, he told me, he spends up to 16 hours fixed to his sofa. He starts around noon, just after he wakes up, and works late into the night and early morning.

No state intelligence agency assigned Mikro this work. He answers to no one and uses methods that are not only ethically ambiguous, but also beyond any kind of democratic oversight and accountability. Nobody even knows what he's doing except for his girlfriend and a motley crew of dedicated operatives. His neighbors just think he's a recluse. To his friends, he's a computer nerd.

Unbeknown to any of them, Mikro is the "operations officer" for GhostSec, a group with the self-declared mission of targeting "Islamic extremist content" from "websites, blogs, videos, and social media accounts," using both "official channels" and "digital weapons." The group claims to have disrupted or taken down more than 133 ISIS-linked websites by overwhelming their servers with fake traffic from multiple sources.[75] (This is called a Distributed Denial of Service, or DDOS, attack.)

More spectacularly, GhostSec also claims to have thwarted a July 2015 jihadist attack on a Tunisian market by passing information to a private security company called Kronos Advisory, which then gave it to the FBI. Michael S. Smith II, one of Kronos's founders, confirmed this over the phone. He made sure to add that GhostSec is "not working for me or with me per se … We are collaborating in gathering and presenting information that is valuable to counterterrorism officials."

Mikro said he played a leading role in uncovering the plot. "I was told by one of my hunters, 'Look into this.' And from there we built up the case." He also showed me a set of screenshots from the dark web listing ISIS donation pages that, he said, were taken down shortly after GhostSec had identified them. He was deliberately vague about how the group came across these pages, why and when they were taken down, and what his role as "operations officer" actually involves.

In February Mikro founded a second group called CtrlSec. It's closely related to GhostSec; both groups originate from Anonymous, and they share personnel and resources. But Mikro told me CtrlSec is no longer affiliated with Anonymous, a non-hierarchical organization that prohibits its members from soliciting financial support from outsiders. "We have a structure," Mikro explained. "We have a leadership, we have roles, and we need money."

CtrlSec's sole mission is to eliminate pro-ISIS accounts on Twitter. A study by the Brookings Institution fellow J. M. Berger and the data scientist Jonathon Morgan found that in the last four months of 2014, at least 46,000 Twitter accounts were used by ISIS supporters, potentially reaching an audience of millions.[76] They also found that ISIS-supporting accounts had an average of about 1,000 followers each and that ISIS supporters on Twitter were far more active than ordinary Twitter users.

Mikro evaded questions about CtrlSec's methods in the same way he evaded logistical questions about GhostSec. When I asked whether CtrlSec uses algorithms to identify pro-ISIS Twitter activity, he was adamant that it does not. Instead, he insisted, every suspect tweet and Twitter account is tracked down manually by one of the group's 28 operatives, many of whom can read Arabic. I asked him what criteria these operatives use to determine pro-ISIS sympathies and he replied, "You need two eyes and brain." When I probed him further, he said, "We are trained to see indicators … Also, we monitor the well-known accounts to pick up new supporters." Mikro claimed that CtrlSec identifies 200 to 600 pro-ISIS Twitter accounts a day.

Once the group is satisfied that it has identified a pro-ISIS account, it adds the account in question to its "blacklist," which it tweets out in automated installments. The group then asks its followers to flag the blacklisted accounts for Twitter. (Under the company's rules, users can be suspended if they "promote violence against others" or post "excessively violent media.") "The purpose of this account is to expose ISIS and Al-Qaida members active on Twitter," explains CtrlSec's Tumblr page. "Whether they should be reported or not isn't our decision: it's your decision."

It's hard to predict just how much it would cripple ISIS if its promoters were banned from Twitter altogether. As *The Atlantic*'s Kathy Gilsinan has argued, ISIS's capacity to mobilize unprecedented numbers of foreign fighters may have more to do with its real-world military successes than the doggedness of ISIS "fanboys" on Twitter.[77] And suspended users frequently return to set up new Twitter accounts.

Still, Berger, one of the authors of the Brookings report, says there is "substantial evidence" that account suspensions seriously limit the group's reach, given how effective Twitter is as an instrument for disseminating information to vast audiences across the globe.[78] In Berger's "6-Point Plan to Defeat ISIS in the Propaganda War," co-authored with the Harvard terrorism scholar Jessica Stern, the sixth and last point is, "Aggressively suspend ISIS social-media accounts."[79] He and Stern conclude that "suspensions do limit the audience for ISIS's gruesome propaganda." Berger has also noted that even when banned pro-ISIS users resume their efforts under new usernames, they suffer from the negative "impact of time lost to the process of creating new accounts and waiting for followers to find them."[80]

Mikro claimed that since February, CtrlSec has helped remove 60,000 to 70,000 pro-ISIS Twitter accounts. These are astonishing numbers (and ones that top Berger and Morgan's estimate of total pro-ISIS accounts). When I pressed Mikro on how he arrived at the figure, he wouldn't elaborate. Early on, he said, he tried to share his blacklist directly with Twitter. "But they never got back to us," he told me. This still exasperates him. "If they would cooperate with us, it wouldn't take more than a couple of days to shut [ISIS] totally out. They are shutting down in waves," he continued. "Suddenly 2,000 accounts are gone, 5,000 accounts are gone, and then [ISIS] can go two weeks with no suspensions, and then 10,000 accounts are gone."

In March, Twitter suspended over 2,000 pro-ISIS accounts,[81] earning one of its founders, Jack Dorsey, several death threats.[82] However, Mikro believes it's no coincidence that "every target they take down has been tweeted by us." (I contacted Twitter to find out whether it has used CtrlSec's lists to identify pro-ISIS accounts for suspension, but I have yet to receive a response.)

As I pressed Mikro on his modus operandi, he showed me a Twitter account that had just made it onto his blacklist. Its tweets contained a lot of ISIS insignia, and I could readily make out the distinctive logo of ISIS's media arm, al-Hayat, in some of the screenshots. Many of the photos depicted the kinds of medieval atrocities that have become ISIS's trademark.

He opened a folder containing a collection of ISIS atrocity porn. "This is what I have to deal with every day," he said, clicking on scores of photos of beheadings and other highly stylized massacres. "I was looking at these over breakfast this morning." One of the photos he showed me was of a child, around 8 or 9, dressed in military garb, holding a severed head. Another was of a head on a spike. I suddenly felt an urge to be elsewhere.

Then Mikro showed me an excruciatingly vivid photo of a severed human neck. It had been sent to his Twitter inbox by a self-professed ISIS supporter and addressed personally to him. There were no words attached, just the gut-wrenching gore. Mikro said he'd lost count of the death threats he'd received. "I don't really take them seriously," he said. Then he added, "I know it's very real, but I can't let it affect me, because I'm up to my neck in shit already with this. If they figure out who I am … they would do anything to come here and take me down." He showed me, with not a little pride, a hit list posted online by ISIS supporters in which CtrlSec held first place.

Before he became a counter-jihadist, Mikro spent years trying to figure out exactly who he wanted to be. He was a boisterous and badly behaved child, always in trouble at school. He said his mother's boyfriend disliked him and threatened to leave her if she didn't put him in foster care. "I woke up one morning and I wanted to go out but noticed the front door was locked. So I asked, 'What's happening?' And my mum told me I was going away for a couple of weeks. But when you're told to pack everything you have, you start to smell that it's more than a week."

He said he "went crazy" and "started kicking down the door. I was going totally maniac and went into my room and started crushing everything. And then the child welfare came, and they actually called the police. And there came a guy with a helmet and shield in through the door, with a couple of police officers behind. They fucking handcuffed me and carried me out to the police vehicle and drove me off to the child-welfare office. I was 12 years old." The "couple of weeks" away turned out to be six years.

Mikro insisted he doesn't feel hostility toward his mother now. She was troubled, he explained, always blowing the rent money to feed her gambling habit. There's clearly more to the story than this, but he was reluctant to say more about it. "I felt rejected," he told me simply. "I still feel it. But I've learned to live with that."

Initially, Mikro moved in with a Christian family, where "I was forced into believing in God." After a year, he was placed with a Muslim family from Turkey and expected to follow the Islamic faith. He recalls being made to fast during Ramadan. "I used to walk to school instead of taking the bus and used the money to buy food because I was so fucking hungry." He said he tried being a Muslim: "I actually found the Muslim belief much more calming than the Christian." But now, he concluded, "Religion isn't for me."

Mikro's placement with the Muslim family didn't last long anyway. After he was caught using drugs, he was transferred to "a house in the middle of nowhere, with a bunch of troubled teenagers." It was there that Mikro's life changed forever. "I remember it really clearly because it has haunted me in every court I have been in." The quarrel was over a girl who had been assaulted by one of the boys in the house. Mikro said he and two friends tried to confront the boy but were stopped by a group of care workers before they could exact revenge. "One of them ... I'm not proud of it, because he was a really nice guy and he was just trying to make us think logically, when I look back at it. We dragged him to the ground and kicked him several times. He cracked, like, six ribs. He didn't break it, but he did serious damage to his spine. He stopped working with youths after that. The doctor said that if we'd kicked him one more time in the chest, he'd be dead."

For this crime, as well as resisting arrest after the incident, Mikro was sent to a high-security adult prison, where he spent six months. He was the youngest inmate there, just 16. Once out, "They put me in an apartment. I had nothing to do. I like drugs. And it was just going downhill from there. I was selling weed—and other heavy drugs."

As I listened to Mikro tell his story, it dawned on me that his biography, with its multiple personal grievances and setbacks and trials, mirrors that of the aggrieved and alienated jihadist. I shared this observation with him, and he readily agreed. "I come from the same shit," he said.

The U.S. Department of State has made its own efforts to beat ISIS at the Twitter game. Earlier this year [February 2015], I interviewed Alberto Fernandez, then in his final week as the head of the State Department's Center for Strategic Counterterrorism Communications (CSCC). Fernandez spoke with disarming honesty and acuity about the myriad difficulties of derailing ISIS's narrative and blunting its appeal among disaffected and marginalized Sunni Muslims. At the time, the CSCC was under fire for its "Think Again Turn Away" campaign, which the terrorism analyst Rita Katz had harshly denounced as inept and "embarrassing" in an article in *Time*.[83] "We don't have a counter-narrative," Fernandez acknowledged. "We have half a message: 'Don't do this.' But we lack the 'Do this instead.'"

CtrlSec's approach is far more straightforward. It is not about countering or repudiating a "narrative." It is not about engaging with the undecided—the so-called "fence-sitters"—about the legitimacy of jihadist violence. It is not about winning hearts or changing minds. Rather, it is about shutting down the message at its source. And unlike the CSCC, CtrlSec has a clear metric for success: suspended Twitter accounts.

One criticism leveled against activists like those involved with CtrlSec is that they're casting too wide a net and targeting non-ISIS accounts. Mikro acknowledged that this happens, but insisted that it's rare and that mistakes are quickly corrected. For example, some parody ISIS accounts that initially fell afoul of CtrlSec were added to the group's "whitelist" to prevent future mistakes.

A related criticism is that Twitter suspension undermines the democratic ideal of free speech. "That's bullshit," Mikro fired back before I could finish articulating the complaint. "Why should somebody who doesn't let other people practice free speech have free speech? We're saving lives."

I tried to get Mikro to tell me more about what's driving him. State counter-terrorism agents are usually paid for their efforts, but this man devotes a huge amount of time and energy to his calling without any financial reward—and at no small personal risk. He told me he was spurred to action by the Charlie Hebdo attacks in January: "I had to do something. You can't kill so many people over a fucking drawing." He realized then, he said, that "sooner or later, if you don't do shit, it's gonna be your problem, too."

But when I asked him what was going on in his life at the time, he said, "I was doing nothing." CtrlSec has clearly filled that void. "I no longer know what else to do," he reflected. "If I didn't do this, I'd do exactly the same thing: I would sit at home, smoke weed all day. Only difference now is that I actually feel like I'm doing something productive." When I asked him how he felt when he heard the news about the thwarted plot in Tunisia, he said, "That was like an orgasm, seriously."

Not long after I returned to the U.K. from visiting him, Mikro sent me a text message. "Something big is happening," he wrote, adding, "it'll be a long night." His ominous words were followed by a smiley face.

The Atlantic, October 8, 2015

Translating ISIS's Atrocity Porn

By ISIS's customary gonzo standards, a recent video [released on January 4, 2016] depicting the execution of five men accused of spying for the British government was relatively tame, and the gore quotient minimal.[84] No one's head was cut off and ceremoniously placed on their contorted and ravaged torso. Nobody was subjected to the horror of being set on fire in a cage; or drowned in a cage;[85] or being run over by a tank;[86] or being tied to the back of a speeding car;[87] or having their heads literally ripped off.[88] For ISIS, the video was, indeed, positively muted.

Yet it remains profoundly disquieting, especially for the Western English-speaking audience at which it was primarily aimed. This, in part, is to do with the British accent of the executioner-in-chief in the video, and what it signals: apostasy, defection. It says, "*I grew up where you grew up, I learned to speak how you speak, and I lived where you lived—and yet I reject you and everything you stand for.*"

What the man—believed to be Abu Rumaysah—with the British accent in fact said was: "Oh British Government, oh people of Britain—know that …

we will continue to wage jihad, break borders and one day invade your land where we will rule by the Sharia …" He also warned: "you will lose this war, as you lost in Iraq and Afghanistan."[89]

This is, of course, a concrete threat, aimed at the British government, its citizens, its armed forces and their collaborators. But the greater threat comes from that British accent, because it raises the spectre of the "enemy within," and undermines confidence in the presumed superiority of Western values: If *this* person has defected, then who else has? And who else *might?* At the same time, the British accent transmits and supports ISIS's narrative of the global "caliphate," with a truly transnational appeal and make-up.

But the chief reason for the disquiet raised by the video isn't the British-accented killer; it's the British-accented *kid*. He appears at the very end of the video, after the victims have been shot. He is very young—around four years old—and is dressed in military-style fatigues. He warns, in English: "We are going to go kill the kaffir (non-believers) over there." Reports suggest that he may be the son of Khadijah Dare, a British woman who left for Syria several years ago,[90] although, for ISIS and its various audiences, his identity is less important than his meaning.

This isn't the first time ISIS has used a child in its atrocity porn. In January last year [2015] it released a video of an angelic-looking Kazakh boy, no more than 10 years old, shooting to death two men, also accused of spying. And in July [2015] it released a video of a mass-execution carried out by a group of teens in Palmyra's Roman Theatre.[91] But this is the first time a child has featured in an ISIS video issuing a threat in English against the British government and people.

What is the child doing and what does he symbolize? He is first and foremost reading a script, and, like the many other children ISIS has hijacked or captured, he doesn't know what he is doing.[92] He is a victim, an instrument of ISIS's brutal and ruthless will. He is also, more crucially for ISIS, a prestige symbol, enlisted to communicate strength and endurance, both to ISIS's rank and file and to their enemies. Given its recent military setbacks and losses, this message has special urgency for ISIS: *We are still here*, the group is saying, *and we will prevail, whatever you throw at us.*

The militarized ISIS child is the perfect vehicle for expressing this point, since he is a graphic symbol of, or testament to, the strength and tenacity of the ISIS worldview, and how it has found root and replication in the very young. He also symbolizes continuity, reassuring existing ISIS fighters that once they have perished in battle their fight will live on through the blood and sacrifice of their young.

This is disquieting enough, but the real disquiet comes from the boundary-transgression the use of the child in this video signifies. Children, the world over, represent innocence and purity and life in all its great potential. Casting a child in a snuff movie is a massive affront to these ideals and the very meaning of childhood. In this sense, it arouses the same disquiet as that provoked by the eroticization of children and pedophilia.

It's hard to know what species of feelings ISIS most wanted to elicit in its British audience: feelings of revulsion and disgust or feelings of fear and terror. The former would suggest a punitive intent with no additional motive, whereas the latter would point to a more instrumental logic, whereby the aim would be to undermine support for military strikes against ISIS, and spread fear among ISIS's own internal enemies who would help facilitate these attacks. It is, of course, eminently possible that ISIS wants to foment both.

What is also unclear is just how effective shock and horror, to say nothing of terror, are as a mode of political communication. Shocking or horrifying images may well capture the headlines, but it's an open question whether they work as tools of intimidation. In the long-run, they may just provoke feelings of anger and the desire for revenge.[93]

National Post, January 25, 2016

The Jihad Will Be Televised

In *Memoirs of an Italian Terrorist,* the author, who purports to have been a member of a left-wing militant group, vividly conveys the excitement and pressures of living underground as a secret operative. There are questions about the book's authenticity—the author, who identifies himself only by the pseudonym Giorgio, declares that "what I write here can't be true, it can only be truthful"—but there's a telling detail in his description of mission preparation. "I would never set out to undertake a proletarian expropriation"—a communist-inflected euphemism for a robbery—"if I didn't feel that I was dressed right."[94]

For today's wannabe jihadists, whether "inspired" or "directed" by groups like ISIS, style—be it in the form of a righteous beard or a voluptuous application of kohl eye makeup[95]—also matters. But perhaps not as much as celluloid, and for a certain kind of Islamized Giorgio the capture of atrocities on film matters almost as much as their actual commission. The British writer Neal Ascherson, in his foreword to *Memoirs of an Italian Terrorist,* referred to the "sinister frivolity of Italian urban terrorism." In the case of ISIS and its so-called "lone wolf" emulators, "sinister narcissism" seems to be the more appropriate formulation.

One evening this month [June 2016], in the French town of Magnanville about 35 miles outside of Paris, Larossi Abballa, a 25-year-old Moroccan Frenchman, ambushed an off-duty police officer outside his home and stabbed him to death. He then broke into the house and murdered the officer's wife with the same weapon.[96] Minutes later he recorded himself live on Facebook with his phone, boasting of his deed and declaring his allegiance to ISIS.[97] A police SWAT team stormed the house and fatally shot Abballa, but his image and voice lived on: ISIS's Amaq news agency, which described Abballa as an "Islamic State fighter," later uploaded to YouTube an edited version of the live video.

Abballa's attack took place less than 48 hours after Omar Mateen slaughtered 49 people at a gay hangout in Orlando, Florida, and wounded many more. Mateen's horrifying legacy is quantitative in nature: No other individual mass shooter in American history has killed more people in a single rampage.[98] Abballa's legacy, by contrast, is qualitative: He is the first terrorist to broadcast live at the scene of his atrocities.[99] And his actions may portend a horrifying new genre of terrorist theater: live streaming political murder. Jason Burke of *The Guardian* was right: "It may not be long," he wrote in February, "before an individual attacker, or a terrorist group, produces a live stream of an attack, with images broadcast from the point of view of the killer."[100] Or rather Burke was partially right: Abballa did not live stream the actual moment of slaughter, although it seems only a matter of time before a terrorist will attempt to do so.

ISIS has revolutionized jihadist propaganda by creating a visually distinct pornography of pain that combines high production values with intimate atrocity. Unlike its predecessor al-Qaeda in Iraq, whose signature production was the IED mash-up video, ISIS has become notorious for staging obscenely graphic, High Definition atrocities. These theatrical events drastically narrow the distance between the viewer and the victim, bringing the latter squarely into the foreground. ISIS doesn't just want to show the viewer the spectacle of a tank or truck exploding; ISIS wants to show the viewer the spectacle of a human body being savaged, up close. It is precisely this quality of horrifying intimacy that is the new element in ISIS propaganda—and a key to its global dissemination. This is the primordial secret, no longer well kept: The killing act is a spectacle people want to see.

Yet for all its malevolent creativity, not even ISIS "central" in Iraq and Syria has live streamed from a murder scene. There are structural reasons for this. To project an image of total power and control in its execution videos, ISIS must make killing look effortless and competent. This calls for heavy post-production editing—and hence rules out the live spectacular. In addition to this, live streaming is precarious from a security perspective, since it risks giving away the location of the atrocity. But for sheer horror, live streaming is hard to beat, because it further narrows the distance between viewer and victim: The killing may be happening in a distant place, but it isn't happening in any distant past. It is happening *now*.

By live streaming from the scene of his crime, Abballa also points to a new and growing trend in jihadist propaganda: the terrorist as auteur.[101] It is likely that Abballa, who had proven links to terrorism, would have watched ISIS propaganda.[102] But he was no mere spectator, and by filming in the immediate aftermath of his attack he propelled himself into the ranks of creator, producing his own brand of do-it-yourself ISIS propaganda.

Facebook quickly removed Abballa's footage and disabled his account. Had it not done so, it is a near certainty that people would have watched in large numbers, transfixed by the horror unfolding in front of their eyes, just as thousands searched online for the beheading video of the American engineer Nick Berg after it was posted online in May 2004. (The video was an early, and then-rare, example of the genre later perfected by ISIS.)

As the anthropologist Frances Larson writes, "There have always been people ready to watch executions, and ready to enjoy the spectacle."[103] Or as Susan Sontag has more piercingly put it, "It seems that the appetite for pictures showing bodies in pain is as keen, almost, as the desire for ones that show bodies naked."[104] One possible reason for this, cited by the intellectual historian Karen Halttunen, is the secret comparison we make between ourselves the person who suffers, and the satisfaction of prizing our own good fortune that results from this.[105] Another possible reason, discussed in J. Glenn Gray's *The Warriors: Reflections on Men in Battle*, is related to what the author calls, invoking the Bible, "the lust of the eye": the urge to see "the novel, the unusual, the spectacular."[106]

"Terrorist attacks," Brian M. Jenkins observed over 40 years ago, "are often carefully choreographed to attract the attention of the electronic media and the international press."[107] The goal is publicity, which is itself a strategic asset that can be used for all sorts of purposes, such as winning recruits or putting an issue on the political agenda. Jenkins also remarked on how the "willingness and capability of the news media to report and broadcast dramatic incidents of violence throughout the world enhances and even may encourage terrorism as an effective means of propaganda."[108] Today, with the advent of the internet and social media, that willingness and capability has increased markedly, and with it a further possibility discussed by Jenkins has materialized: namely, ever "more extravagant and destructive acts" of terrorism.[109]

It is easy to condemn the news media for its fascination with terrorism and for "playing into the hands of the terrorists" by giving them the publicity they crave. Yet audiences, too, collude in this. We denounce the killers, yet we are riveted by their awesome violence and their convoluted life-histories.[110] They are the classic folk devil we love to hate—and endlessly talk about. Terrorists know this and draw encouragement from it, as does the international news media with which they are in a dark symbiosis. Which is why the jihad will be televised—and you and I will be watching.

The Atlantic, June 28, 2016

ISIS and the Little Monsters

The so-called Islamic State has seemingly done the impossible: earlier this month [January 2017] it released what is arguably its most shocking and abhorrent atrocity video yet.

This is quite a statement, of course: ISIS has made a lot of truly shocking and abhorrent atrocity videos. Some of these depict mass beheadings, burnings, drownings and stonings—all in horrible High Definition close-up. The new video, titled "Made Me Alive with His Own Blood," features the murder of a broken and defenceless man at the hands of a three-year-old boy. A. Three. Year. Old.

There is something unedifying about rating ISIS videos for their shock impact, just as there is something off about marvelling at their "slickness" and sophistication. But the latest atrocity video represents a qualitative shift in depravity, and it is important to understand why and what it means.

It is well known that ISIS has created a vast and sophisticated apparatus for recruiting and indoctrinating children into its brutal ideology, and this isn't the first time ISIS has used children as executioners in its videos. One of these, released in January 2015, showed a 10-year old Kazakh boy shooting to death two men accused of spying. Another, released in July that same year, showed boys as young as 13 or 14 executing 25 Syrian soldiers in an amphitheatre in the ancient city of Palmyra.

But this latest atrocity video features not a boy, but a very young child. This is new: a radical innovation in political atrocity that goes beyond the paradigm of what we conventionally understand as terrorism. For this isn't terrorism, commonly understood. This is *horrorism*: a form of violence so monstrous and transgressive that it corrupts our most fundamental notions of what it means to be human and civilised.

According to the political philosopher Adriana Cavarero, who has written a book on the subject, horrorism "has nothing to do with the instinctive reaction to the threat of death," and everything to do with "an instinctive disgust."[111] Horrorism, in other words, arouses not fear or terror, but rather a deep repugnance that sickens us to our stomachs.

And few things are as disgust-evoking as the image of a three-year-old shooting to death a helpless and traumatised man. There are two central reasons for this. First, it violates our deepest beliefs about the innocence of children. For ISIS, the militarised child reflects the power and durability of its ideology: the caliphate may be shrinking,[112] but its essential foundations are in good condition. For everyone else, this child represents the defilement of a purity to which we accord an almost sacred status.

Second, it presents a grotesque asymmetry: between the smallness of the killer and the magnitude of the deed he is forced to commit. It just doesn't add up: murder is such a heinous act, and yet here is a killer who has only just learned to walk and can barely hold a gun.

The image of the infant jihadist unnerves in other ways, too, subliminally reminding us of that most horrifying of all monsters: the demonic child. In *Evil Children in the Popular Imagination*, the English scholar Karen J. Renner estimates that there are over 600 films in which "some kind of arguably evil child" is portrayed, with almost 400 made since 2000.[113]

One of the most disquieting movies in this genre is Stanley Kubrick's 1980 adaptation of Stephen King's novel *The Shining*. The central character of the movie—Jack Torrance, played by Jack Nicolson—descends into madness and tries to kill his wife and son. But it's the son, Danny, who is the more unnerving presence, seemingly in communion with a silent and ominous supernatural force. He sees and hears things. And what he sees and hears is horrifying, like the two little Grady girls, who in one second invite him to come and play and in the next lie on the floor in a pool of blood, having been butchered to death. Or like the elevator whose doors release an ocean of dark blood.

Children, as Stephen King has observed, can be "uncivilised and not very nice." They are unruly and impressionable, and in some ways strange and "other." So it's not surprising that they serve as a repository of our fears. The monstrous child motif in horror movies mercilessly plays on these. And so, it seems, does ISIS, with its endless stream of videos featuring the so-called "cubs of the caliphate."

One of the biggest stories on ISIS since it came to global prominence in mid-2014 centred on three British teenage schoolgirls who had absconded to Islamic State-controlled territory in February of 2015. One classmate described the girls as "studious, argumentative and driven."[114] The youngest, who was 15 at the time, apparently used to be a fan of the reality TV show *Keeping Up With the Kardashians*. Another had reportedly danced "in her teenage bedroom" the night before she left for Syria.

Yet, for all their reported ordinariness, the girls had somehow fallen under the "spell" of ISIS to become "jihadi brides." According to Britain's then-Prime Minister David Cameron, they had been "brainwashed in their bedrooms."[115] Keith Vaz, the then-chairman of Parliament's Home Affairs Select Committee, said in a special hearing to which the families of the girls were invited that what had happened was "every parent's nightmare."[116]

This story, despite the haziness of the details about the girls' motives and how they became radicalised, was instantly generalised into a moral fable about innocent children and their vulnerability to ISIS's ideology. But what it really resembled was a script from a horror movie about teenage girls and demonic possession: a shadowy, evil force had inscribed itself into their minds—via an electronic screen—and turned them into sex-mad, husband-chasing, ideological fanatics, whose parents could no longer recognise them. They were once just "ordinary teenagers." And then they entered the jihadist twilight zone and became "jihadi brides," whose mouths frothed with monstrous bile.

As the caliphate shrinks, ISIS's ability to conduct large-scale terrorist attacks will correspondingly diminish. But it will continue to horrify us with its sickening videos of jihadist children, stirring up deep, primordial fears about our own mysterious and ever-so impressionable children.

Vice, January 31, 2017

Why Do We Want to Watch Gory Jihadist Propaganda Videos?

What does prolonged exposure to jihadist online propaganda do to us?

One popular answer, especially among politicians, is that it radicalizes our thoughts and transforms us into terrorists.

A more nuanced answer, put forward by terrorism scholars, is that while sustained exposure to extremist online material is not in itself a sufficient cause of radicalization, it can reinforce existing assumptions and beliefs that are already tending toward the extreme.

Yet in even the most robust scholarship on online radicalization, there is a conspicuous lack of data on how the most important variable in online radicalization—namely, the audience for extremist material—understands and engages with that material.[117]

For the past 18 months, I have been conducting research on how young adults in the West perceive and react to Islamic State propaganda videos. I myself have watched hundreds of hours of these videos, including scenes of horrifying violence and cruelty. Without a doubt, this has been detrimental to my spiritual well-being; I've had night terrors. Yet none of this was imposed on me. I willingly—sometimes excitedly—exposed myself to this material, including and especially the very worst of it. This has given my research a personal dimension: Why do I want to watch? What is it about the Islamic State that so captivates me?

Last September [2016], the criminologist Jack Cunliffe and I started an online survey to test audience responses to official English-language Islamic State videos. The idea behind the survey was simple: Ask ordinary young adults to watch these videos—which we edited to exclude scenes of graphic violence—and then get them to tell us about that viewing experience.

Despite the ethical and legal challenges in doing this research (Britain's 2006 Terrorism Act makes it a criminal offense to disseminate terrorist propaganda), our survey went ahead. We collected more than 3,000 responses and will be presenting our findings at the Terrorism, Crime, Culture conference in Copenhagen this week [October 5, 2017].[118]

Around 1,300 survey respondents were from North America and about 1,000 were from Britain. The remainder came from all over the world. Their mean age was 30, with a big clump—around 1,800—between 18 and 26. Most (67 percent) were male. Thirty-six percent identified as having no religion, 17 percent identified as Christian and 4 percent identified as Muslim.

A vast majority—93 percent—reported a negative attitude toward the Islamic State, and just 1 percent said they had a positive view of the group. Six percent reported that they were neutral. Of the 34 people who reported a positive attitude toward the Islamic State, five were Muslims.

It did not surprise us that a vast majority of respondents expressed a negative attitude toward the Islamic State or that those who held a positive view of the group said almost uniformly positive things about the videos embedded in the survey. Nor was it surprising that most respondents were impressed by the technical quality of the Islamic State videos. They are sophisticated and movie-like in style.[119]

What did surprise us was that a significant number of those who held a negative attitude toward the Islamic State were still receptive to its utopian message, while still larger numbers exhibited a curiosity about watching the kind of "slick" and horrifying atrocity porn for which the group has become notorious.

We were furthermore surprised by respondents' reported exposure to the Islamic State's videos. Fifty-seven percent said they had watched an Islamic State video before, beyond clips shown on TV and in online news material. Of this number, an even more remarkable 46 percent said they had seen more than 10 Islamic State videos. This may well say more about the selection biases of our sample than about young adults' exposure to the Islamic State—or it may not. A recent Policy Exchange report showed that the ease with which Islamic State videos can still be viewed on the internet, despite the pushback from social media companies, is quite remarkable.[120]

Responding to a clip from an Islamic State video in which a handsome, strong-looking fighter hands out toys to young children dressed in colorful clothes, around a third of respondents expressed positive judgments about the physical strength and moral character of the fighter. And a not insignificant number—28 percent—said the video gave them a "warm feeling," and this percentage drops to only 26 percent when restricted to those who proclaim to feel negatively about the Islamic State.

This was in marked contrast to respondents' reaction to a clip from a mass-beheading video in which a group of Islamic State fighters marches Syrian Army captives to their execution. Just 3 percent of our respondents said the video overall made them "feel good." A vast majority reported feelings of discomfort, disgust and fear.

Still, only 11 percent of our survey respondents said that the video bored them, suggesting that for the majority, while staged mass beheadings may be unpleasant to watch, they nevertheless make for compelling viewing. Indeed, when asked if they wanted to view the video to its grisly completion, 33 percent said yes. Less than half—44 percent—said definitively that they didn't want to see the video to the end.

Given the nature and size of the sample, our survey is not representative and does not warrant firm generalizations about young people's engagement with Islamic State videos. But it does yield some suggestive findings, not least of which concerns the dark power of this propaganda.

In *The Anatomy of Disgust* the legal scholar William Ian Miller observes that "something makes us look at the bloody auto accident, thrill to movies of horror, gore, and violence; something makes porn big business and still draws people to circus sideshows."[121] It isn't clear what that something is, but it can be certain that the Islamic State understands the basic dynamic, because for all the disgust, discomfort and fear that its beheading videos evoke, something makes us—or many of us, at least—want to look.

Perhaps more important, our survey suggests that even among those who hold a negative view of the Islamic State, the softer image of the group cultivated in so much of its propaganda seems to resonate positively among a significant number of people.

The broader question of how exposure to the Islamic State's online content features in the radicalization of jihadists is not answered in our research. It may, in fact, be unanswerable, given how difficult it is to disentangle the myriad causal threads in the complex process by which someone becomes radicalized. But there is still much that can be learned about the role and affective impact of jihadist propaganda.

The New York Times, October 5, 2017

Inside Europol's Online War Against ISIS

In January [2018] I travelled to Europol's heavily fortified HQ in The Hague to interview members of the EU's Internet Referral Unit (IRU), an innocuous-sounding name for a group that spends most of its time trawling the internet for beheadings, bomb-making manuals, hysterical incitements and all the rest of it.

Despite the recent collapse of ISIS's "caliphate" in Syria and Iraq, the IRU is still busy. And, in any case, ISIS has far from gone away. Just a few months ago its Sinai faction released a new 23-minute video,[122] and around the same time ISIS's media centre al-Hayat—famed for its "slick" English-language videos—released a clip showing what appeared to be a woman fighting in frontline combat.[123]

The IRU was established by Europol—the law enforcement agency of the EU—in July 2015. Its main business is to spot jihadist online material and then flag this to the relevant internet service provider for removal—although it doesn't have any legal power to compel the internet providers to follow its requests. Still, according to a July 2016 Europol press release, in the first year of the IRU's operation 91 percent of the total content referred—over 11,000 pieces of material across some 31 online platforms in eight languages—was removed following requests from the IRU.[124]

The IRU is a small operation, with around 30 members. I spoke with four of them to find out what they do and how they cope with the stress of watching copious amounts of jihadist propaganda. For security reasons they cannot be identified by their real names—I can't even tell you where they're from or how old they are—so I've used pseudonymous first names throughout.

What is an average day like at the IRU? Usually, it starts with an alert of web-links to check. The material on them is then assessed, and if it's deemed referable a referral will be made. The assessment, along with the relevant content, is then uploaded to the "Check-the-Web Portal," Europol's giant digital library of jihadist online propaganda.

What kind of content does the IRU flag? The priority, *Anna explained to me, is anything that threatens violence against European countries and civilians. But the IRU also refers non-violent extremist material, which, in the case of ISIS, can be anything from a photo report of an old dude picking grapes to a video describing the structure of the caliphate. Not all the internet platforms the IRU works with are willing to censor this kind of stuff—and some, Anna told me, only suspend graphically violent material. I gently suggested that these companies may have a point, and that "extreme" ideas should be protected under the principle of free speech, but Anna was adamant: it's all pernicious, because it's all part of the same recruitment drive.

What the IRU doesn't flag is non-jihadist propaganda. According to *Celine: "We don't go out of the terrorist organisations that were listed by the EU, and we don't go for material produced by terrorist organisations that are not calling for violent jihad ... Not left, not right, no other kind of terrorism, only violent jihad." This will no doubt be seen as controversial by those who think the counter-terrorism efforts of Western governments, especially those of the Trump administration, are disproportionately focused on Muslims.

The IRU has good relationships with most of the internet companies it works with, but Telegram—ISIS's preferred secure messaging app—isn't one of them. Anna told me that the company rarely responds to referral emails. In September 2015 Telegram's founder and CEO, Pavel Durov, reportedly mocked calls to remove ISIS channels from the app: "I propose banning words. There's evidence that they're being used by terrorists to communicate," he said in a post on the Russian social networking site VKontakte.

On November 18, 2015, just days after the Paris attacks—and following mounting political pressure from Western governments—Telegram removed 78 pro-ISIS channels from its platform.[125] This was a departure from its previous hands-off approach, and in response ISIS supporters declared war on Telegram. But they didn't leave the platform; they just stopped using its public channels, and moved to private ones instead, which are harder to monitor. This, Anna said, has made the IRU's job a lot more difficult, because you need an invitation to join a private channel, or to be added by the person who created it.

As part of an ongoing research study on the attractions and repulsions of violent images, I've spent the last year interviewing people who take voyeuristic delight in viewing the very worst of what the internet has to offer: videos of beheadings, torture, suicides and other things I cannot possibly mention here.

Like a first love, they all fondly remember their first gore video: the one that made them cringe and want to look away, all the while beckoning them to look ever closer; the one that enraptured them and made them search for more. And everyone has their favourite: the most shocking and sickening video they have ever seen; the one that delivered the all-elusive cringe they felt on watching their beloved, unforgettable first.

At the IRU, it's the same, minus the amorality. All the operatives I spoke with could recall the first atrocity video they saw on the job, and within a heartbeat they could all name the video that most shocked and sickened them.

"I don't know if you can make a hierarchy in the most disturbing stuff," said Celine, "but for me the worst are the ones with the children. When you see a kid of two years old with a gun, executing someone in a playground in Syria, this is insane, disgusting, horrible."

*Nicolas, the only male member of the team I spoke with, mentioned the same video: "Actually, the most shocking video is this tiny kid in the playpen. They give him a gun and let him shoot someone in the head. When you see kids it's always hard, because they're victims too."

For Anna, the one ISIS video she can't forget is of a beheading of a Russian intelligence agent: "This is a video I remember because you see his face, and there are tears running from his eyes, he's speaking really calm, he doesn't seem nervous—and then they execute him. But they show it in detail."

And for *Layla, the worst of the worst is a video of a mass beheading of Syrian Army troops. "It made me sick, literally—I threw up," she said. "Everybody in that video is trapped, the prisoners, but also the foreign fighters because you see their faces, they can't go back, it's over for them. Everybody's trapped, except the guy ["Jihadi John"] in the balaclava."

"My job," Layla added, "is to look at that knowing that I couldn't do anything."

If you're going to do this line of work, it's pretty clear what you need. You need a high tolerance for blood and gore, and an equally high tolerance for boredom and bullshit: most ISIS videos, for all their widely touted "slickness" and narrative skill, are monotonous and annoying, often with ridiculously portentous voice-overs.

Back in 2014, when ISIS videos felt trailblazing and hair-raising, I must confess to a shameful feeling of exhilaration every time a new major release was announced—but that feeling soon faded, and now I can barely watch the stuff. "We have to watch it, all the way through," said Celine when I alluded to the temptation to hit the fast-forward button.

What else do you need? You need to be battle-hardened from a daily grind of real-life violence, so that its online incarnation doesn't look quite so horrifying. "For me," Anna confided, "I'm coming from law enforcement, so I've seen some stuff already … Let's say I had a tough job before." Celine echoed this: "I was already exposed to the violence of jihadi terrorist organisations." She recalled the immediate aftermath of a horrific suicide attack she had witnessed prior to joining the IRU. "This was way more difficult than watching the videos."

You need to be able to compartmentalise, so that the day-job doesn't bleed over into the life-job. "I'm just trying to delete this the moment I see the image," Anna said, referring to ISIS beheading videos, adding, "I'm not taking this home with me." Or, as Celine put it, "I know how to close the door."

Crucially, you also need a sense of humour: you need to be able to laugh at the humourless jihadi be-headers and blowhards. "I do make black humour, but it depends on who I'm with," Nicolas said, without going into detail. Layla gave me the details, of which I can only report the following:

"There was another video in which a foreign fighter was being interviewed, and a guy walking in the background suddenly fell into a hole—it was Monty-Pythonesque," she said, laughing. "We watched that many times."

Celine relayed a similar story:

> There were two guys claiming an attack, but they still needed to kill two people … We were disturbed by the beheading and the nonsense of the narrative. I was sitting next to my colleague and he said, "But the guy [one of the ISIS executioners] has mascara on, no?" We then started joking about how you need to be fresh and young when you do the jihad. This is stupid, but it helps.

Members of the IRU also use a range of distancing techniques to shield themselves from the abyss they're looking into. One such technique is to routinise the work of watching, so that it becomes a mechanical, programmed operation, where the focus is on the segmented detail of the video rather than on the cruelty and suffering depicted in it. "I have to put on my professional hat," Celine told me. "I need to be precise: we are collecting evidence—it is important to pay attention to the detail, the camera they used, the way it was filmed, where it was filmed, the behaviour of the person acting, the clothes, every detail has an importance."

Similarly, Nicolas said: "I know how the video will end, but the gory part of the video I'm not interested in. I look at it not as a voyeur—I'm not a voyeur. What I'm looking for is: what's his discourse? What's the message he wants to deliver? So I focus more as an investigator, and not as a person getting affected by what I'm watching. So, from the beginning, can I identify a person? Can I identify an environment behind? Who's the hostage? And I do abstraction … I never put a face on the dead body."

Nicolas said he learned this last technique from a surgeon he knew in his previous job as a cop. "If you put a face on the body, you will get affected."

Another technique is to apply what Layla called "filters." For videos, Layla said, "you can watch it first without the sound, and then you can listen to it without watching it, so you don't associate the images with the sound." Does this work? Not for beheadings: "The sound-effects are very good, the gurgling and everything."

In a recent survey on ISIS videos I carried out with the criminologist Jack Cunliffe,[126] we found that 57 percent of our 3,000 respondents had seen an ISIS video before, beyond clips shown on TV and in online news material. Of this group, 46 percent said they had seen more than ten ISIS videos. This may well say more about the selection biases of our sample than about young adults' exposure to ISIS—or it may not. Either way, it's a remarkable statistic. And what cannot be doubted, despite the recent pushback from social media companies, is the ubiquity and accessibility of ISIS-related content on the internet.

One survey respondent, an American-Muslim woman in her early twenties who contacted me about the survey, told me:

> They've [ISIS] really upgraded *nasheeds*. It's not your father's nasheed music. It's not boring, like those al-Qaeda propaganda vids, or really any Arabic political videos. That German nasheed was fire. Twerk-able. Milly Rock-able. Overall, all of their videos seem surreal. I have a hard time believing they're some crazy-ass terrorist group. It looks like an action film. It was hard for me to be scared, even though some were graphic. Sometimes I had to remind myself that this is real, created by a real terrorist group.

The German nasheed she was referring to was the soundtrack to a graphically violent 2015 ISIS video calling for jihadist attacks on Western cities. Has this woman become desensitised, a passive consumer of the pornography of pain? Or is ISIS-staged violence so preposterously monstrous and slickly-produced that, for Western audiences, it doesn't look properly real?

For counter-terrorism experts and policy-makers, the most urgent question about ISIS videos is whether they are radicalising. But a no less important issue is the spiritual cost they incur on the countless number of people who come into contact with them. It is probably incalculable.

"We have faith in what we do," Nicolas said. But, for all the IRU's efforts, the tide of jihadi-snuff culture can't be stopped. And, for the rest of us, it may already be too late.

*Names have been changed.
Vice, April 10, 2018

Chapter 2

THE MEANING AND APPEAL OF JIHADIST VIOLENCE

Terrorism with a Human Face

It's all in the face, apparently. Just check out that terrifying mug shot of Mohammad Atta, the so-called "ringleader" of the 19 hijackers who staged the 9/11 attacks. His face, wrote the novelist Martin Amis in a short story about Atta, was "gangrenous" and "almost comically malevolent."[1] Hateful, too:

> The detestation, the detestation of everything, was being sculpted on it, from within. He was amazed that he was still allowed to walk the streets, let alone enter a building or board a plane. Another day, one more day, and they wouldn't let him. Why didn't everybody point, why didn't they cringe, why didn't they run?

In his investigative study *Who Killed Daniel Pearl?*, Bernard-Henri Levy described Pearl's convicted murderer, the British-Pakistani Omar Sheikh, as "handsome," his face showing no "vice or malice though somewhat veiled."[2] He looked "intelligent and rather frank … a strong chin under a well-trimmed beard, a good man it would seem, slightly tart smile, an intellectual demeanor, very Westernized—nothing, in any case, that signals the obtuse Islamist, the fanatic."

So it's not, apparently, all in the face, although the implication in Levy's portrait, as in Amis's fictionalized account of Atta, is that it should be, and that Pearl's killer was somehow an aberration.

The idea that human evil is inscribed into the body and face of the criminal offender has deep roots, and is in fact the animating throb behind modern scientific criminology and its founding document, Cesare Lombroso's *The Criminal Man*, published in 1876.[3] It is also an underlying assumption in much of the news coverage of the Kuwaiti-born Londoner Mohammed Emwazi, who was exposed recently as the ISIS executioner "Jihadi John."[4]

Lombroso was convinced he had found the root causes of crime after studying "the skull of a brigand" and finding in it "a very long series of atavistic abnormalities."[5] Against the prevailing theology at the time, he concluded the "criminal man" was not innately sinful, still less possessed of the devil, but genetically abnormal, a subhuman throwback to an earlier, less advanced, stage of human evolution, proof of which could be found in his beastly appearance ("crooked noses, sloping foreheads, large ears, protruding jaws, dark eyes").

Lombroso's work has since been discredited, "relegated to the status of a myth," in the words of the renowned criminologist Sir Leon Radzinowicz,[6] and is liable to occasion more mirth than serious intellectual consideration among criminologists and their first-year undergraduate students. But its spirit is alive and well in popular discourse on terrorism and in the fervent reaction to the description of Emwazi as a "beautiful young man" by Asim Qureshi, the director of the human-rights group CAGE, who knew him.[7] It is also present in the perplexity, voiced in many news reports, over how Emwazi transformed from a smiling and reserved child to the demonic black-clad masked executioner of the ISIS snuff movies. How could an "angelic"-looking schoolboy[8] become "Jihadi John," the monster with the sadistic swagger and malicious eyes?

People who seriously challenge the social and moral order, the sociologist Harold Garfinkel argued, threaten the unity of that order and must therefore be excluded from it.[9] Sociologists like to call this "othering," a process which, as Garfinkel showed, involves "ritually separating" the transgressor from the conventional order by publicly reclassifying him as inherently bad or loathsome— and above all *different*. He is "made strange," Garfinkel wrote, so as to preserve the gap between "them," the vile ones, and "us," the virtuous ones.

Emwazi challenges the social and moral order. To put it mildly. Far more than, say, Abu Bakr al-Baghdadi, the Iraqi-born ISIS leader challenges the social and moral order. This is because Emwazi spent most of his life in Britain, in the secular West. Despite his Kuwaiti background and heritage, he was socialized or "acculturated" here, not over there. He went to school here, played football here, went to university here, talked London-street tough here, and wore baseball caps here.[10] He was one of us. And then something happened, he became radicalized and embraced violent jihad, he rejected the society he had grown up in, and he went to Syria and started murdering people in the name of God.

Emwazi, in other words, is a renegade, a person who defects from one group to an opposing group. He is, to use a phrase from Lewis A. Coser's discussion of political defection, "the enemy from within," threatening the confidence and very identity of the "in-group":[11] because if Emwazi can be converted to ISIS, then why not others from among us? This, together with his horrible proficiency with a serrated six-inch blade, is why Emwazi haunts the West's collective psyche—and why he must be demonized and, to use Garfinkel's terminology, "made strange" in the form of the cartoonish "Jihadi John."

In the 1940s, anthropologist Edward Evan Evans-Pritchard studied how the Nuer of modern-day South Sudan reacted to the birth of a deformed child. Reflecting on his findings, Mary Douglas wrote:

> [W]hen a monstrous birth occurs, the defining lines between humans and animals may be threatened. If a monstrous birth can be labelled an event of a peculiar kind, the categories can be restored. So the Nuer treat monstrous births as baby hippopotamuses, accidentally born to humans and, with this labelling, the appropriate action is clear. They gently lay them in the river where they belong.[12]

Emwazi is *our* monstrous child. And the outright condemnation and opposition that has greeted the acknowledgment of his human qualities speaks to how desperately we want to separate him from ourselves. This goes a long way toward explaining why so many are resistant to Qureshi's description of Emwazi as a "gentle, kind" and "beautiful young man." That account humanizes him and hence draws us closer to him, to this "monster." One need not accept CAGE's blame-shifting to recognize this essential point.[13]

"Some newspaper stories," the late Christopher Hitchens wrote in a 2007 *Slate* article, "quite simply write themselves."[14] He was specifically referring to the journalistic tendency in news reports on serial killers to record the disbelief of the killer's neighbors and acquaintances, who "feel duty-bound to say that this has come as a great shock, not to say a complete surprise, and that the guy next door seemed perfectly decent—if perhaps a little inclined to 'keep to himself.'" This reportorial protocol is also closely adhered to in news stories on terrorists, where expressions of shock—he seemed like such "a nice lad who could get on with anyone"—are invariably attributed to neighbors and acquaintances of the terrorist in question. It is fast becoming the dominant script in the story of Emwazi, as evidenced in Friday's CNN report on the video of the teenaged Emwazi in a school playground.[15] "But for the people who knew him it is difficult to fathom that the football-loving teenager they knew as Mohammad Emwazi has emerged as the man behind the mask," the report concluded. This kind of incomprehension casts a sharp light on deep-seated assumptions about terrorists and other comparable folk devils in our culture: that they should be immediately recognizable as two-headed monsters who live in cesspools and feed on small children. Or something resembling that.

"Yes," wrote Elie Wiesel, "it is possible to defile life and creation and feel no remorse. ... To go on vacation, be enthralled by the beauty of a landscape, make children laugh—and still fulfil regularly, day in and day out, the duties of a killer."[16] How profoundly and horribly true this is.

Killers, too, can act in decent and humane ways. It is just that we rarely like to admit it—unless of course they kill in defense of the good, as we subjectively define it. Hannah Arendt famously argued in her study of Adolf Eichmann that ordinary people are capable of extraordinary evil.[17] Arendt's emphasis was on the "banal" face of human evil. But there is no reason why evil cannot also have a beautiful face.

The Atlantic, March 8, 2015

What Exactly Is the Allure of Islamic State?

"She used to watch *Keeping Up With the Kardashians* and stuff like that, so there was nothing that indicated that she was radicalized in any way—not at home." So said Sahima Begum in her testimony before the House of Commons Home Affairs Select Committee in London this month [March 2015].[18] She was speaking about her sister Shamima, 15, who together with Kadiza Sultana, 16, and Amira Abase, 15, absconded from England last month to Turkey, eventually crossing the border into Syria.[19]

Begum's statement was meant to sound exculpatory. *Keeping Up With the Kardashians*, a brash, shameless reality TV show about young wealthy socialites, is emphatically not *Although the Disbelievers Dislike It*, an Islamic State video released in November [2014] depicting the beheading of 22 Syrian soldiers. Had Sahima said her sister "had an IS flag on her wall," the media would have castigated the family for doing nothing to stop Shamima's radicalization. The emphasis on Shamima's quotidian interests served to immunize the family from outside censure, as well as forestall further interference from law enforcement.

This isn't to say that Begum's comment was not sincere, and there is no evidence to suggest that the family's shock and disbelief has been fabricated. Neither, however, was it exactly unscripted. In fact, it closely adhered to what is fast becoming a standard narrative in news reports on terrorists, in which family, friends and former teachers are filmed or quoted expressing their amazement at how the ordinary person they knew could have committed such an outrage.

He was such "a nice lad who could get on with anyone," said one neighbor. And, no, the subject of this bromide wasn't the "quiet and reserved" and "polite" Mohammad · Emwazi,[20] the Kuwaiti-born Londoner who was exposed recently as the Islamic State executioner "Jihadi John." It was another Mohammad: Sidique Khan, one of the four British men who carried out the July 7, 2005, London bombings.[21]

Like serial killers, terrorists have become the new everyman next door who, according to the script we have written for them, transform, without warning, from angelic-looking children into megalomaniacal monsters.

How does this transformation happen, if that's even what it is?

Foreign militants in Syria would probably say that nothing but their conscience and sense of justice "drove" them to join Islamic State. Reportage on Shamima Begum and her two co-conspirators, meanwhile, has tended to focus on how they became "brainwashed."[22] The emphasis is on how outsiders, like the Scottish "jihadi bride" Aqsa Mahmood, who is now in Syria and is thought to have been in touch with one of the girls, manipulated them. In these accounts, there is no sense of agency, of actual persons with real desires. More crucially, the implicit assumption is that Islamic State is a repulsive place that no normal person would want to even visit.

This needs revising. Islamic State may look like a dystopia, but this is not how wannabe fighters see it. And while their jihadi talk may sound crazy, their longings may not be wholly different from those that have prompted other radical departures.

In his memoir *The Warriors: Reflections of Men in Battle*, J. Glenn Gray, a U.S. intelligence officer in World War II, writes that "the majority of us, restless and unfulfilled, see no supreme worth in our present state. We want more out of life than we are getting and are always half-ready to chance everything on the realization of great expectations."[23] Gray confesses that in his early manhood he longed for one more war in which he might participate: "Though I never spoke of such a wish, and regard it today with considerable dismay, I cannot deny that it was an important part of the aspirations of my youth."

Philip Caputo says something nearly identical about his own motives for enlisting in the U.S. Army prior to the outbreak of the Vietnam War. "I wanted a chance to live heroically. Having known nothing but security, comfort and peace, I hungered for danger, challenges and violence."[24]

It is not inconceivable that Shamima Begum and her two fellow travelers were animated by the same desires and impulses, and were searching, above all, for an escape from their humdrum everyday lives and for transcendence of self through total commitment to a sacred cause.

Sahima Begum prefaced her remark about her sister's TV habits by saying, "My sister was into normal teenage things." But while *Keeping Up With the Kardashians* makes for perfectly conventional TV viewing, the reality it depicts, with its larger-than-life characters, is far from "normal." On the contrary, it is a window into a distant, albeit fabricated, world.

The Islamic State is both a terrorist organization and insurgent army. It is also, like the best reality TV, a fantastically compelling viewing spectacle. We watch aghast at its moral depravity—but we watch nonetheless, transfixed by atrocity. The Islamic State show is slick and exciting, and there are twists and turns. It is also edgy and, with its cast of sword-wielding, horse-riding, hair-raising holy warriors, profoundly exotic, offering a version of reality that is a stark counterpoint to life in the West.

For some, this carefully crafted spectacle is powerfully seductive and—entirely unlike the Kardashian world—seemingly attainable. Islamic State tells us: Come to the land of the caliphate. *Do not live under kuffar. Exchange your meaningless life for the beauty and security of Islamic State. Reinvent yourself. Find peace and belonging and happiness.*

Perhaps Shamima Begum, in between keeping up with the Kardashians, had also found time to watch last August's soulful 22-minute Islamic State video *Eid Greetings from the Land of Khilafah,* in which a contingent of mostly English-speaking émigrés wax lyrical about the spiritual satisfactions of living in the Islamic State, all the while beseeching their audience to join them.

In recent months, debate over Islamic State has centered on one large question: namely, how Islamic is it?[25] A potentially richer question about Islamic State is how much it owes not to Islam, but to more universal desires and longings—and how, more practically, it exploits these in what is arguably the most compelling reality TV show on earth.

Los Angeles Times, March 28, 2015

What Motivates Terrorists?

One of the most frequently asked questions about terrorism is also the most intractable. Why? Why do they do it? Why do people join terrorist groups and participate in acts of terrorism?

There are as many answers to this question as there are terrorist groups, and everyone from clerics to caustic cab drivers seems to have a confident opinion on the subject, as though the interior world of terrorists can be easily mined and mapped. But this confidence is often misplaced, given how little scholars actually know about terrorism and the people who are involved in it.[26] It also betrays an epic obliviousness about just how difficult it is to access the internal, subjective desires and emotions that shape the outer world. Instead of asking why people join terrorist groups and commit terrorist atrocities, a more worthwhile starting point for explanation is to ask *how*.

One culturally prevalent answer to the why question is that terrorists are "driven" or "pushed" to do it, and that the decisive driving or pushing agent is pathology. This answer has evolved in recent years in line with advances in knowledge and moral sensibilities. In terrorism studies in the late 1960s, it was not uncommon for scholars to conceive of pathology as a psychological abnormality or affliction rooted inside the individual.[27] Since the 1980s, this idea has fallen into disrepute, and the scholarly consensus now holds that the roots of terrorism lie not in the individual, but in the wider circumstances in which terrorists live and act.

This reflects a broader consensus in the social sciences about violence: namely, that it is "socially determined," a product of deeper historical, economic or cultural forces over and above the individual.[28] It is perhaps best summarized by the renowned social psychologist Albert Bandura. Drawing on studies of violence from across the human sciences, Bandura concluded that "it requires conducive social conditions rather than monstrous people to produce atrocious deeds."[29] Social scientists argue about the nature and impact of the "social conditions" in question, but few would question the essential point that violence, however personalized or idiosyncratic its expression, is primarily rooted in historical structures or social relationships, not individuals, still less their "pathological" mindsets.

This consensus is also reflected in much liberal-left commentary about terrorism, especially of the jihadist variant. For example, in some quarters of the "radical" left it is asserted that the roots of jihadist terrorism lie not in Islam but in the myriad historical crimes and injustices of Western, and specifically U.S.-driven, imperialism—most notably, in the post–9/11 era, the 2003 invasion of Iraq.[30] Jihadist violence, from this perspective, is an inevitable reaction fueled by Muslim anger and vengeance; and Westernized jihadists, far from rejecting the civilized norms and ideals proclaimed by the West, are in fact alienated from a West that excludes, demeans and harasses Muslims.

The scholarly consensus on violence has a lot going for it. It humanizes the perpetrators of violence by insisting on their ordinariness and contextualizing their actions. It obliges people to reflect on their own possible shortcomings and vulnerabilities, and how, in different circumstances, they too could do monstrous deeds. And it compels people to recognize that they do not act in a social vacuum, and that what they think, feel and do is powerfully shaped by the broader historical circumstances in which they are compelled to live and act. Moreover, Westernized jihadists, as a recent report cogently suggested, assuredly *are* alienated and feel that they do not belong in a secular world that often mocks and challenges their religion and identity as Muslims.[31]

But the consensus can't divest itself of the idea of pathology. Rather, it simply relocates the notion, tracing the causes of violence to pathological "background factors" operating on the violent. No doubt this is a more illuminating and edifying narrative than that sketched out in earlier psychological accounts. But its explanatory power is limited, because, as the eminent sociologist Jack Katz has convincingly argued, "whatever the validity of the hereditary, psychological, and social-ecological conditions of crime, many of those in the supposedly causal categories do not commit the crime at issue, ...

many who do commit the crime do not fit the causal categories, and ... many who do fit the background categories and later commit the predicted crime go for long stretches without committing the crimes to which theory directs them."[32] Or as the British writer David Aaronovitch once joked, "Why don't black lesbians blow up buses? Aren't they alienated enough?"[33]

One of the most sensitive and profound explorations of terrorism in recent years comes not from a scholar, but from a novelist. Philip Roth's *American Pastoral* is a murder mystery in which the focal point is not the who, but the why. The protagonist, Seymour Levov, is a successful businessman whose 16-year-old daughter Meredith ("Merry") blows up a post office to protest the Vietnam War, killing a bystander. All Seymour can think about is why Merry did it. She was an adored only child who grew up in a privileged and decent family in the idyllic hamlet of Old Rimrock, New Jersey. Seymour is desperate to locate "the wound" that caused Merry's violence. Was it her stutter? Was it that anomalous kiss on the mouth he gave her one summer when she was 11 and he 36? Or was it the mysterious firebrand Rita Cohen who radicalized her?

As the novel progresses, Seymour's disbelief gives way to clarity. But it is a negative clarity. "He had learned the worst lesson that life can teach—that it makes no sense," Roth writes.[34] He had learned that his daughter "was unknowable," and that "there are no reasons," that "reasons are in books." In capturing Seymour's efforts to understand the disaster that befalls his family, Roth holds up to scrutiny conventional efforts to explain terrorism—and exposes just how imaginatively restricted and simplifying they can be.

Do terrorists have reasons for committing atrocities? They certainly reel off any number of reasons in their pronouncements,[35] but, as law professor Stephen Holmes has observed, "private motivations cannot always be inferred from public justifications."[36] Sometimes people do what they do for the reasons they profess. Sometimes not, because what they do is motivated by reasons that are too dark, shameful, or bizarre to be openly acknowledged. Sometimes people do things that are so morally contentious that when called to account they are liable to excuse or justify, rather than to explain, their actions.[37] Terrorists unquestionably fall into this category.

And sometimes people do what they do without the slightest sense of knowing why. I once met someone who robbed a liquor store in his teens. He was caught and did jail time for it. This person is now an accomplished writer. Doing that stick-up was a hinge moment in his life and today, some 30 years later, he still cannot make sense of it. The motive simply eludes him.

Terrorism scholar John Horgan has made a similar point. "The most valuable interviews I've conducted [with former terrorists] have been ones in which the interviewees conceded, 'To be honest, I don't really know,'" he writes.[38] "Motivation is a very complicated issue. To explain why any of us does anything is a challenge." It's a challenge further compounded by the fact that some actions are informed by multiple motives, and even if these can be reliably identified it is often difficult to disentangle them and calculate their respective causal weight.

As Horgan suggests, a more manageable and useful question to ask about terrorism is not why, but how—and when and where? How did this specific person come to join this specific organization? What networks helped facilitate the act of joining, and where and how were these networks accessed or sought out?

Because these questions are about the circumstances of terrorism, and not the interior world of terrorists, they are not only more intellectually tractable for scholars, but also more directly relevant to efforts to prevent or stop terrorist recruitment. Law-enforcement agents can't disrupt a motive, but with the right intelligence and skills they may be able to disrupt a network of terrorist recruiters. Marc Sageman's work on Western "leaderless" jihadists demonstrates the promise of this kind of approach. Although Sageman has some interesting things to say about the why question, the strength of his research lies in showing just how decisive social and kinship networks are in the radicalization process.

This isn't to suggest that the why question should be abandoned, but rather that those who ask it better appreciate the magnitude of the question and acknowledge the possibility that some momentous life decisions will remain forever opaque and mysterious—not only to outside observers, but also to the people who take them and must live with the consequences.

The Atlantic, June 9, 2015

Pilgrims to the Islamic State

In *Political Pilgrims*, the sociologist Paul Hollander exposes and excoriates the mentality of a certain kind of Western intellectual, who, such is the depth of his estrangement or alienation from his own society, is predisposed to extend sympathy to virtually any opposing political system.[39]

The book is about the travels of 20th-century Western intellectuals to the Soviet Union, China and Cuba, and how these political travelers were able to find in such repressive countries a model of "the good society" in which they could invest their brightest hopes. Hollander documents in relentless and mortifying detail how this utopian impulse, driven by a deep discontent with their own societies, led them to deny or excuse the myriad moral defects of the places they visited.

But the significance of *Political Pilgrims* extends far beyond its immediate subject matter, and its insights may help to illuminate the mentality of that most recent and disconcerting set of pilgrims: namely, the Western migrants to the Islamic State, whose estrangement from their own societies primes them to idealize the so-called Islamic State and overlook or justify its terrible human-rights abuses.

It is estimated that around 4,000 people have left their homes in the West to migrate to ISIS.[40] Many have become jihadist fighters in the apparent hope of achieving martyrdom. A significant number—over 550 women[41]—seem to have gone to become mothers and raise the next generation of jihadist "lions." Some have left to put their medical expertise to use,[42] and others to help in whatever capacity they can. Their motives are as mixed as their backgrounds. Indeed, the striking fact about these new pilgrims is that they don't fit any single profile. They represent a broad spectrum of humanity, from former rappers[43] and gangbangers[44] to grandparents[45] and gifted students.[46]

On the face of it, they share little in common with the rarefied intellectuals of *Political Pilgrims*. Yet their estrangement from Western society and the force of their belief in an alternative system far superior to it, evidenced in interviews they have given and other forms of personal testimony, suggest that they share certain discontents and susceptibilities with the subjects of Hollander's study.

Among the countless examples of folly cited by Hollander is Sidney and Beatrice Webb's tome *Soviet Communism: A New Civilization?*, in which the Soviet penal system is praised for—wait for it—its progressive spirit. The second edition of this book, from which, as the historian Robert Conquest noted, "the question mark was triumphantly removed," was published in 1937—"at precisely the time," Conquest observed, that "the regime was in its worst phase of gloomy, all-embracing terror."[47]

How could the Webbs and others like them have gotten it so wrong? They were clearly foolish, but they were not stupid. Indeed, writes Hollander, many of the intellectuals in his survey were widely revered for their fierce intelligence and lively skepticism. Hollander contends instead that they *wanted* to be deceived about the failures and depredations of the societies they visited. And this, he theorizes, was in turn because, psychologically, they needed to believe in the existence of a perfect social system that not only exemplified their deepest ideals but also gave voice to their deepest misgivings about their own societies.

"Wishful thinking," the sociologist Karl Mannheim wrote, "has always figured in human affairs. When the imagination finds no satisfaction in existing reality, it seeks refuge in wishfully constructed places and periods."[48] Hollander approvingly reproduces this quote in his introduction to *Political Pilgrims*, and one of the great merits of his book is the clarity and force with which it shows how desire can supersede and subvert critical thinking.

The recent migrations to ISIS, just like the political pilgrimages before them, are yet further testimony to the power of wishful thinking and how desire can trump reason.

Earlier this month [July 2015], it was reported that a family of 12 from Luton, England—including, according to the BBC, "a baby and two grandparents"[49]—had made the journey to Syria.[50] It was the second family believed to have left the United Kingdom for the Islamic State since May. Was the family coerced or, as one relative has suggested, manipulated into going to Syria?[51] Were they the victims of some collective psychosis? Not a chance, if a press release purportedly from the family is to be credited.[52] The BBC acquired the statement from an individual claiming to be an Islamic State fighter, though the media organization could not verify its authenticity.

"None of us were forced against our will," it said, describing a land "free from the corruption and oppression of man-made law … in which a Muslim doesn't feel oppression when practicing their religion. In which a parent doesn't feel the worry of losing their child to the immorality of society. In which the sick and elderly do not wait in agony, tolerating the partiality of race or social class."[53] It also derisively alluded to the "so-called freedom and democracy" of Western states.

The statement, as the scholar Shiraz Maher pointed out, clearly serves a propagandistic purpose, and it could well be a fabrication.[54] But it also accurately reflects the sentiments expressed by other Western migrants who have made the journey to Syria, and who in their social-media postings have mocked the notion that they have been "brainwashed" into joining ISIS. Furthermore, it distills two intimately connected themes that are essential for understanding the mentality of the Western migrants: estrangement and utopian hope.

ISIS's caliphate project, because it offers a bracing utopian alternative to Western secular society, speaks directly to those who feel their lives are worthless, spiritually corrupted, empty, boring, or devoid of purpose and significance, and who see no value in their own societies. It promises, in short, salvation and ultimate meaning through total commitment to a sacred cause. "I don't think there's anything better than living in the land of Khilafah," [caliphate], said one British jihadist in a video, *Eid Greetings from the Land of the Khilafah*, released last summer [2014] by ISIS's media arm. "You're not living under oppression … You're not living under *kuffar* [unbelievers] … We don't need any democracy … All we need is shariah."

Similar themes come out strongly in a recent report[55] on female Western migrants.[56] Based on the social-media postings of self-identified migrants apparently within ISIS-controlled territory, the authors found that estrangement from Western society and anger at perceived injustices against Muslims worldwide, together with a strong sense of religious calling and an unwavering faith in the rectitude of the newly emerging caliphate, form the basis for why these women journey to ISIS.

From this, it is clear that their departures owe as much to perceived corruption and oppression at home as to a desire to see in the Islamic State a utopian society free of any such secular perversions. This may also explain how, despite all the evidence, Western migrants to the caliphate can ignore or discount the mountain of incriminating evidence against ISIS, and risk everything to join it.

In Britain, where Prime Minister David Cameron just this week introduced a counterterrorism strategy as part of what he called "the struggle of our generation,"[57] debate over ISIS and its recruitment methods has become unhelpfully polarized. On the one side are those, including British officials, who portray ISIS recruits as "vulnerable" or impressionable youth who, despite their murderous intentions or actions, are actually victims.[58] On the other side are those, often academics and human-rights activists, who similarly argue that ISIS recruits are victims, but of oppressive government policies and actions rather than sinister jihadist groomers.[59] The problem with both lines of argument is that they deny the agency of those who join ISIS, and obscure the religious idealism that motivates them.

One of the biggest challenges associated with counter-messaging efforts against ISIS is how to prompt would-be migrants to rethink their favorable perceptions about the group and its self-proclaimed state. This is less a problem of finding the "right" narrative than of reconfiguring individual human desire, because it is possible that, at some deep psychological level, would-be migrants to ISIS *want* to be deceived about its widely reported depredations. As Christina Nemr, a former U.S. counterterrorism advisor, recently observed, people "push 'threatening information' away in favor of information that confirms their own beliefs."[60]

It is hard enough to sway those who have yet to make up their minds about ISIS—the so-called "fence-sitters." But it is monumentally harder to sway those who, because of their idealism and estrangement from their own societies, want or need to see the best in ISIS.

The Atlantic, July 24, 2015

The Challenge of Jihadi Cool

If you want to get a sense of what attracts Westernized Muslims to ISIS, you could do worse than listen to one of its sympathizers, as opposed to its legion of opponents, who are liable to pathologize the group's appeal as an ideological contagion that infects the weak,[61] instead of taking it seriously as a revolutionary movement that speaks to the young and the strong-minded.[62]

Check out, as just one of many examples, the Twitter user "Bint Emergent": an apparent ISIS fangirl and keen observer of the jihadist scene. (Bint Emergent has not disclosed her identity, or gender, but *bint* is an honorific Arabic word for girl or daughter; like *umm*—mother in Arabic—*bint* features prominently in the Twitter display names of female ISIS sympathizers.[63])

"Jihadis," she explains on her blog BintChaos, "look cool—like ninjas or video game warriors—gangstah and thuggish even—the opposition doesnt."[64] She concedes that "There aren't a lot of jihadist 'poster-girls' displayed—they all wear niqab [face veil], but sometimes its tastefully accessorized with an AK-47 or a bomb belt." By contrast, "Team CVE [a reference to Countering Violent Extremism, or Anglo-American counterterrorism entrepreneurs whose role, state- or self-appointed, is to challenge "extremist" narratives]," consists "mostly [of] middle-aged white guys with a smidgin of scared straight exmujahids [ex-jihadists] and a couple middleaged women."

"Jihadis have cool weapons. And cool nasheeds [a cappella hymns],"[65] she continues. They also have "young fiery imams that fight on the battle-field," whereas Team CVE "has ancient creaky dollar scholars …" Most importantly:

[S]alafi-jihadism made being pious cool. It became cool to quote aya [verse] and study Quran. And CVE has absolutely no defense against this … I love jihadi cant—dem, bait, preeing, binty, akhi [brother] … its like Belter dialect in the Expanse. And it borrows from all languages— because jihad draws from all races and ethnicities. The voice of youth counterculture and revolution for an underclass. Like ghetto culture in the US—the inexorable evolution of cool.

Bint Emergent reveals little to nothing about who she is, and without that crit-ical context it's difficult to assess her credibility. A lot of what she says in her blog posts is arcane and rambling, and she insists at the top of her prolific [and now suspended] Twitter feed that "im not necessarily proforma pro-#IS"—a statement seemingly contradicted by the sympathetic tone she often adopts toward the group.

And yet Bint Emergent's words, and especially her reflections on ISIS's countercultural appeal to young people, are worth considering. "The bottom line," she asserts in one blog entry, "is that the Islamic State is the classic scifi underdog battling a seemingly all powerful Evil Empire America against impossible odds—and in the very best scifi tradition—*they are winning*."[66] "Besides," she observes in another entry, "IS [Islamic State] has a bottomless youth recruitment pool for the next 35 years, and like IS says, the fighting has just begun. You Are Not Prepared."[67]

She is scathing about U.S. counterterrorism efforts against ISIS, and dismisses the State Department's "Think Again Turn Away" campaign[68] as "the most utterly clumsy and doomed propaganda effort since sexual abstinence campaigns."[69]

In a blog post titled "Embracing Apocalypse I: the Islamic State and the Prophetic Methodology," she expresses particular admiration for a black-and-white photo of an ISIS fighter on the streets of Kobani, Syria.[70] He is nonchalantly holding a machine gun, with an arm raised triumphantly in the air. Behind him is a scene of utter devastation, in which orange flames—the only color in the photo—and thick smoke cascade from a truck and building. The fighter depicted is reportedly Abu Ahmad al-Tunisi.[71] "This iconic photo," she writes, "distills the whole conflict into one image for me. To glory in apocalypse, to embrace it …" It also distills a possible contradiction or discrepancy: Abu Ahmad al-Tunisi is wearing, in addition to a thick, righteous beard, what appear to be a pair of Nike trainers. Nike is a large American corporation, and the distinctive Nike swoosh is a symbol of American urban cool—or, at least, it used to be. Apocalypse, Bint Emergent goes on to say, unconvincingly, is "a wholly alien concept for the west." But the idea of the righteous, brand-wearing badass certainly isn't.

In a chapter on "Warrior Values" in John Archer's edited collection *Male Violence*, the psychologist Barry McCarthy cites the Japanese samurai as the most obvious exemplar of this idea: He is "unflinching in the face of danger, strong and energetic, cunning in tactics though honorable, proficient with his weapons as well as in the arts of unarmed combat, self-controlled, self-confident and sexually virile."[72]

The cross-cultural appeal of this figure is hard to deny, as Richard E. Nisbett and Dov Cohen make clear in their study *Culture of Honor.* "The world over, men are sent out to sacrifice and to die, not for such purely instrumental purposes as deterrence; rather they are motivated by what they and the community expect good, honorable men to do."[73] "There is," indeed, Nisbett and Cohen remark, "a romance and an allure to the Masai warrior, the Druze tribesman, the Sioux Indian, the Scottish chieftain …"

For those who are bewitched by it, there is also a romance and an allure to the jihadist warrior. In a recent article, "The Soft Power of Militant Jihad," the jihadism expert Thomas Hegghammer touches on this and the wider "jihadi culture" of fashion, music, poetry, and dream interpretation.[74] "Jihadis," he writes, "can't seem to get enough anashid [nasheeds]. They listen to them in their dorms and in their cars, sing them in training camps and in the trenches, and discuss them on Twitter and Facebook." "Jihadi culture," he elaborates, "also comes with its own sartorial styles. In Europe, radicals sometimes wear a combination of sneakers, a Middle Eastern or Pakistani gown and a combat jacket on top. It's a style that perhaps reflects their urban roots, Muslim identity and militant sympathies." Hegghammer concludes that, "As the West comes to terms with a new and growing threat … we are not only confronting organizations and doctrines, but also a highly seductive subculture."

The genius of ISIS propaganda is how skillfully it imbues the idea of jihad not only with traditional notions of honor and virility, but also a strong undercurrent of oppositional, postmodern cool.

CVE practitioners can't possibly hope to challenge the glamor, energy and sheer badassery of violent jihad as an ideal, still less the wider emotional resonance of the warrior ethos on which it draws. But they can reasonably hope to subvert ISIS's claim to embody that ideal. What isn't yet clear is at precisely whom CVE programs should be targeted, how their counter-messaging should be framed and delivered, and, crucially, by whom. Vague references to those "at risk of" or "vulnerable to" radicalization, and to "credible voices" who can offer alternatives, do little to help in this regard. Challenging ISIS's bona fides as the true inheritor of jihad is also fraught with peril, in that it may play into the hands of other jihadist groups who profess that mantle. The bigger challenge—as Alberto Fernandez, the former coordinator of the U.S. State Department's Center for Strategic Counterterrorism Communications, noted when I interviewed him earlier this year [2015]—is how to create a counter-narrative that is not merely negative but boldly affirmative, offering a vision that is just as exhilarating and seductive as that of jihadists.[75] "The positive narrative," he said, "is always more powerful, especially if it involves dressing in black like a ninja, having a cool flag, being on television, and fighting for your people."

The problem for CVE is that in an ironic age in which few "grand narratives" remain,[76] no one—except perhaps for the jihadists and their supporters—really knows what that narrative is anymore.

The Atlantic, December 24, 2015

Reborn into Terrorism

In 2014, Abdelhamid Abaaoud, the organizer of the November 2015 Paris attacks, appeared in a video,[77] driving a pickup truck with a mound of corpses in tow. Speaking to the camera before driving off, he said: "Before we towed jet skis, motorcycles, quad bikes, big trailers filled with gifts for vacation in Morocco. Now, thank God, following God's path, we're towing apostates." This was a derogatory reference to his victims, who, in his mind, were renegades from the Muslim faith and thus legitimate targets for slaughter. But it was also a telling allusion to his own irreligious past, before he found God and joined ISIS and started murdering people.

Indeed, Abaaoud was once a wayward soul with a rap sheet. His sister Yasmina told *The New York Times* that Abaaoud didn't show any particular interest in religion prior to his departure for Syria, and "did not even go to the mosque."[78] But he had gone to prison several times, and it was apparently there, like so many Western jihadists,[79] that he grew radical.

Brahim Abdeslam, who blew himself up in the Paris attacks, seems to have been intimately acquainted with criminality as well: The bar he owned in Molenbeek, Brussels was shut down by police a week before the attacks over concerns about the illegal sale of drugs there.[80] And Brahim's brother Salah, a suspected Paris assailant who remains at large,[81] was not your typical finger-waving ideological fanatic: He reportedly visited gay bars[82] and was more likely to be seen rolling a joint than a prayer mat.

According to a recent *Washington Post* article, Abaaoud and his crew of assassins represent a "new type of jihadist"—"part terrorist, part gangster," who uses "skills honed in lawbreaking" for the ends of "violent radicalism."[83] "European jails have been breeding grounds of Islamist radicals for years, particularly in Belgium and France," the *Post's* Anthony Faiola and Souad Mekhennet write. "But recently, criminality and extremism have become even more interwoven, with recruits' illegal behavior continuing even after they are shown 'the light' of radical Islam."

This is an acute observation, although it's scarcely surprising that Westernized recruits to ISIS are just as deviant and lawless as their patrons in Syria and Iraq—the true originators of punk jihad, where anything goes and nothing, not even the weaponization of children,[84] is off-limits. After all, the spiritual founder of ISIS, Abu Musab al-Zarqawi, was a violent thug both before and after his embrace of Salafi jihadism.[85]

Like Abaaoud and Zarqawi, Siddhartha Dhar[86] (a.k.a. Abu Rumaysah[87]), the latest British-accented ISIS recruit to gain notoriety for his suspected role in the group's videos, also broke dramatically with his past: He was a Hindu before gravitating toward radical Islam, although, unlike Abaaoud and Zarqawi, Dhar didn't have a history of violence, robbery or drug-dealing, and hadn't done any jail time. Instead, he rented out bouncy castles to the "*kaffirs*" he came to loathe.[88]

These biographical traits have cropped up in numerous studies. In his survey of 31 incidents of jihadist terrorism in Europe between September 2001 and October 2006 Edwin Bakker found that at least 58 of the 242 perpetrators of these attacks—or 24 percent, a "strikingly high number," he says—had a criminal record prior to their arrest for terrorism-related offenses.[89] According to a study by Robin Simcox, of 58 individuals linked to 32 ISIS-related plots in the West between July 2014 and August 2015, 22 percent had a past criminal record or were in contact with law enforcement.[90]

Simcox also found that 29 percent of these individuals were converts to Islam. Converts, he reported, accounted for 67 percent of American Muslims involved in committing or planning an ISIS-related attack—"a significantly disproportionate percentage, considering that they comprise only 20% of Muslims throughout the entire United States." Converts are similarly overrepresented among convicted British jihadists. According to Scott Kleinman and Scott Flower, converts constitute an estimated 2 to 3 percent of Britain's 2.8 million Muslims, yet "converts have been involved in 31% of jihadist terrorism convictions in the UK from 2001 to 2010."[91]

What is it about ISIS, and militant Islamist groups in general, that makes them attractive both to criminals and to converts or born-again Muslims?

In *The True Believer*, published in 1951, the philosopher Eric Hoffer suggested that mass movements hold a special appeal to "sinners," providing "a refuge from a guilty conscience."[92] "Mass movements," he wrote, "are custom-made to fit the needs of the criminal—not only for the catharsis of his soul but also for the exercise of his inclinations and talents."[93] This also applies to jihadist groups like ISIS, which promise would-be recruits not just action and violence, but also redemption.

In his 2005 study of al-Muhajiroun, a banned Islamist movement based in Britain with reputed connections to ISIS, Quintan Wiktorowicz detailed the multiple material and social costs attached to what he calls "high-risk Islamic activism."[94] He mentioned one al-Muhajiroun document in which members are sternly warned to refrain from behaviors ranging from "listening to music and radio" and "window shopping and spending hours in the market," to "hanging out with friends" and "joking around and being sarcastic." The organization's activism, Wiktorowicz observed, is "fast-paced, demanding, and relentless." It also bristles "against the mainstream," generating a "kind of excitement often found in counterculture movements rebelling against the status quo." Many members, he noted, "seem to enjoy their role as 'outsiders.'"

But more crucially, Wiktorowicz argued, al-Muhajiroun promotes the idea of spiritual salvation—socializing its members to believe that their sacrifices in the here-and-now will be rewarded in the hereafter.

High-risk, high-intensity Islamist activism, in other words, seems tailor-made for the needs of criminals and ex-cons, providing them with a supportive community of fellow outsiders, a schedule of work, a positive identity, and the promise of cleansing away past sins.

Can the same be said for converts to Islam or born-again Muslims?

A common line of argument among scholars is that converts to Islam are insufficiently knowledgeable about their new faith and thus acutely vulnerable to extremist interpretations of Islam, which they lack the intellectual or theological resources to counter.[95] While this explanation seems intuitively plausible, it assumes that converts to Islam know less about their newfound religion than Muslims who were born and raised into it. Yet the evidence for this claim is shaky, and at odds with studies showing just how engaged and well-versed many converts are in debates over matters of faith.[96] The idea that converts, lacking in religious knowledge, are peculiarly susceptible to demagogic manipulation also carries the implication that those with a deep knowledge of Islam are unlikely to join jihadist groups. This, too, is a contentious point—and it's unclear whether it could even be empirically established, given how contested Islamic knowledge is. More contentious still, this logic essentializes Islam as inherently pacifist, suggesting that some true or proper understanding of the faith would serve as a repellent against deviant jihadist interpretations. But what Islam is or isn't is an open (and indeed volatile) question; there is not one "true" Islam, but a plurality of Islams, each competing for epistemological hegemony.

A more promising explanation lies in the social situation of converts in the West, and their status as apostates or defectors from the non-Islamic faith or secular world into which they were born and acculturated. In an illuminating article on "court Jews and Christian renegades," the sociologist Lewis A. Coser wrote, "The renegade is, as it were, forever on trial." Indeed: "He must continually prove himself worthy of his new status and standing."[97]

Converts to Islam are perennial outsiders, fully belonging neither to the Muslim communities into which they convert nor to the communities they leave behind. They are "doubly marginalized," as Kate Zebiri puts it in her study *British Muslim Converts*. This, more than any cognitive failings on their part, may explain the nature of their vulnerability to jihadist groups, which offer potential recruits not only belonging, but also seemingly irrefutable proof of commitment to the faith: self-sacrifice and ultimately death. It may also make them more lethal as jihadist talent, since their eagerness to prove their new commitment may push them to ever greater extremes.

Yet this hypothesis depends on the assumption that the converts in jihadist groups were in any meaningful sense converts to Islam prior to becoming jihadists, rather than the other way round: that they converted to jihadism before, or at the same time as, they became Muslims, so that their conversion to Islam was, as the political scientist Olivier Roy recently argued, "opportunistic" and thus a *consequence* of, and not an antecedent to, their conversion to jihadism.[98]

One way of clarifying the sequencing in these situations would be to look closely at the convert's social milieu and the circumstances in which he or she converted to Islam. According to Roy, the "second-generation Muslims and native converts" who dominate the European jihadist scene were "radicalized within a small group of 'buddies' who met in a particular place (neighborhood, prison, sport club)" and who "recreate a 'family,' a brotherhood," often with biological ties. They are, he says, in the first instance attracted not to "moderate Islam," but to the radicalism of violent Salafism, and correspondingly, "almost never have a history of devotion and religious practice."

In short, Roy argues, echoing the findings of Marc Sageman[99] and Scott Atran,[100] radicalized European youth, disaffected from their own societies, are not seeking Islam, but "a cause, a label, a grand narrative to which they can add the bloody signature of their personal revolt."

Hoffer reminds us how deeply personal that revolt can be. "A mass movement," he wrote, "particularly in its active, revivalist phase, appeals not to those intent on bolstering and advancing a cherished self, but to those who crave to be rid of an unwanted self."[101] For today's repentant criminals and restless converts, whose "innermost craving is for a new life—a rebirth," the all-immersive and all-redeeming jihadist project seemingly offers the perfect solution.

The Atlantic, January 25, 2016

Is There Any "Logic" to Suicide Terrorism?

In his edited collection on "suicide missions," the sociologist Diego Gambetta described his childhood admiration for Pietro Micca, a solider in the artillery regiment of the Duke of Savoy in what is now northern Italy.[102]

"In 1706, as the French were besieging Turin," Gambetta wrote, Micca "realized that a party of the besiegers had succeeded in penetrating the network of tunnels that were part of the city citadel, and would have no doubt been able to take it." Instead of trying to save himself, Micca heroically fought back, sacrificing himself for his comrades and city: "Despite having too short a fuse to run away in time, Micca ordered his companion to go before blowing himself up with a few barrels of gunpowder so as to destroy and block the tunnels."

Micca's memory lives on, and he is commonly regarded in Turin as a war hero. (A museum there is dedicated to him.) But the difference between Micca's actions and those of the Brussels suicide bombers[103] could not be more different. First, and most obviously, by Gambetta's account Micca had no wish for martyrdom. On the contrary, Gambetta wrote: "Losing his life was a pure cost to him, not a means to achieve anything pertaining to his own self, not even a heavenly reward." Second, his act was not intended to impress an audience. It was, rather, purely instrumental in purpose: to stop the French assailants, regardless of his deed being known.

Micca, Gambetta suggested, "could be dubbed a proto-suicide bomber." But is he a paradigmatic one? The political scientist Robert Pape, to judge by Uri Friedman's recent interview with him,[104] might think so. It is just over a decade on from the publication of his seminal study on suicide bombing,

Dying to Win: The Strategic Logic of Suicide Terrorism, in which he argued that "the bottom line is that suicide terrorism is mainly a response to foreign occupation."[105] From a dataset of 315 suicide attacks from 1980 to 2003, Pape concluded that strategic logic, rather than ideology or religion, explains 95 percent of all suicide attacks around the world. They are "organized, coherent campaigns" to compel a modern democracy to withdraw military forces from a group's domestic territory. "Suicide terrorism," he wrote, "is mainly a strategy to compel democracies to make concessions that will enable a community to achieve self-determination."[106]

Given that neither the United States nor its Western democratic allies occupy territory in Iraq or Syria, and given also that ISIS constitutes the occupying force in parts of those two countries, how does Pape's explanatory model—based on pre-ISIS datasets—apply to the recent attacks in Belgium? Friedman summarizes Pape's view in this way:

> ISIS has trained its sights on countries like Belgium, France, Russia, and Turkey because the U.S. coalition's air and ground campaign, along with military operations by Russia and its ally, Syrian President Bashar al-Assad, have significantly eroded ISIS territory in Syria and Iraq in recent months.[107]

Friedman quotes Pape as saying, "ISIS is now losing in Iraq and Syria—they're losing actually quite badly—and so they're now in a position where they're trying to change a losing game." In other words, per Friedman: "The less in control the organization is at home, the more it strikes at targets abroad." This would suggest that the Brussels attack, just like the Paris attack before it, had a strategic logic: to compel the U.S.-led coalition against ISIS to stop its bombing campaign against the group, its assets, and—in particular—its territory. This certainly appears to be Friedman's understanding of what he describes as "Pape's secular thesis," according to which "Brussels was being targeted for the participation of Belgium, and European countries more broadly, in the anti-ISIS coalition."

There is, however, a problem with this thesis and the broader explanatory account on which it draws: It obscures or minimizes the various non-coercive purposes to which suicide terrorism can be put.

A suicide attack might, for example, be intended as punishment for some real or imagined past offense or wrong, and not calculated to achieve anything beyond that. Belgium, as Friedman points out, "has participated in air strikes against ISIS in Iraq, but not Syria." It is clear that ISIS's leadership views Belgium as a deserving target of retributive punishment for its role in these strikes—and perhaps also because it sees the country as part of a wider cesspool of satanic wrongdoing. But it isn't clear the attacks were informed by any strategic logic, and it's possible that ISIS just wants Belgium to suffer and feel pain. Certainly, ISIS has taken some heavy hits recently, most notably the reported killing of senior commander Omar al-Shishani earlier this month [March 2016].[108] Attacking Belgium, a soft target if ever there was one,[109] is certainly one way of leveling the score.

Another possibility is that a suicide attack may be intended simply to gain maximum attention. Publicity, the philosopher Jeremy Waldron has observed, "is itself a strategic asset" for a terrorist group, which "it can use for all sorts of purposes, not just for the narrow range of intimidatory purposes."[110] "It may be used," he writes, "to win recruits, or to put an issue on the political agenda, or to attract international attention to some situation which the terrorist manages to associate with the campaign." Or, more pertinently in the case of ISIS, given its recent military setbacks and defections, the publicity associated with suicide attacks may be used to fortify wavering followers. As the terrorism expert Clint Watts has argued:

> Recent European attacks, viewed from afar, might imply that the Islamic State is stronger than ever, but it's the reverse: The group desperately needs to show signs of success to shore up its ranks and inspire international popular support. And since those wins are harder to come by in Syria and Iraq, they have started looking elsewhere.[111]

Connected to this is the idea of what the sociologist Mark Juergensmeyer has called "performance violence."[112] Referring to the 9/11 attacks and other "dramatic displays of power," he wrote that "these creations of terror are done not to achieve a strategic goal but to make a symbolic statement." They are, he contended, theatrical expressions of rage and empowerment, an attempt to shake off feelings of humiliation and impotence.

This seems very close to Frantz Fanon's notion of violence as a form of therapy for the perpetrator, particularly where he has suffered ignominy and dishonor at the hands of others. As Fanon famously wrote:

> To shoot down a European is to kill two birds with one stone, to destroy an oppressor and the man he oppresses at the same time: there remain a dead man, and a free man … At the level of individuals, violence is a cleansing force. It frees the native from his inferiority complex and from his despair and inaction; it makes him fearless and restores his self-respect.[113]

Or, as Juergensmeyer put it, performance violence is "empowering in a special way," not because it leads to "conquests of territory or personnel in the traditional definition of military success," but because it's a "sacred drama" in which the perpetrators are dramatically elevated to the status of epic and heroic figures in a cosmic battle.

A further possibility is that a campaign of suicide bombing seeks to provoke the targeted state into responding in ways that will be perceived as repressive and unjust in the eyes of the international community, undermining the state's self-image as a model of freedom and human rights. This seems to be one of ISIS's goals. In an audio message issued by ISIS's al-Furqan Media last May [2015], ISIS's leader Abu Bakr al-Baghdadi warned:

> [I]f the Crusaders today claim to avoid the Muslim public and to confine themselves to targeting the armed amongst them, then soon you will see them targeting every Muslim everywhere. And if the Crusaders today have begun to bother the Muslims who continue to live in the lands of the cross by monitoring them, arresting them, and questioning them, then soon they will begin to displace them and take them away either dead, imprisoned, or homeless. They will not leave anyone amongst them except one who apostatizes from his religion and follows theirs.[114]

Notice that this message has nothing to do with defending territory or compelling the cessation of coalition airstrikes. Rather, it is about fomenting discord between Muslims and non-Muslims in Europe, or in ISIS's terminology, eliminating "the gray zone," a liminal—and, as ISIS sees it, fundamentally corrupt[115]—public space in which Muslims and non-Muslims peacefully co-exist, and maximizing division.[116] It may in fact be the case that, despite the complexities in deciphering what ISIS "really" wants,[117] ISIS's aim is to provoke an intensification of military hostilities, leading to a violent apocalyptic denouement in which it believes it will triumph. It is beside the point just how fanciful that aim is.

The idea that ISIS's decision to launch attacks in Europe is a direct response to its imperiled position at home makes intuitive sense, as does the notion that it is targeting coalition states to coerce them into withdrawing from the coalition. But it is not the only possible scenario. Not all suicide terrorism is Pietro Micca-style suicide terrorism, although Pape's worldview seems to preclude him from acknowledging that.

The Atlantic, March 29, 2016

What If Some Suicide Bombers Are Just Suicidal?

When Brahim Abdeslam bespattered himself in a restaurant in last November's Paris attacks he didn't much look like a man, to borrow the title of Mia Bloom's seminal study of suicide bombing, *Dying to Kill*.[118] He looked, rather, like a man killing to die. If there is a script for doing a jihadist suicide mission, as there now assuredly is, Brahim Abdeslam wasn't following it. He didn't cinematically burst through the doors screaming "allahu akbar." He didn't condemn the restaurant's patrons in bloodcurdling religious language nor profess his avenging motive for Muslims or God. He didn't smile, beatifically, in anticipation of all those black-eyed virgins awaiting him in paradise. Instead, he appeared to trudge dejectedly toward death, covering his face in what may have been a gesture of shame just before detonating his deadly load. Or at least that's how it looked from the CCTV footage of the scene released recently.[119] Miraculously, no one else was killed in the attack, although many sustained injuries.

From the perspective of ISIS, this footage is a total PR disaster: a grainy, low-definition testament to a pitiful suicide mission in which not a single "kaffir" or unbeliever was killed. As an item of atrocity porn, and by ISIS's usual exorbitant, Vimto-hued standards,[120] it is almost banal. And, like the recent footage taken from the headcam of an ISIS fighter killed in battle against Kurdish Peshmerga troops in northern Iraq,[121] the emotion it arouses is more pity than terror, still less awe. But given the pressures ISIS is now under, following several bruising military defeats and intensifying aerial bombardment from the American-led coalition,[122] the PR disaster of one of its "martyrs" looking decidedly un-martyr-like and abject is the least of its current woes.

Was Brahim Abdeslam's abjectness just a figment of the CCTV footage, or was Brahim Abdeslam actually abject? His mother, Faklan, certainly seems to think it was the latter. Her son, she told a reporter, "did not mean to kill anyone."[123] According to a cousin, he took his own life because of "stress." In an interview with the British tabloid *Daily Mail*, Abdeslam's former wife, Naima, who was married to him for two years until they separated in 2008, said "his favourite activities were smoking weed and sleeping. He often slept during the day. The number of joints that he smoked was alarming. Despite his diploma as an electrician, he found no job, it made him lazy."[124] He was also, she said, religiously lax and neither prayed nor attended a mosque, although he did reportedly "keep Ramadan because his family forced him to." This suggests that far from being an ideological fanatic, Brahim Abdeslam may have been depressed. Of course it is impossible to know this with any degree of certainty, since so much about his life remains opaque. And it is clearly naïve to take at face value the testimony of a dead jihadist's relatives, since they have an obvious interest in expressing incredulity about how their ever-so-normal, soccer-playing, Kim Kardashian-loving, Chelsea-supporting, Vans-sneakers-wearing[125] kin could have joined ISIS. But it is not entirely beyond the bounds of possibility that Abdeslam was more interested in ending his own life than those of others—which, in the end, is exactly what he did.

In Islam, as in Christian and Jewish traditions, suicide is generally prohibited: Only God has a right to take the life he has granted. For those who are suicidal, one way of getting around this prohibition would be to sign up to a cause that rhetorically redefines suicide as a communal act of heroic self-sacrifice. As Stephen Holmes puts it in a chapter of the edited collection *Making Sense of Suicide Missions:*

> The social stigma of suicide probably deters some clinically depressed youths in Muslim societies from taking their lives. But the ideal of militant jihad gives them a way to circumvent this taboo. By enlisting in a [suicide mission], a suicidally depressed individual can kill himself with social approval. All he has to do is agree to kill an enemy of Islam in the process.[126]

Even if Brahim Abdeslam was in fact secretly an atheist and didn't believe for a second that he would forever burn in hell for taking his own life, he would still have had a strong interest in presenting his death as an act of religious martyrdom, in the hope that this would forestall the shame that a suicide for personal reasons would have elicited from the wider community of Muslim believers in which he and his family lived. The fact that he didn't succeed particularly well in conveying this impression, since he didn't kill anyone, is beside the point.

Or is it? In *Making Sense of Suicide Missions*, Diego Gambetta acutely remarks, referring to the classical Islamic distinction between "facing certain death at the hands of the enemy and killing oneself by one's own hand," that "as the links between [suicide missions] and their effects becomes tenuous the sacrifice gets murkier."[127] "Why," he adds by way of illustration, "should anyone sacrifice his life for killing a couple of retired Israelis? What exactly is the benefit in that? Why not just leave a parcel bomb and leave?" Gambetta goes on to discuss the views of the Shia cleric Sheikh Hussein Fadlallah, who insisted that the only observable proof that the perpetrator of a suicide mission is not taking his life for a suicidal or self-centered purpose is the number of people he kills or the devastation he causes. "This shows," Gambetta elaborates, "that dying is not itself the purpose but a true sacrifice by a genuine martyr."[128]

It's unlikely that we will ever know Abdeslam's true motives, given how difficult it is to access the dark interior world of another person's self—even more so if that person is dead. But he would not be the first terrorist to kill himself because he no longer wanted to live, masquerading personal suicide as martyrdom.

According to Adam Lankford, in an article published in *Studies in Conflict & Terrorism*, "there are many reasons to think that both event-based and psychological risk factors for suicide may drive the behavior of suicide terrorists."[129] Lankford bases this assessment on a sample of 75 individual suicide terrorists "who may have exhibited … classic suicidal traits." He also draws heavily on an even smaller sample of 15 Palestinian would-be suicide bombers via the work of Ariel Merari,[130] a retired professor of psychology at Tel Aviv University. According to Merari's findings, 53 percent showed "depressive tendencies" (melancholy, low energy, tearfulness), compared to 21 percent of the organizers of suicide missions and 8 percent of the insurgents who engaged in non-suicide attacks. Merari also found that 40 percent of the would-be suicide bombers displayed suicidal tendencies, whereas none of the terrorist organizers were suicidal.[131]

Lankford's argument, however, is deeply controversial—and not least because of the limited sample on which it is based.[132] In fact, the balance of the scholarly evidence suggests that suicide terrorists are, for the most part, psychologically normal individuals who kill and die for a cause they regard as sacred and for comrades with whom they share a deep bond.[133]

It is also a well-established research finding that terrorist groups actively screen out depressed or pathological individuals, due to their unreliability. As Rex Hudson explains, discussing the "highly selective" recruitment procedures of most terrorist groups:

> Candidates who exhibit signs of psychopathy or other mental illness are deselected in the interest of group survival. Terrorist groups need members whose behaviour appears to be normal and who would not arouse suspicion. A member who exhibits traits of psychopathy or any noticeable degree of mental illness would only be a liability for the group, whatever his or her skills. That individual could not be depended on to carry out the assigned mission.[134]

This, however, doesn't seem to uniformly apply to ISIS, which on matters of recruitment, and distinctly unlike its jihadist competitor al-Qaeda, shows a striking level of permissiveness, admitting almost anyone to its ranks. And given the widely advertised sadism of the group, it is more than likely that not a few of its recruits are mentally unhinged in some way.

Does the scholarly consensus—that suicide terrorists are psychologically "normal individuals"—apply to Brahim Abdeslam? Was he unconditionally committed to a sacred cause, as well as to his comrades? He was obviously, at some point, bewitched by ISIS, reportedly watching ISIS videos while kicking back with a beer and a joint in the cafe he used to run with his brother Salah in

Molenbeek.[135] Bewitched enough, also, to have gone to Syria, only to return to try and kill his fellow Europeans in Paris. What isn't yet clear, and may never be, is whether that bewitchment was driven by a death wish or an ultimate cause that he truly believed in, to the extent that he was prepared to die for it.

The Atlantic, May 5, 2016

What's the Right Way to Think About Religion and ISIS?

In his *Atlantic* article on "What ISIS Really Wants" last March [2015], Graeme Wood insisted that "the Islamic state is Islamic. *Very* Islamic."[136] Wood's detractors have been similarly emphatic, arguing that ISIS is a perversion of the Islamic faith.[137] For Wood's critics, secular politics, far more than religion or religious ideology, is the key to understanding the existence and appeal of jihadist violence.

In the immediate aftermath of the Orlando massacre in June [2016], the same arguments resurfaced. According to one line of thinking, the shooter Omar Mateen was a repressed homosexual and his actions are inexplicable without understanding the psycho-social—and hence fundamentally secular—roots of his hatred toward the LGBT community.[138] Correspondingly, "radical Islam" had little to do with the massacre, and Mateen's professed allegiance to ISIS was merely a smokescreen and a way of aggrandizing himself. This would suggest that the Orlando massacre was about secular hate, not religious terror, not radical Islam, not ISIS.

An alternative viewpoint is that Mateen was a lone-wolf terrorist, whose actions were inspired, if not directed, by ISIS,[139] and who took to heart the Islamic State spokesman Abu Muhammad al-Adnani's injunction to carry out attacks in the West during Ramadan.[140] Moreover, according to this viewpoint, Mateen's decision to target the LGBT community in particular, as opposed to unbelievers more broadly, is perfectly explicable in terms of ISIS's murderous homophobia.

These discrepant positions—one emphasizing the secular origins of ISIS-related violence, the other emphasizing its theological roots in "radical Islam"—reflect a deeper difference over the role of ideology in social and political life.

In fact, the ongoing "is ISIS Islamic?" debate is, in effect, a debate between idealists and materialists, and it long predates the current controversies—or more recent ISIS-related atrocities in Bangladesh, Iraq and elsewhere. In *England in the Age of the American Revolution*, published in 1930, the British historian Sir Lewis Namier warned about public figures who summon high moral principles to explain their own actions, and insisted that such professed ideals will be *ex post facto* rationalizations that have little or nothing to do with those individuals' actual motives for acting.[141] Indeed, for Namier, like the Marxist historians he claimed to despise,[142] the ideals invoked by politicians were mere epiphenomena, deployed to conceal intentions of a very different and often inadmissible kind. Namier and his followers were castigated by less hard-headed historians for their cynicism. Herbert Butterfield, for example, argued that many public figures are "sincerely attached to the ideals" in whose name they proclaim to act.[143]

The clash over the role of ideology in human affairs also formed a crucial sub-textual thread in the debate between Christopher Browning and Daniel Goldhagen over the nature and origins of the Holocaust. According to Goldhagen's *Hitler's Willing Executioners*, the "ordinary men" who shot and murdered Jews or else assisted in their deportation to the death camps did so because they had internalized "a Hitlerian view of Jews, and therefore believed the extermination to be just and necessary."[144] Against this, Browning, in *Ordinary Men*, argued that German soldiers killed Jews not because they were virulently anti-Semitic, but because there were powerful "situational factors" in operation that caused them to kill Jews.[145] For Browning, far more important than ideology was conformity to the group or peer pressure: the desire for praise and career advancement, and the fear of being seen to be weak or cowardly for not killing. Commenting on the contrasting explanatory worldviews behind these two conflicting accounts, the philosopher Nick Zangwill wrote, "Goldhagen, in somewhat Hegelian style, thinks that ideology drove at least this segment of history; Browning, in somewhat Marxist style, thinks that ideology did not drive at least this segment of history."[146]

The same division can be seen today in arguments over ISIS, where one set of protagonists insists that ideology in the form of radical Islam is the key to understanding the group's violence, whether directed, inspired or branded, and the other argues that materialist factors, like political grievance or political self-interest or social networks, override any ideological-religious dimension.

According to the Namierite reading of ISIS, the group's rise to power is a story of political state failure in Iraq, where jihadists, in collaboration with ex-Baathists from the previous Saddam Hussein regime, were able to exploit Sunni disaffection and seize territory and resources. Ideology, according to this story, did not drive this historic advance, but rather was, like the territory itself, annexed and refashioned for ISIS's own political purposes. Dalia Mogahed, for example, argued, *contra* Graeme Wood, that "a violent reading of the Quran is not leading to political violence. Political violence is leading to a violent reading of the Quran."[147] Or as *The Atlantic*'s Kathy Gilsinan paraphrased Mogahed: "It's not ISIS's interpretation of Islamic texts that drives its brutality—it's the group's desired brutality driving its interpretation of the texts."[148] In this view, ideology legitimizes ISIS's violence, but it doesn't cause it.

The Namierite reading also extends to the individuals who perpetrate violence in ISIS's name. The British journalist Mehdi Hasan, for example, has pointed out that "it isn't the most pious or devout of Muslims who embrace terrorism, or join groups such as ISIS."[149] Referring to two British men who purchased copies of *Islam for Dummies* and *The Koran for Dummies* prior to joining a jihadist group in Syria, Hasan wrote: "Religion plays little, if any, role in the radicalisation process."

This view has gathered considerable traction since Wood's article was published last year. Writing after the Brussels attacks in March, *The Washington Post*'s Ishaan Tharoor argued that "radicalization is driven less by religious fervor than by more local factors, and it is shaped also by ties to gangs and other criminal activity."[150] Although Tharoor referred to the "complexity" of the causes of jihadist radicalization, he declined to identify religion as a salient variable in the causal mix. Far more important, he suggested, quoting Cas Mudde, an associate professor at the School of Public and International Affairs at the University of Georgia, is the story of how Europe "has created the conditions for the resentment that drives the terrorists."

On the other side of this argument are those who insist, in somewhat Hegelian style, to echo Zangwill, that there is direct relationship between belief and action, and that the former inexorably drives the latter. "Believe," the atheist philosopher Sam Harris has written, "that you are a member of a chosen people, awash in the salacious exports of an evil culture that is turning your children away from God, believe that you will be rewarded with an eternity of unimaginable delights by dealing death to these infidels—and flying a plane into a building is only a matter of being asked to do it."[151] Ayaan Hirsi Ali, a former Muslim who is now among Islam's more prominent critics, similarly contended that the "cause of [jihadist] terrorism" lies in "the ideology of radical Islam." She also wrote contemptuously of the view that religion "is a mere smokescreen for underlying 'real' motivations, such as socio-economic grievances."[152]

But in their rush to either blame or exonerate Islam, participants on both sides of this debate have contrived to ignore what to non-politicized ears must sound like a thundering platitude: Namely, that people who engage in jihadist violence may have mixed motives for doing so, and that these may be both secular and religious in character. As Peter Bergen recently observed, summarizing his research on jihadist activism in the United States since September 11, 2001:

> I found that the perpetrators were generally motivated by a mix of factors, including militant Islamist ideology; dislike of American foreign policy in the Muslim world; a need to attach themselves to an ideology

or organization that gave them a sense of purpose; and a "cognitive opening" to militant Islam that often was precipitated by personal disappointment, like the death of a parent. For many, joining a jihadist group or carrying out an attack allowed them to become heroes of their own story. But in each case, the proportion of the motivations varied.[153]

There is a further sense in which the division between the ideological (or religious) and the material (or secular) is artificial. Even if jihadists in the first instance are motivated by worldly goals, like fame or political grievance, they nevertheless seek to legitimize their violence through an appeal to a religious ideology that, as Graeme Wood has convincingly demonstrated, has a basis, however controversial and contested, in Islamic texts and history. If they did not have recourse to such an ideology, and if such an ideology found no support among a broader constituency, however small, their capacity for violently acting out would be restricted—or grafted on to another culturally available cause. As the intellectual historian Quentin Skinner has postulated, critiquing both Namier and his antagonists, "Any course of action will be inhibited to the degree that it cannot be legitimized."[154] Accordingly, Skinner argued, "any principle that helps to legitimize a course of action will therefore be among the enabling conditions of its occurrence."[155] More succinctly: Ideology is not a sole cause; but it is a cause, insofar as it legitimizes and hence facilitates any course of action.

Omar Mateen, whoever he was and whatever he wanted, needed the warrant of combative Islamic martyrdom, however shakily interpreted, to justify his act of suicidal mass slaughter. And in ISIS he found it. This warrant may not have given him the desire to kill. It may not have led him to kill when he did, who he did, and where he did. But it gave him the moral license, however hallucinatory, to do it, and thus directly facilitated his murderous plan. This is why ideological-religious motifs, as much as personal and political motives, must feature in any adequate attempt to fathom the conundrum of jihadist violence.

The Atlantic, July 12, 2016

ISIS in the Caribbean

This summer, the Islamic State published issue 15 of its online magazine *Dabiq*.[156] In what has become a standard feature, it ran an interview with an ISIS foreign fighter. "When I was around twenty years old I would come to accept the religion of truth, Islam," said Abu Sa'd at-Trinidadi, recalling how he had turned away from the Christian faith he was born into.

At-Trinidadi, as his *nom de guerre* suggests, is from the Caribbean island of Trinidad and Tobago (T&T), a country more readily associated with calypso and carnival than the "caliphate." Asked if he had a message for "the Muslims of Trinidad," he condemned his co-religionists at home for remaining in "a place where you have no honor and are forced to live in humiliation, subjugated by the disbelievers." More chillingly, he urged Muslims in T&T to wage jihad against their fellow citizens: "Terrify the disbelievers in their own homes and make their streets run with their blood."

For well over a year and a half now, Raqqa, the so-called "stronghold" of the Islamic State in Syria, has been subjected to sustained aerial bombardment by U.S., French and Russian war planes.[157] Yet still there are people making the long and precarious 6,000-mile journey from Trinidad to Syria in an effort to live there. Just three days before the release of *Dabiq* 15 [July 31, 2016], eight were detained in southern Turkey, attempting to cross into ISIS-controlled territory in Syria.[158] All were female, and they included children.

In a recent paper in the journal *Studies in Conflict and Terrorism*, John McCoy and W. Andy Knight posit that between 89 and 125 Trinidadians—or Trinis, to use the standard T&T idiom—have joined ISIS.[159] Roodal Moonilal, an opposition Member of Parliament in T&T, insists that the total number is considerably higher, claiming that, according to a leaked security document passed on to him, over 400 have left since 2013.[160] Even the figure of 125 would easily place Trinidad, with a population of 1.3 million, including 104,000 Muslims, top of the list of Western countries with the highest rates of foreign-fighter radicalization; it's by far the largest recruitment hub in the Western Hemisphere, about a four and a half hour flight from the U.S. capital.

How did this happen?

In a 1986 travelogue essay about Saint Lucia, a Caribbean island north of Trinidad, Martin Amis described the place, condescendingly, as "both beautiful and innocuous, like its people."[161] "Even at its most rank and jungly," he continued, "St Lucia has a kiddybook harmlessness."[162] This is all very far from Trinidad, where away from the tourist spots at Maracas beach and the Queen's Park Oval Cricket ground, you can feel an edge and menace on the streets, especially after dark.

On the night I arrived in St. Augustine, a town in the northwest, there was a double murder. The number of murders for the year was already 77, and it was still only February. This was unprecedented, even for Trinidad, where the "overall crime and safety situation" is currently rated by the U.S. State Department as "critical," with 420 murders in 2015.[163] By late June, when I made a second trip to the island, the number of murders for 2016 had soared to 227, a 15 percent increase on the 196 murders over the same period in 2015. Last month, on November 11, it reached 400.

In 2011, the government declared a state of emergency, in response to a wave of violent crime linked to drug trafficking and intelligence reports warning of an assassination plot against the then-Prime Minister Kamla Persad-Bissessar and senior members of her cabinet.[164] At-Trinidadi, along with several others, was detained on suspicion of colluding in the alleged plot. In *Dabiq*, at-Trinidadi alludes to this, but denies any involvement. "That would have been an honor for us to attempt," he acknowledged, "but the reality of our operations was much smaller." He also credited a Muslim scholar named Ashmead Choate as a formative spiritual influence. Choate, a fellow Trini and former principal of the Darul Quran Wal Hadith Islamic School in Freeport, central Trinidad, reportedly left for Syria between 2014 and 2015. According to at-Trinidadi's testimony in *Dabiq*, Choate, who was detained alongside him during the state of emergency, was killed fighting in Ramadi, Iraq.

Prior to 2011, the last state of emergency in T&T was declared in 1990, when, on July 27, a group of black Muslims, the Jamaat al Muslimeen, stormed into the nation's Parliament in the capital city of Port of Spain and tried to overthrow the government, shooting then-Prime Minister Arthur Robinson and taking members of his cabinet hostage.[165] Around the same time, another group of Muslimeen gunmen forced their way into the studio of the nation's only TV station. At 6:30 p.m. the Muslimeen's leader Yasin Abu Bakr came on television and announced that the government was overthrown. This was premature: Six days later, the Muslimeen surrendered, and the government regained control. But history was made. As Harold Trinkunas of the Brookings Institution remarked to *The Miami Herald*, Trinidad is "the only country in the Western Hemisphere that has had an actual Islamic insurrection."[166]

In a telling comment his *Dabiq* interview, at-Trinidadi references this cataclysm in T&T's recent history, alluding to "a faction of Muslims in Trinidad," who "attempted to overthrow the disbelieving government but quickly surrendered, apostatized, and participated in the religion of democracy, demonstrating that they weren't upon the correct methodology of jihad." In Trinidad, the Muslimeen is widely excoriated as a "militant" group, yet it is instructive that at-Trinidadi condemns it for not being militant enough, and for not practicing the right kind of Islam.

The Islamic scene on the island is divided: There is the Indo Islam of the East Indians, who first came to Trinidad in the mid-19th century as indentured slaves, and there is the Islam of the Jamaat al Muslimeen, whose members, many of whom were formerly Christians, are almost exclusively black. These two groups do not tend to mix, still less intermarry. But both, in their different ways, are far from the Salafi Islam that the Trinidadian criminologist Daurius Figueira believes has infiltrated T&T. Figueira, who is Muslim, has written widely on drug trafficking in the Caribbean and, more recently, on the jihadist ideologues Abu Muhammad Al-Maqdisi and Anwar al-Awlaki.

He attributes the growth of Salafism on the island to Saudi proselytizing. "They've spent money and brought in all these Wahhabi scholars from Mecca," he told me when I visited him. "They've passed on the doctrine, then they've started to take the young males and send them to Mecca, and then they come back to Mecca and they continue, so now you don't even need to send missionaries again." The most visible sign of this infiltration, he said, is the hijab: Before the Saudis' missionaries came, Muslim women in Trinidad didn't wear it, but now he said it's relatively commonplace. Figueira was keen to dissociate the Jamaat al Muslimeen from the militant Salafis whom he believes are sympathetic to ISIS. "If you have any understanding of the Jamaat al Muslimeen," Figueira said, "you'll understand that Islamic State will have nothing to do with them because the Muslimeen does not pass the test by Islamic State to be a Salafi jihadi organization."[167]

In a research paper on the Jamaat al Muslimeen, published in the *British Journal of Criminology*, the sociologist Cynthia Mahabir describes how the Muslimeen, after 1990, transformed itself from an idealistic social movement— "a fraternity of 'revolutionary men of Allah'"—into an criminal enterprise, or "Allah's outlaws," to use the title of Mahabir's paper.[168] Figueira puts it like this: "Yasin [Abu Bakr] would never get involved with Islamic State and recruit [people] and send them to Syria, because it's bad for business! They on a hustle, they're hustlers, they looking for a living." According to the analyst Chris Zambelis, this hustle has allegedly involved gangland-style slayings, narcotics and arms trafficking, money laundering, extortion, kidnapping, and political corruption."[169]

On the two occasions when I was in Trinidad earlier this year I tried to meet Yasin Abu Bakr, but he was unable to see me. However, I did meet his urbane and charming son, Fuad, who leads a political party called New National Vision. Fuad, who has inherited his father's height and striking looks, showed me around the Muslimeen compound on the outskirts of Port of Spain. He spoke of his father with great warmth and affection, describing him as "a genuinely good person" who has spent his life defending the underdog and fighting injustice.

From what I'd read about the compound,[170] I had expected to see Abu Bakr's scowling security detail policing the joint, but they were nowhere to be seen. Instead, while I was waiting outside in the carpark with my noticeably nervous East Indian cab-driver, who remained inside his locked and glacially air-conditioned car, I was surveilled by a group of giggling girls, no more than 7 or 8 years old, from an Islamic school on the site. The compound was quiet, and has clearly seen better days. "This place was full, it was a community, people lived here, people were coming in droves," Fuad said, referring to the period just before the attempted coup in 1990. (Afterward, the group declined due to internal feuds and law enforcement's massive curtailing of their activities.) He also spoke wistfully of a period of "communal living, even community justice." "If you had an issue, you came to the imam, and he would send his guys and they would sort it out."

Tentatively, I asked Fuad about ISIS and whether there were recruiters in T&T working for the group. According to local news reports, the recruitment hubs are located in Rio Claro in the southeast and Chaguanas in central Trinidad.[171] "Listen," he said, "there are facilitators, people who are there [in Syria], they communicate to friends. Trinidad is small and the Muslim community is even smaller, so it's basically friends, people you know, who are saying to you, 'you know, do you want to come?' No big, bad recruiter." Yet this not quite the picture I received from one source within the Ministry of National Security, who said there was one particular imam playing the role of "big, bad recruiter."

The source, who spoke on condition of anonymity, said the Trinis who had gone to Syria since the outbreak of the civil war included an entire community of Muslims from Diego Martin, a small town north of Port of Spain. "An *entire* community," he repeated. He also claimed that some leavers had received military training in Trinidad before they left. "There is mujahideen training, or there has been mujahideen training going on in T&T, since about 2007. I was made aware of that in 2009." He received this information, he said, from a trusted confidant from within the Muslim community, and added that it wasn't the Muslimeen, but a more radical faction of Salafis that had splintered from them. I had heard this rumor many times when I was in Trinidad, but this was the first time I'd heard it from a source within the security services. Mark Bassant, an investigative TV journalist in Trinidad, also suspects that some of those who have gone to Syria have undergone weapons training in Trinidad.

When, in the summer of 1498, Christopher Columbus approached the shores of Trinidad, he would have been struck by the richness of the island, with its tropical climate, flowering vegetation, flashing birds, rivers and waterfalls. For more recent visitors, who reach the island by air, it is the richness of Trini culture, vividly exemplified in its annual carnival in February. To outsiders, Trinidad can look like a paradise. But for those many Trinis who are blighted by its high crime rate, rising unemployment, pockets of abject poverty and endemic corruption this proposition is routinely put to the test. This may explain why Islam, with its call to end corruption and oppression and to return to a simpler, more just society, appeals to so many of those from whom Trinidad's myriad blessings are withheld. But this doesn't get us any closer to understanding why so many Trinis have been captivated by the brutal Islam of ISIS.

A more immediate question, and one that's easier to answer, is how so many were able to leave Trinidad to join ISIS. The answer to this is that they were allowed to. Nobody was stopping them. In fact, this was state policy. It was state policy when the conflict first started in Syria, in 2011, and it is still state policy in late 2016.[172] As Roodal Moonilal flatly explained to me, over a drink in the Hyatt in downtown Port of Spain, "ISIS is not proscribed in T&T, meaning that you can go and train with ISIS for 2–3 years and come back here with all the rights and privileges of a citizen of T&T."

Gary Griffith, who served as Minister of National Security between September 2013 and February 2015, told me, when we met earlier this year, that his "concern as Minster of National Security was not them [fighters from T&T] going across—they were free to go across, if they wanted—my concern was to ensure that they do not come back." Griffith is particularly critical of his successor and political opponent Edmund Dillon, for what he sees as Dillon's evasiveness in dealing with the issue of returnees from Syria. Griffith, by contrast, is emphatic: "They should not be allowed re-entry … If they know that it's a one-way ticket to hell, that is the ultimate deterrent." He also expressed indignation that his own proposal to create "a counter-terrorism intelligence unit" for monitoring terrorist threats, launched when he was minister, was blocked by the current government. Dillon, he said, has "a good heart and means well." But "he's burying his head in the sand. He thinks God is a Trini." Dillon did not respond to my numerous requests for comment.

In addition to turning a blind eye to ISIS recruitment, the current government has done little to challenge the spread of Salafi Islam in in the country. Moonilal believes that this, more than derailing ISIS recruitment networks, is the greatest security challenge facing T&T. Yet there are few signs that it will be taken up any time soon.

"We have beautiful sunshine, we have oil and other natural resources, arable land, we have a blessed country," Fuad Abu Bakr told me. But it evidently wasn't enough for at-Trinidadi. A woman identifying herself as his mother told the Trinidad *Express* that, since he left, "His life is better. He has purpose."[173]

The Atlantic, December 8, 2016

How a British College Student Became an ISIS Matchmaker

In March last year [2015], less than two months after arriving in Syria, Umm Muthanna al-Britannia tweeted a picture of herself wearing a burqa and brandishing an AK-47. It was captioned: "Living the life of real freedom." Yet not so long ago she was enjoying a very different kind of freedom, hooking up with guys, wearing make-up and listing her favourite activities online as: "Jamin wid my gyalsz, Sleepin, Munchin, & SmoOkiin."

Umm Muthanna's real name is Tooba Gondal, a 22-year-old French-born, British-Pakistani woman who grew up in East London. Until late 2014 she was a student at Goldsmiths University, taking a degree in English. Today, she is in Raqqa and a widow to a husband who died last year fighting for ISIS. Her father, Mohamed Bashir Gondal, has told reporters that his daughter is alive and in Syria, but has said little else, and hasn't responded to several interview requests for this article.

A prolific Twitter user, Umm Muthanna hasn't posted since mid-March [2016], but in one of her last tweets she paid homage to her deceased husband, Abu Abbas al-Lubnani, an ISIS fighter from Lebanon and ringleader of an online recruitment operation that targeted women and girls in Britain, encouraging them to fly to Syria to become "Jihadi brides" and give birth to the next generation of ISIS militants.[174] Like fellow British citizen Sally Jones—a.k.a. Umm Hussain, the former punk from Kent who left for Syria in 2013[175]—Umm Muthanna is a propagandist and recruiter for ISIS. "Sisters," she tweeted last September, "if you're serious about *Hijrah* [migration to the Islamic State] yet stuck in *Dar ul Kufr* ["land of disbelief"] for whatever reason, know there is a way out for you. Contact me privately."

Earlier this year Umm Muthanna enthused about attending a military training camp where she had practiced using firearms. Now that ISIS has reportedly reversed its policy on sending female recruits into battle,[176] there is a possibility she'll get to put that training into practice—something it appears from previous tweets she would be keen to do. On the evening of the Paris attacks last November [2015], in which 130 were killed by ISIS operatives, she took to Twitter to announce: "Wish I could have seen the hostages being slaughtered last night with my own eyes. Would have been just beautiful."

Umm Muthanna al-Britannia, in other words, is a piece of work. But who is Tooba Gondal?

This remains something of a mystery—and even more unclear is how Tooba transformed into Umm Muthanna al-Britannia. According to an anonymous former classmate quoted in the *Mail on Sunday*, Tooba smoked at school, had secret boyfriends and adored boy bands. Then, about two years ago, "she started posting verses of the Koran on Twitter and talking about religion."[177]

What is clear is that Tooba, like many ISIS recruits, is a "born again" Muslim, having lived a secular life before returning to Islam. "Alhamdulillah for Islam," she tweeted in November 2014, "how lost and astray I was before I had this blessing in my life, and how everything makes sense …" Her Facebook page marks the exact date of her religious awakening or rebirth: "November 16, 2012: The day Allah guided me to Islam, Alhamdullilah."

This awakening was a hinge-moment in her life. And it was so full with meaning and significance that she made an audio-recording in which she tried to convey exactly what it meant to her. She made this available on personal request to scores of her Twitter followers in 2013, two years before she left for Syria. I obtained a copy from someone who received it at around that time. Approximately 40 minutes in length, it provides a vivid insight into the early days of her metamorphosis, and intimates at the strong-headedness and emotional volatility that can be discerned in her subsequent persona as Umm Muthanna.

"Firstly, I will give some background on how I used to think and behave, without revealing my sins too much," she begins, recalling that it was "Year 9 [age 13 to 14] where I started to, you know, go totally off track. I started smoking, got into the habit where it became addiction. And then hanging around with bad company and guys and doing all sorts of *haram* [forbidden] things. But it wasn't to such a bad extent until I got to college. Then I had that freedom, you know? I wore whatever I wanted. As time went on it was getting worse—piercings—without even thinking what I was doing. You know, there was no *haya* [modesty], no limit."

In the recording she notes that her family are practising Muslims. "But I was never home to realise this; I never connected with them," she says. "I believed in Allah and that was it. Nothing resembling a Muslim. Now I realise, of course, I was lost. Every time I thought about Islam I would put it to the back of my mind, and every time I thought about covering up I would put it to the back of my mind and think, 'Nah, that's not me, that's not who I am.'"

It wasn't until that day in 2012, when she would have been 18, that Tooba reverted to Islam. She was in a college tutorial on animal welfare and slaughter for the fast-food industry, and took issue with her "atheist teacher" saying electrocution was the most humane method to kill an animal.

"The halal way is best," she said in response. "Then, as the argument proceeds, we both get very passionate [...] It gets so heated that he takes it to another level, *Subhanallah*. He says these exact words, which I cannot forget. Ever. To this day I remember, and every day I think it sinks in my heart so deep. He goes: 'Who are you to say anything about Islam when you choose what you want to follow and disregard everything else?' Next thing he said: 'Do you pray five times a day?'—this is in front of the whole class—and I sit there shocked. And then I'm like, 'How dare you ask me this question? I will not answer to you, I will not answer to you. I will only answer to Allah on the day of judgment!'"

At this point in the recording, Tooba bursts into tears. "Never have I said these words before," she says. "As soon as these words came out of my mouth my heart sank, and then straight away, at that moment, the bell went and I quickly left the classroom alone. I looked down at what I was wearing and I started thinking, 'How will I stand in front of Allah like this? I've never done anything good in my life.'"

Later that day she approached a fully veiled Muslim from her class and asked her questions about her faith and her jilbab, the long and loose-fitting garment she was wearing; Tooba liked the fact it was "tailored." The following day her friend brought one in for her to try on, as well as a headscarf. "I literally fall in love," she recalls of the moment she saw her reflection in the mirror. "I feel like a new person … I felt so pure and clean and happy."

Before leaving the toilet she took the cigarettes from her bag and threw them in the bin. Then she took all her piercings out and discarded them, too. Her first walk through college dressed in the jilbab was difficult. "I got so many looks," she recalls. "But at the college gates I see my best friend. This is the tightest girl—I've been through thick and thin with her. I thought, 'Hold on: just this morning I was just like her, chilling with the guys, smoking, dressed like that—so how would she react when she sees me?' But I just thought, 'I have to do this, I have to face her.' As soon as she saw me she said: 'What the fuck are you wearing?' to my face. And I went quiet; I didn't have nothing to say to her. But then in my head I was thinking, 'How dare she say this to me— she's meant to be my friend.'"

She remembers one of the boys in the group telling her she wouldn't last two days. "I said to him, 'OK, we'll see,' and then I walked off. Allah showed me exactly who my real friends are. Since that day," she says, "I stopped every-thing that was haram."

But at what point did Tooba start believing in ISIS's fringe version of Islam, and what was the epiphany or turning-point, if any, that led her to embark on her journey to Syria just over two years later? The recording provides no clues, but what's certain is that this didn't happen overnight. In May 2013 Tooba was tweeting about how she pitied "poor atheist souls," but by the end of 2014 she was justifying the slaughter of non-Muslim civilians. In the six months prior to leaving for the caliphate there is a discernible change in the theme and tone of her tweets. They are mostly about Syria and show a new and unguarded belligerence, with some openly condoning ISIS atrocities, including the beheading in October 2014 of Alan Henning.

At some point in 2014 she began to hero-worship the American jihadist cleric Anwar Awlaki, disseminating his theological and political statements on Twitter. Awlaki, a member the al-Qaeda affiliate in Yemen, was killed in a drone strike in 2011. Tooba's admiration for Awlaki brought her to the attention of the now disbanded U.S. State Department's Center for Strategic Counterterrorism Communications (CSCC), whose role was to "counter-message" ISIS and its vast cadre of online supporters. In a tweet about Awlaki, dated October 29, 2014, Tooba said, "We will never forget you! America killed you but you are in highest ranks." The CSCC tweeted back: "Awlaki—another hypocrite held up as a model of piety—visited prostitutes at least seven times."

By the end of 2014 Tooba had fully absorbed ISIS's ideology, and her estrangement from mainstream British society was total. What's unknown is which came first: the estrangement or the ideology. In a flurry of tweets on November 21, 2014,[178] she reported on an incident in one of her university seminars. The subject under discussion was feminism, and when the tutor asked the feminists present to raise their hands, Tooba's un-raised hand drew attention. "Everybody turned to me basically," she wrote. "I explained if you knew your place as a woman, if there was Sharia implementation … These feminists are deluded!" Referring to the icy reaction of her fellow students, she wrote, "they already think I am an alien, being the only Muslim woman covered from head to toe so who cares." It is evident from this, and many other telling tweets, that she felt she didn't belong in Britain and that her place as a pious Muslim was constantly under scrutiny and suspicion.

A persistent theme in her Twitter postings is worldly corruption. In February 2013 she even uploaded to an audio-file sharing site a nine-minute recording in which she passionately warns against what she sees as the dangers and seductions of the material world—or "duniya," as she calls it.

"As a Muslim," she says, "I have to live within certain limits; I can't just do what I want to do and what all my desires tell me to do … I will not allow the materialist world to become my sole source of happiness and fulfilment […] Why is it we find Muslims committing these sins and wrongdoings, violating the laws of Allah, using intoxications, going gambling, going to clubs? Is it because we put more emphasis on this duniya? […] We have to keep strong and firm—we must obey Allah, even if it's against our own selves."

Another recurring theme in her online posting is sexual propriety. On September 19, 2014, she went on Facebook and shared the following post: "I have ZERO men on my Facebook and I will keep it that way. Why allow any males to be my 'friend' on here only allowing them to comment and inbox me. If it can all be avoided that is better, rather than complain later as to why men keep interacting. I don't get any interaction from males of any kind on here. #NoFreeMixing applies online as much as it does anywhere else. Same goes to the lowering of the gaze."

This, you sense, has a deeply personal element to it, reflecting a revulsion against the person she once was: a carefree party girl who was more interested in dating than *dawah*, or proselytising. In *The True Believer* Eric Hoffer wrote that "a mass movement, particularly in its active, revivalist phase, appeals not to those intent on bolstering and advancing a cherished self, but to those who crave to be rid of an unwanted self," and who "see their lives as irredeemably spoiled."[179] This, you also sense, is what ISIS meant to Tooba: an escape-route from a reviled self. Redemption. Yet another rebirth.

It is suspected that Shamima Begum—one of the three east London schoolgirls who left for Syria in February of 2015—had, just days prior to her departure, communicated with the notorious ISIS recruiter Aqsa Mahmood (a.k.a. Umm Layth), a young Scot who was one of the first 60 or more British women to defect to ISIS since 2013.[180] Tooba's Twitter feed in the weeks prior to her departure suggests that she too may have been in contact with Mahmood. It seems unlikely that Mahmood radicalised Tooba, but she may have helped her plan her trip. It also remains unclear what role the ISIS recruiter Abu Abbas al-Lubnani, who Tooba married, played in both her radicalisation and journey to Syria.

In September of 2014 Tooba launched a blog entitled "From Darkness to Light." On the opening page she described herself—in florid script over a photograph of the Eiffel Tower—as a "student, a sister and most importantly a *muslimah*." In her first post she promised: "My unique and very much emotional story of how I came to Islam will be released. Stay tuned guys …"

It never came. She abandoned the blog, only to return to social media just months later as Umm Muthanna al-Britannia, poster-girl for the so-called Islamic State.

Vice, December 20, 2016

Osama bin Laden's Secret Masturbation Fatwa

In January, the U.S. government released 49 new documents seized in 2011 from Osama bin Laden's compound in Abbottabad, Pakistan.[181] Among the items—the fourth and final batch of bin Laden documents made public since 2012—is a letter addressed to a senior colleague in North Africa in which the now-deceased al-Qaeda leader raises "a very special and top secret matter":

> It pertains to the problem of the brothers who are with you in their unfortunate celibacy and lack of availability of wives for them in the conditions that have been imposed on them. We pray to God to release them. I wrote to Shaykh/Doctor ((Ayman)), [al-Zawahiri], and I consulted with Shaykh ((Abu Yahya)) [al-Libbi].
>
> Dr. Ayman has written us his opinion … As we see it, we have no objection to clarifying to the brothers that they may, in such conditions, masturbate, since this is an extreme case. The ancestors approved this for the

community. They advised the young men at the time of the conquest to do so. It has also been prescribed by the legists when needed, and there is no doubt that the brothers are in a state of extreme need.[182]

It is well-known that bin Laden was a fastidious and overbearing micro-manager.[183] But few would have suspected that it extended *this* far. And although it has been widely reported that he was in possession of a porn stash at his Abbottabad compound, it will no doubt come as a surprise that bin Laden, the foremost jihadi of his generation, had thought long and hard (no pun intended) on the issue of masturbation, as has current al-Qaeda leader Ayman al-Zawahiri.

Bin Laden's edict, though, raises more questions than it clarifies: If knocking one out in times of "extreme need" is permitted, how does one define the emergency of "extreme need": Is it a week, a month, or a mere day of celibacy? Alas, bin Laden's letter doesn't shed any light on these burning questions.

All of this is good, harmless fun, of course. But the sexual torment of jihadis is no laughing matter, and may even help explain the genesis of their violence.

In the immediate aftermath of the 9/11 attacks, the evolutionary biologist and world-famous atheist Richard Dawkins poured scorn over the notion that the 19 hijackers were motivated by thoughts of injustice. On the contrary, he insisted, what they really wanted was to get laid. Referring to the "martyr's reward of 72 virgin brides," he claimed that "testosterone-sodden young men too unattractive to get a woman in this world might be desperate enough to go for 72 private virgins in the next."[184]

A more nuanced version of this argument holds that suicidal jihadi violence is rooted in the sexually repressed atmosphere endemic across the Muslim world and in Muslim communities in the West. In both, sexual activity outside of marriage remains taboo—especially for women. According to this argument, the stigma and barriers attached to premarital sex create a frustration that, in some men, boils over into murderous violence. As Christopher Hitchens succinctly put it in his anti-theist polemic *God Is Not Great*, "[jihadis'] problem is not so much that they desire virgins as that they *are* virgins."[185]

This argument draws support from a rich reservoir of anecdotes about jihadis and their ideologues. For example, the Egyptian thinker Sayyid Qutb, who is widely credited as a formative ideological influence on bin Laden, was notoriously disgusted by sex. Yet, few subjects so vigorously aroused his interest and fascination. In one of the articles he wrote about his experience studying abroad in the United States between 1948 and 1951, he registered his revulsion at "the American temptress," with her "expressive eyes and thirsty lips," "round breasts ... full buttocks ... shapely thighs and sleek legs."[186]

In the same article, he expressed his shock at a dance in a church, where "the atmosphere was full of desire." The novelist Martin Amis contended that Qutb's sexual desires, which he was unable to satisfy, "made him very afraid, and also shamed him and dishonoured him, and turned his thoughts to murder."[187]

The so-called ringleader of the 9/11 attacks, Mohamed Atta, was also obviously sexually repressed. He willingly enlisted in a mission that would end his life and those of countless others, but he was terrified of women, refusing to date them or to even shake their hands. In his will, he instructed that his body be prepared for burial by "good Muslims" and that no woman was to go near it. Women, for Atta, as for Qutb, were dangerous and dirty: a source of sin and spiritual contamination.[188]

One of the big problems with linking sexual repression to jihadism, however, is that not all jihadis are sexually frustrated. Moreover, of all those countless Muslims who are sexually frustrated very few become jihadis. There can be little doubt that Atta was sexually tormented—but for every Atta, there is an Abdulaziz al-Omari, another of the 9/11 hijackers, who was married and had a daughter. It is of course possible that al-Omari was sexually bored with his wife. But, unlike Atta, he was not a virgin, and there is no evidence that he was sexually repressed.

Another problem with this linkage is that it forecloses the countervailing possibility that *exposure* to sex—as much as sexual repression—can be a cause of murderous religious violence.

One of the most striking facts about the current wave of European jihadis in Syria and Iraq is their prior secularism, before their conversion to militant Islam. According to the French sociologist Olivier Roy, "they almost never have a history of devotion and religious practice."[189] On the contrary, they engaged in drinking and dope-smoking, and many had a criminal record before becoming jihadis.

Mohamed Lahouaiej-Bouhlel, who killed 86 people last year [2016] in a horrific truck rampage in Nice, France, had a criminal record. He also reportedly drank alcohol, used drugs, gambled, and neither prayed nor fasted. And according to French prosecutor François Molins, he had a "wild" sex life, dating both men and women. One former classmate recalled: "Mohamed was a womanizer, a sexual obsessive … It's all he talked about—that was his principal characteristic."[190]

Lahouaiej-Bouhlel's rapid radicalization remains shrouded in mystery. But it would be unwise to discount the role of his reportedly rapacious sexuality and the possible shame he may have internalized about this in his transformation into a jihadi killer.

Sexual torment also features in life stories of female members of terrorist groups. Mia Bloom, in her extensive research on women and terrorism, argues that women's involvement is driven by a range of overlapping motivations, including revenge, redemption, relationships, and respect. Discussing the Chechen "Black Widow Bombers," who committed suicide attacks against Russia, Bloom points out that many were victims of rape. This, she observed, inflicted an additional wound: the shame of sexual degradation. Paraphrasing one woman who had abandoned her suicide mission at the last minute, Bloom writes: "If you sacrificed your life in the name of Allah and killed some infidels, you would go straight to heaven regardless of your previous sins."[191]

The fixation of Western female Islamic State supporters with sexual propriety may also betray a deeper sexual discontent. In early 2015, I began a year-long investigation into a prominent female British Islamic State recruiter and propagandist who left East London for the Syrian city of Raqqa, the group's de facto capital, in late 2014. This 22-year-old woman, who was born into a Pakistani Muslim family, had lived a very secular life for most of her teenage years and reverted to Islam just two years before her departure for Syria.

According to her testimony, expressed in an audio recording of her "reversion" story, she had previously been something of a sexual libertine. It was clear that this had shamed her. Among the various subjects that most animated her in her many and now-defunct pro-Islamic State Twitter accounts, sexual modesty was foremost. So it is possible that this women's defection to the Islamic State wasn't an "escape" from patriarchal family control,[192] still less a quest for sex, but an escape from sex and the corruption of a sexually permissive society to which she had once succumbed.

Sexuality is so fundamental to a person's sense of self and self-identity that any account of radicalization that does not take it seriously must be considered inadequate. Jihadism, of course, cannot be reduced to sexuality. But neither can sexuality—repressed or untethered—be wholly discounted as a possible catalyst in the development of jihadi zealots. And bin Laden himself clearly saw it as an important factor regulating their effectiveness.

Foreign Policy, February 1, 2017

ISIS Will Fail, but What About the Idea of ISIS?

The Islamic State is claiming responsibility for the London attack that left three people and the attacker dead on Wednesday [March 22, 2017]. "It is believed that this attacker [Khalid Masood] acted alone," Prime Minister Theresa May said, adding that the British-born man, already known to authorities, was inspired by "Islamist terrorism."[193] For its part, ISIS called the attacker its "soldier" in a report published by its Amaq news agency in both Arabic and English.[194] The caliphate, it seemed, was eager to signal to a broad audience that it was as busy and effective as ever. The facts, however, tell a different story.

Back in 2014, God was on the side of ISIS—or so it appeared, and so ISIS claimed, with some plausibility. The speed and scope of its ascent was extraordinary. In mid-June it seized Mosul, Iraq's second-largest city, and in the following months it annexed a Britain-sized swath of territory crossing Syria and Iraq. In his historic June 29 statement, in which he declared the restoration of the caliphate and announced Abu Bakr al-Baghdadi as its leader or caliph, ISIS spokesman Abu Muhammad al-Adnani said:

> It is a hope that flutters in the heart of every *mujahid* [one who does jihad] and *muwahhid* [monotheist] … It is the caliphate—the abandoned obligation of the era … The sun of jihad has risen. The glad tidings of good are shining. Triumph looms on the horizon. The signs of victory have appeared … Now the caliphate has returned … Now the dream has become a reality.[195]

Al-Adnani also warned ISIS fighters that they would face "tests and quakes," and the next few months proved him right about that. But he couldn't have been more wrong about the "triumph" part.

In early 2015 ISIS was at the height of its powers, but since then it has lost about 45 percent of its territory in Syria and 20 percent in Iraq—and with it a vast source of wealth generation.[196] According to research conducted by the International Centre for the Study of Radicalisation (ICSR), ISIS's "annual revenue has more than halved: from up to $1.9b in 2014 to a maximum of $870m in 2016."[197] At the same time, the flow of foreign fighters to the caliphate has plummeted, from a peak of 2,000 crossing the Turkey-Syria border each month in late 2014 to as few as 50 today.[198] The U.S.-led anti-ISIS coalition has reportedly killed more than 10,000 ISIS fighters,[199] including key figures among ISIS's leadership, most notably its senior strategist and spokesman Abu Muhammad al-Adnani.[200] And last month [February 2017] Iraqi government forces took complete control of Eastern Mosul.[201]

More than two and a half years after al-Adnani's statement, "the sun" of ISIS's jihad would appear to be setting. Far from becoming an entrenched reality, ISIS's self-declared caliphate is desperately hanging on for survival and will in all probability return to the dreamscape from which it came. God, it turns out, has switched sides and deserted ISIS—or so it seems, and so ISIS's enemies can claim, with some plausibility.

It's far too early to be writing ISIS's obituary, but it seems likely that the group will lose its hold on Mosul and its de-facto capital of Raqqa in northern Syria by the end of the year, although much will depend on what role the United States takes on in coalition efforts to defeat the group.

What will happen to ISIS—both as a physical entity and as an idea—once it is removed from its territorial bases in Iraq and Syria?

The expert consensus seems to be that ISIS as a physical entity will retreat into the desert, where it will regroup in some form or other, just as it did after the U.S.-led surge in Iraq in 2007.[202] Whether such a retreat will spell the end of ISIS in the long term will depend crucially on the political situation in Iraq. If nothing is done to change the power balance between Sunnis and Shia, and if Sunni civilians are massacred out of misplaced revenge for ISIS atrocities, there is every possibility that ISIS will again return and resume a footing among Sunni communities.[203] As Hassan Hassan put it in *The New York Times*, if there is no Sunni group in Iraq that can "fill the void left by the Islamic State," then ISIS "will once again emerge from the desert."[204]

A return to the desert will almost certainly make it harder for ISIS to mount large-scale attacks on Western targets, although it may intensify the desire to mount such attacks as a way of signaling continuing relevance and resilience to the wider jihadist community. And although surviving foreign fighters may seek to return to their countries of origin to launch attacks there, incidents of remotely guided lone wolf attacks[205] in the West may actually decline, given the diminishing symbolic rewards a degraded ISIS is able to provide distant would-be-martyrs.

Loss of territory will also, as Georgetown's Bruce Hoffman recently observed, greatly reduce ISIS's global appeal, making it difficult to recruit and retain supporters.[206] Indeed, it may even, as political scientist Mara Revkin suggested in *The New York Times*, "trigger a credibility crisis from which the group may never fully recover,"[207] given that ISIS's self-avowed status as the world's preeminent jihadist actor is based almost entirely on its control of territory and ability to govern.

The other point of consensus is that the destruction of the caliphate will not spell the end of the caliphate as an *idea*; it will live on not only in the minds of surviving ISIS members, but also as a free-floating ideological meme in contemporary global culture. ISIS analyst Charlie Winter, for example, has argued that one way in which this meme will be preserved is through ISIS's massive digital propaganda archive. "The caliphate idea will exist long beyond its proto-state," Winter wrote.[208]

No doubt there will be some ISIS foreign fighters for whom territorial defeat of the caliphate will spark a spiritual crisis, prompting disaffection from ISIS and disillusionment with its animating ideology.

But for many others, especially those true believers whose core identity is intricately and indissociably bound up with ISIS, it will spark disaffection from neither the group nor its animating ideology. For these diehards, ISIS will remain the divinely ordained real deal whose setbacks are merely temporary and whose ultimate triumph is guaranteed. It's not that God has abandoned the *mujahids* in favor of the infidel; rather, it's that trial and torment are inevitable on the path of jihad, and must be endured. Even if territorial defeat does occur, it will not be a "true" defeat, as al-Adnani explained in his last recorded massage in May 2016: "Whoever thinks that we fight to protect some land or some authority, or that victory is measured thereby, has strayed far from the truth … O America, would we be defeated and you be victorious if you were to take Mosul or Sirte or Raqqa? … Certainly not! We would be defeated and you victorious only if you were able to remove the Quran from Muslims' hearts."[209]

For others still, territorial defeat of the caliphate may prompt defection from ISIS, but not from its worldview. In John Horgan's research on former terrorists, many belonged to this category: "disengaged" but not "deradicalized."[210] "Often," Horgan wrote, "there can be physical disengagement from terrorist activity, but no concomitant change or reduction in ideological support."[211]

There is some evidence to suggest that many former ISIS members are disengaged but ideologically committed. "Many of the ISIS deserters I have met in Turkey," Revkin wrote, "still identify as jihadists who want to establish some form of shariah-based governance, but they became disillusioned with ISIS when they saw that the group was failing to follow its own strict rules."[212]

A report by the ICSR echoed this: Among a sample of 58 ISIS defectors, only a few had renounced their "commitment to the jihadist ideology," whereas "for the majority, the critique of [ISIS] continued to be framed in jihadist and/or sectarian terms."[213] Terrorism researcher Amarnath Amarasingam categorized ex-ISIS foreign fighters as "disengaged returnees," writing, "While they may rescind their allegiance to a particular militant group, they remain committed to the broader cause of jihadism."[214] According to German authorities, 48 percent of German fighters linked to ISIS and al-Qaeda returning from Syria and Iraq (274 in total) were still devoted to the cause of jihad.[215]

The history of Western supporters of Soviet communism testifies to a similar phenomenon: Although many renounced their membership in the Communist Party and acknowledged its failures, they did not renounce their commitment to the ideals of communism. In *The End of Commitment*, the sociologist Paul Hollander called these unrepentant comrades "the unwavering," those whose "deep attachment to ends and ideals persists in the face of disillusioning experiences."[216] By way of example, he cited the British social historian E. P. Thompson, who, in a 100-page "Open Letter" to the Polish philosopher and ex-communist Leszek Kołakowski, expressed his allegiance not to the Communist Party, "but to the Communist movement in its humanist potential."[217]

Hollander also discussed the case of British historian Eric Hobsbawm, who, though he recognized the flaws inherent in existing communist societies, remained resolute in his commitment to the ends of communism. "The dream of the October Revolution," Hobsbawm wrote in his 2002 autobiography *Interesting Times*, "is still there somewhere inside me ..."[218]

For Hollander, such formidable intransigence, as exemplified by Thompson, Hobsbawm, and a host of other left-leaning intellectuals, is a testament to the power of utopian ideas—and their extraordinary capacity to inspire and retain allegiance even after history has decisively repudiated them.

This intransigence is also a testament to the need to believe—or rather, as the English writer Stephen Spender put it in his contribution to *The God that Failed* (a classic volume of essays by famous ex-communists), "the unwillingness of people to believe what they did not want to believe, to see what they do not want to see."[219]

History will assuredly repudiate ISIS, just as it has decisively repudiated the utopian experiment of Soviet communism. But the idea of the caliphate will remain, despite its tarnished association with ISIS. Just as unrepentant communists said of their utopian vision of a classless society, today's caliphate supporters can say: *The caliphate never failed—it was never tried.*

The Atlantic, March 23, 2017

The Islamic State's Shock-and-Bore Terrorism

It was the advent of the second plane, sharking in low over the Statue of Liberty," wrote Martin Amis.[220] "[T]hat was the defining moment." He was referring to United Airlines Flight 175, the second plane that smashed into the World Trade Center on September 11, 2001. "That second plane looked eagerly alive, and galvanised with malice, and wholly alien," Amis ruminated, adding: "For those thousands in the south tower, the second plane meant the end of everything. For us, its glint was the worldflash of a coming future."

9/11 was a terrible moral outrage. But it was also a terrific visual event, shocking in its destructive immensity.[221] As the philosopher Lars Svendsen puts it, drawing on a distinguished lineage of thinking that goes back to Edmund Burke and Thomas De Quincey and finally to Aristotle: "Violence can give rise to aesthetic delight, even though we find it morally deplorable."[222]

Not all violence, though. In fact, according to the sociologist Randall Collins in his study on the subject, most violence—the violence of everyday life in bars, nightclubs, kebab joints, betting shops, pool halls and jail yards—is so banal and lacking in competence that aesthetic repulsion is the more likely response in those who witness or view it: "[It] is more ugly than entertaining," Collins writes, and thus a world away from the balletic and beautifully choreographed violence of Hollywood movies.[223] Or as Amis memorably captured it in a 1994 *New Yorker* article on screen violence: "In life, the average fistfight, for instance, lasts about a second and consists of one blow. The loser gets a broken nose, the winner gets a broken hand, and they both trudge off to the outpatient clinic. Thus the great Stallone joins the queue at the trauma unit, while Chuck Norris fumbles with his first-aid kit. It just wouldn't play."[224]

Historically, terrorist violence has sought to transcend the quotidian and reach for the spectacular and the catastrophic, showing an acute appreciation for what plays. There are structural reasons for this: Terrorism is intended to communicate a political message to the widest possible audience.[225] That message often takes a coercive form—"do this or feel the pain"—but not always: Sometimes a terrorist atrocity is intended solely to punish a group for its past crimes and injustices (real or perceived) and isn't calculated to achieve anything beyond that. In both cases, however, the message must properly resonate. It must be heard, or else it is pointless. And what ensures resonance or a hearing is the lethality of the attack. Lethality is also a crucial element in the coercive structure of terrorism, for unless a substantial dose of pain and mayhem has already been effectively delivered the threat of more violence isn't fully credible. As the philosopher Jeremy Waldron remarks in an essay on the uses of terrorism: "By imposing [violence] in advance, [the terrorist] demonstrates that he already has the ability and the will to impose harms of the kind he is threatening to impose in the event of non-compliance."[226]

Over the past few years, however, terrorism in the West—often committed at the hands of those claiming affiliation with the Islamic State—has deviated from this essential logic and tended toward the banal and the commonplace. This is reflected not only in the lowly scale of recent attacks but also in the stunning crudity of the weapons enlisted in their commission, as well as in the rank mediocrity of the human capital executing them. If, as the terrorism expert Brian M. Jenkins classically observed more than 40 years ago, "terrorism is theater,"[227] the current theatrical offerings are distinctly half-assed affairs, featuring a cast of B-movie wannabe thespians who can barely remember their poorly scripted lines or why they signed up for the low-budget caper in the first place.

One reason for the shift away from the spectacular is practical: In the West, at least, it's now much harder for terrorists to carry out large-scale atrocities against civilians and symbolic landmarks.[228] This is one of the legacies of 9/11. Political elites' sudden sensitization to the threat of terrorism produced a dramatic securitization of the public and—notoriously—private space. Terrorists, it would seem, have more or less given up on using fully loaded passenger jets as missiles. It's just too difficult, too hard a target to crack.[229] They may not yet have given up on using chemical weapons, but thus far no terrorist group has managed to pull off a mass casualty chemical attack against Western targets.

Another reason for the shift is historical: Terrorism, like every other professional activity in the wider culture, has succumbed to the unstoppable forces of democratization. Terrorism, at least up until the emergence of al-Qaeda in the late 1990s, used to require a talent for violence and subterfuge. It also used to require a *casus belli*, both for the terrorist and the organization to which they belonged. Now, it seems, it just requires a willingness to kill and die.[230] Indeed, now, just about any village idiot can aspire to become a martyr to a cause that politically makes no real sense and that they barely understand.

The Islamic State, more than any other terrorist group, is at the forefront of this development, embracing anyone who can wield a kitchen knife, drive a vehicle, don a vest, or push a button. Even al-Qaeda, which is commonly regarded among experts as an "elite" group, succumbed to these forces,[231] extending a hand to that bumbling imbecile Richard Reid,[232] who is currently serving a life sentence in an American supermax prison for trying and failing to ignite explosives in his shoes on an American Airlines flight from Paris to Miami in December 2001. Terrorism was once the profession of "masterminds" and exotic outsiders; now, with the rise (and fall) of the Islamic State, it has become a playground of punks and losers.[233]

As terrorist groups have become more permissive in their recruitment policies, the scale and sophistication of their attack planning have correspondingly reduced, ushering in a new style of violence that is more squalid than spectacular. Flying planes into tall and iconic buildings, for example, doesn't seem to be on the Islamic State's agenda, but the most brutal beheadings, knifings, shootings and vehicle rammings most definitely are. "If you can kill a disbelieving American or European, then … kill him in any manner or way however it may be," declared Islamic State spokesman Abu Muhammad al-Adnani in September 2014.[234] "Smash his head with a rock, or slaughter him with a knife, or run him over with your car, or throw him down from a high place, or choke him, or poison him," he suggested, setting the template for the recent wave of attacks in the West.[235]

This injunction says more about the Islamic State's declining power and immiseration than it does about its fanatical savagery, although it speaks volumes about this, too. The Islamic State, for all its capabilities and reach, hasn't gotten even close to manufacturing an international terrorist atrocity on the scale and ambition of 9/11. Its most lethal attack in the West was the killing of 130 people in Paris in November 2015. It can still wreak carnage, as the July 2016 attack in Nice, France, amply testified, but it has yet to unleash the sort of cosmic, iconic attack that befits its tough, apocalyptic talk. And although the low-level international atrocities it inspires generate shock and intense, if fleeting, publicity, these outrages are poor at disseminating terror beyond the epicenter of the actual carnage, because the emotions they elicit in the wider audience watching from their TV screens or cell phones are primarily ones of anger and disgust. This is the inherent tension in the Islamic State's current "just terror" strategy:[236] Extreme and transgressive brutality attracts global headlines, but it also brings with it a surfeit of revulsion that crowds out and silences the terror.

And because of the sheer frequency of these attacks they have become normalized in the wider culture, from the ritual of "breaking news" coverage to that of the official reaffirmation of the sanctity of whatever belief system the terrorist acted in the name of.[237] This has created a kind of terror fatigue:[238] a desensitization to atrocity images, and a pornographic lust for ever more prurient details about each new atrocity[239] and the person or persons who carried it out.[240] It has almost made terrorism boring. Almost certainly, it has made it less terrifying.

One of Hannah Arendt's great insights was that the perpetrators of evil, far from being exotically and voluptuously monstrous, are often banal and anemic nonentities. Of the Nazi bureaucrat Adolf Eichmann, she wrote that he was "neither perverted nor sadistic ... [but] terribly and terrifyingly normal"[241]— and hence utterly disproportionate to the enormity of the evil for which he was partially responsible.

There seems to be no such disproportion between perpetrator and deed in the recent wave of terrorist attacks in Europe and the United States. Like Eichmann, the authors of these attacks are mostly ordinary and unremarkable people: the terrorists next door. Far from being "masterminds," they are often misfits, loners or losers. And, also like Eichmann, they appear to have no clear motives at all, other than a generic desire to participate in "something historic, grandiose, unique."[242] But they are not, as Eichmann and his fellow Nazi bureaucrats undoubtedly were, the architects of a dementedly sophisticated evil on the scale of the Holocaust or a 9/11.

The vileness of their attacks is not in question, but there is something stunningly prosaic in how they were conceived and carried out. They are parochial, devolved, amateurish, ugly and uncinematic. They do not create a theatrical spectacle or any overarching narrative. They leave no memorable visual mark on the culture, like, say, the implosion of the Twin Towers. They are as liable to arouse feelings of incredulity and disgust as feelings of fear and terror. They do not change a thing politically. One attack is indistinguishable from another;

the perpetrators are never remembered because each is rapidly eclipsed by the next. "Who," journalists Christopher Dickey and Nadette de Visser acidly remarked, referring to a 31-year-old French national,[243] "will remember the fool who tried to blow up a bunch of gendarmes [on June 19, 2017] on the Champs-Élysées with an improvised suicide car bomb, but only managed to asphyxiate and immolate himself, stumbling half-fried into the street before collapsing and dying?"[244]

For all these reasons, the Islamic State's brand of international shock-and-bore terrorism is a miserable, monumental failure. And in this it is possible to discern a perfect symmetry between the terrorist and the deed.

Foreign Policy, July 27, 2017

The "Softer" Side of Jihadists

"Yes," Elie Wiesel, "it is possible to defile life and creation and feel no remorse. To tend one's garden and water one's flowers but two steps away from barbed wire ... To go on vacation, be enthralled by the beauty of a landscape, make children laugh—and still fulfil regularly, day in and day out, the duties of [a] killer."[245]

Wiesel, a Holocaust survivor, was referring to the ordinary Germans who willingly participated in the destruction of European Jewry in World War II, riffing on a point that has since become conventional wisdom in geno-cide studies and the criminology of collective violence: that, by and large, the perpetrators of mass killing are "normal" people, neither monsters nor sadists, whose capacity for evil coexists with their capacity for good.

Thomas Hegghammer's recent book, *Jihadi Culture*,[246] seems to concur with this: "Yes, it is possible to saw off heads and feel no remorse. To produce third-rate poetry but two steps away from one's sex slave. To sing and pray—and still fulfil regularly, day in and day out, the duties of a jihadi warrior." Actually, this quotation is nowhere to be found in Hegghammer's book, because I made it up. But it does capture the book's central thesis: that jihadi militancy "is about more than bombs and doctrines. It is also about rituals, customs, and dress codes. It is about music, films, and storytelling. It is about sports, jokes, and food."

If jihadists were not so bloodthirsty outside of their downtime, this thesis wouldn't be nearly so jarring or disquieting. But, as Wiesel reminds us, "It is possible to fire your gun at living targets and nonetheless delight in the cadence of a poem, the composition of a painting ..."[247] Or, as in the case of Abu Musab al-Zarqawi, the late leader of al-Qaeda in Iraq, the predecessor to ISIS, it is possible to enjoy your work as a proficient beheader of "infidels" and "apostates" and still partake in a good cry: Zarqawi was known in jihadi circles as both "the Slaughterer" and "He Who Weeps a Lot," the latter being a reference to his inclination to emote and cry during prayer.[248]

And weeping, evidently, is quite a thing among jihadists. So, too, are poetry recitation, hymn singing, dream interpretation, and a whole gamut of other things that serve no obvious strategic purpose. This is the "soft" face of jihadism that *Jihadi Culture* aims to understand, drawing together a range of contributions—on poetry, music, iconography, cinematography, dream interpretation and martyrology—from some of the world's leading "jihadologists."

As a work of scholarship, *Jihadi Culture* is original and ground-breaking, blazing the trail for a social anthropology of jihadi culture that doesn't yet really exist. It is also a work of studied scholarly open-mindedness that foregoes the considerable opportunities for making fun of a culture that takes itself very seriously indeed. (Hegghammer, in his own downtime, is not immune to the joys of laughing at jihadists. Check out, for example, his @ BoredJihadi Twitter account, in which there is a running joke about jihadi training montages. But there is not a trace of this in his scholarship.)

At the heart of *Jihadi Culture* is a deep appreciation for the centrality of culture to jihadi groups, and how it serves not only to bind its members together but also to attract new acolytes. For Hegghammer, jihadi groups are far more than just organizations with doctrinal beliefs; they are also living subcultures that provide emotional rewards to those who participate in them. This is no mere academic matter, for, as Hegghammer suggests, understanding what these rewards are and how jihadi groups meet them "can shed new light on why people join extremist groups."[249]

In the concluding chapter, Hegghammer asks, "What do jihadis do when they are not fighting?"[250] This seems like a straightforward and inconsequential question, yet it is anything but, because it has such a strong bearing on the decisive question of what role (if any) religion, and Islam in particular, plays in the decision-making and behavior of jihadists.

According to one school of thought, religion plays very little role in the motivational structure of jihadism, and explains neither why people join nor why they remain in jihadi groups. Often this claim is made by foregrounding secular psychological states or motives, like alienation, the search for identity or meaning and belonging, outrage over political injustices, and a host of sensually charged desires related to excitement, risk-taking, and sadism. Or it is made by portraying jihadists, variously, as opportunists who exploit religion for political ends, closeted libertines who hide behind a veil of piety, or as cretinous neophytes who know little about their religion.

Jihadi Culture offers a sustained and strongly argued corrective to this school of thought by showing that jihadis spend most of their downtime on devotional and recreational practices that are saturated with religious meaning and content. "It may be true that many militants have a non-observant past," writes Hegghammer, "but my investigation suggests that once they are in a militant group, they take ritual observance very seriously."

"We should not assume," Hegghammer adds, "that their belief is less intense just because they know little about theology." In this, Hegghammer is in agreement with Graeme Wood, who has trenchantly argued against the inclination, common among those who downplay the role of religion in the motivation of jihadists, to "confuse duration of piety for depth of piety; religion for religiosity; and, most tellingly, orthodoxy for belief":

> But that is not how religion works, and it is certainly not how ISIS works. Often, the ISIS foreign fighter is newly pious; he arrives at his piety as a Hemingway character once said he arrived at bankruptcy: slowly, then all at once. He is sometimes inconsistent in his practice. (These very failings, and his own self-hatred over them, are often what drive him into ISIS's redemptive embrace in the first place.) He isn't learned—most people are not, including most pious people—and he consciously rejects the mainstream. Rejecting it is not error. It is the point.[251]

Jihadi Culture is also a vigorous corrective to tabloid-fueled fantasies of jihadists as bloodthirsty monsters. But is it a little *too* insistent as a corrective to these fantasies, a little *too* appreciative of the more soulful aspects of jihadi culture?

On the opening page of the book, Hegghammer writes that "jihadis have a rich aesthetic culture that is essential for understanding their mindset and worldview." "Rich," as journalist Andrew Anthony observed in his profile of Hegghammer, is an odd word choice for a culture that is immersed in prohibition, censure and repression.[252] It is also an unfortunate word choice, because "rich" is a term that morally shades the thing it describes, lending it a positive valence.

This is emblematic of a larger problem with *Jihadi Culture*. So keen is Hegghammer to correct the tabloid construction of jihadists as one-dimensional brutes that he risks going too far in the opposite direction. This is not to say that he excuses—or, still less, justifies—jihadi culture. But the account he offers is an unmistakably favorable one. It is also consonant with the one that jihadists themselves would like to propagate.

Reading *Jihadi Culture*, you will find that jihadists "love poetry," "weep a lot," "talk regularly about dreams," "value personal humility, artistic sensitivity, and displays of emotion," and spend an inordinate amount of time listening to hymns and praying. What you will not read about is the secret, subterranean culture of jihadi groups. Hegghammer makes a big point about jihadists weeping, but it's likely that they masturbate with as much frequency and ferocity as they weep. There's probably also a lot of illicit gay sex in jihadi camps.[253] And there's good evidence to suggest that there's a fair amount of drug-taking among jihadists.[254] But you won't read about any of this in *Jihadi Culture*, because it's so heavily reliant on the idealized jihadi presentation of self in the form of jihadi personal memoirs.

In his classic work *Folk Devils and Moral Panics*, the sociologist Stanley Cohen warned against the danger of being "too respectful" in decoding the "subcultural detritus" of deviant groups—of being too reverential toward "the musical notes, hair styles, safety pins, zips, and boots."[255] This was a reference to 1980s British skinhead culture, and the "deferential care" and "exaggerated contextualization" with which some Marxist-inspired deviance scholars approached it. Cohen, in elaborating on his point, quoted a passage from Claude Levi-Strauss's *Tristes Tropiques*: "While often inclined to subversion among his own people and in revolt against traditional behavior, the anthropologist appears respectful to the point of conservativism as soon as he is dealing with a society different from his own."[256] For Cohen, the core task of the sociologist of deviance is to "understand without being too respectful."[257] If there is a tension in *Jihadi Culture*, it is that it leans too far in the direction of the latter.

In his critique of the Howard Becker School of deviancy sociology, which sought to identify with the deviant and take his side,[258] the radical sociologist Alvin Gouldner noted his impression that "their pull to the underdog is sometimes part of a titillated attraction to the underdog's exotic difference and easily takes the form of 'essays on quaintness.'"[259] Gouldner then went on to accuse Becker of romanticism, comparing him to "the zoo curator who preeningly displays his rare specimens."

It would be unfair to level the same accusation against Hegghammer and his fellow jihadologists, but the charge of sentimentalism is not entirely unwarranted. It's also easy to see how research papers on jihadi dream interpretation and blog posts on jihadi embroidery can be derided as "essays on quaintness." The effect is not unlike that of well-meaning efforts to expose the ordinariness of right-wing extremists:[260] The emphasis on the quotidian serves to obscure the grotesqueness.

The Atlantic, November 30, 2017

Chapter 3

HOW NOT TO THINK ABOUT ISIS

The *Zoolander* Theory of Terrorism

Who knew that *Zoolander* would eclipse *The Siege* as the most prescient Hollywood movie about jihadist terrorism?

The Siege, scripted by Lawrence Wright—who went on to author a ground-breaking study of al-Qaeda called *The Looming Tower*[1]—is a pre-9/11 drama about a wave of jihadist atrocities in New York and the human-rights catastrophe thereby entrained, including the introduction of martial law and the internment of Arabs across the city. *Zoolander*, released just weeks after the 9/11 attacks, is by contrast a comedy about an imbecilic male model who is brainwashed by an outlandish criminal organization to carry out an act of international terrorism.

The movie is inane and frivolous, if occasionally funny. But the brainwashing narrative it parodies is fully earnest, and shows up in some of the more sensational reportage on Western recruits to ISIS, especially the so-called "jihadi brides."[2] Consider, for example, the case of the three East London schoolgirls who absconded from England in February to join the self-proclaimed "caliphate" in Syria. Shamima Begum, 15, Kadiza Sultana, 16, and Amira Abase, 15, were just ordinary teenagers with ordinary teenage enthusiasms—until, as Prime Minister David Cameron put it, they had their "minds poisoned by this appalling death cult."[3]

The *Daily Mail* constructed a similar story. In one report, it claimed that the girls had been "ruthlessly groomed online" and were "brainwashed in their bedrooms."[4] It noted that both Begum and Sultana were prolific Twitter users, and that Begum had followed scores of pro-ISIS accounts, giving her "access to a torrent of appalling images and footage." It quoted Begum's sister as saying, "We love her, she's our baby. She's a sensible girl. … [ISIS is] preying on young innocent girls and it's not right."

This infantilizing narrative is the same one that the parents of Aqsa Mahmood—the 20-year-old ISIS propagandist from Scotland investigated for potential connections with the three schoolgirls—offered to explain their own daughter's radicalization: "She may believe that the jihadists of ISIS are her new family but they are not and are simply using her … Our daughter is brainwashed and deluded."[5] Writing in *The Guardian*, Humaira Patel—herself a female Muslim student from East London—similarly reflected on how the three schoolgirls had been "led astray by people with no morals" and had fallen "prey to a form of virus spreading through the Internet, brainwashing young women and men in the name of religion."[6]

The idea that jihadists are brainwashed or somehow manipulated isn't just a media trope. It also appears to be a foundational tenet of one of the most lauded counter-terrorism initiatives in the world today[7]—the Mohammad bin Naif Counseling and Care Center in Saudi Arabia—even though the center's official materials make no reference to the term "brainwashing."

The center, established in 2004, purports to "de-radicalize" jihadists—or, as the center prefers to call its detainees, "beneficiaries"—through an extensive program of religious re-education. It also provides psychological counseling, convenes classes in creative writing and artwork, and helps with post-treatment resettlement. Underpinning this is the worldview that jihadists are misguided about the authentic nature of Islam and their religious obligations, and that these lost souls must be returned to the correct path. All this comes out clearly in the research of my doctoral student Mohammad Almaawi, who has undertaken an empirical analysis of the center's practices and philosophies. One staff member told Almaawi that the majority of detainees were, in his view, "simpletons" whose youth—most are in their early 20s—and "lack of knowledge [made] it easy for extremists to target them and influence their way of thinking." The solution to extremism, this staff member said, lay in the propagation of "true" Islam, by which he apparently meant the apolitical and conservative version defined by the center and the Saudi state.

Harvard terrorism scholar Jessica Stern encountered similar views among staff members in 2010, following her own visit to the center. "A Saudi official," she wrote, "told the group of us who visited ... that the main reason for terrorism was ignorance about the true nature of Islam."[8] She observed that "the guiding philosophy" behind the center's efforts "is that jihadists are victims, not villains, and they need tailored assistance—a view probably unacceptable in many countries."

In the context of Western counterterrorism policy, the Saudi initiative may look like an innovation. But the rhetoric surrounding it in fact mirrors that of anti-cult groups in America during the late 1970s. In their research on the "cult scares" of that era, Anson Shupe and his colleagues noted that the notion of "brainwashing," and the reverse process of "deprogramming," formed the centerpiece of anti-cult activism and legitimized the physical abduction of cult members to protect them from the "demonic" embrace of the cult and its manipulative gurus.[9] Shupe's co-author David Bromley has argued that the "captivity narrative" promulgated by anti-cult groups framed the cult member as a dupe, a naive innocent "subjected to overpowering subversive techniques."[10] According to Bromley, anti-cult activists believed that through deprogramming they could liberate cult members from mental enslavement and convert them back to normality, helping them disavow "the cult-imposed personality" and return to their "natural, pre-cult personality."

The idea that terrorists are brainwashed ostensibly serves as an objective and value-free causal explanation: X became a terrorist because of Y's bad influence. Only it's not just that. It also serves as a delegitimizing device since it contains the unmistakable and highly moralized implication that joining a terrorist group (or a group proscribed as such) isn't actually a conscious choice predicated on reasons. It is, rather, an occurrence orchestrated by others, a process that takes place without the knowledge of the person who undergoes it. Terrorists, in other words, are suckers, fools, the instruments of someone else's will and evil designs.

This idea also promotes the reassuring myth that the roots of terrorism lie away from and beyond a given moral order. It allows people to believe that it is not their own revered texts, revered institutions, revered cultures, or deepest aspirations and values that produce terrorists, but reviled outsiders who occupy the shadows and exploit the vulnerable and the simple-minded.

But what scholarly research on terrorism overwhelmingly shows is that terrorists, in the main, are not only *not* crazy,[11] but also *not* stupid.[12] Furthermore, it shows that people who join terrorist organizations tend to do so because they believe they are defending what they see as a just cause. They join because they want to, and because they think that what they are doing is right and necessary. And in the case of Westernized jihadist "wannabes," many, as Scott Atran and Marc Sageman have observed,[13] are self-recruiters who actively seek out violent action before they become fully radicalized into the ideology of jihadist Salafism.

A potentially richer discourse for talking about terrorism is one that takes terrorists seriously not as dupes but as autonomous moral agents who feel the gravitational pull of terrorist organizations, allow themselves to be seduced by their message, and make themselves available as potential recruits, willing to sacrifice themselves for the cause and the group. Understanding this, and not how they have been "brainwashed," is the graver and more urgent explanatory project.

Terrorism is primarily a moral, and not an intellectual, failure: a violation of our common humanity and the sanctity of all human life. Terrorist groups invest great energy in ideologically justifying their depredations and rank criminality, casting themselves as defenders of the good. The key task for any de-radicalization program is to expose this fallacy and confront terrorists with the fundamental inhumanity of their actions. One way of doing this is to bring them into direct contact with the human pain and suffering they unleash. There is strong evidence to suggest that this works in conventional criminal-justice settings, and that offenders who are brought face-to-face with their victims are less likely to reoffend.[14] It may yet work for terrorists, but only if we first credit them with the moral and intellectual abilities we so readily ascribe to ourselves.

The Atlantic, May 12, 2015

The Pre-Terrorists Among Us

Philip K. Dick's *The Minority Report* is a short story about a dystopian future in which there are "no major crimes," but a mass of imprisoned "would-be criminals." This is thanks to "Precrime," a criminal-justice agency whose preventive efforts are directed by a trio of mute oracles called "precog mutants." The inherent and dark illiberalism of this approach is not lost on Precrime's chief John Anderton, who concedes, "We're taking in individuals who have broken no law." The film adaptation of the story was described by the film critic Peter Bradshaw as an "allegory for a hi-tech police state which bullies villains and law-abiding citizens alike with self-fulfilling prophecies of wrongdoing."[15]

To a certain degree, the future Dick envisioned has already arrived. It comes in the form of "Countering Violent Extremism" (CVE), a set of "non-coercive" counterterrorism initiatives—embraced in the United States, the United Kingdom, and elsewhere—aimed not only at de-radicalizing or disengaging convicted terrorists, but also at preventing "at risk" individuals from becoming terrorists in the first place.[16]

Unlike Precrime, CVE doesn't license the mass imprisonment of would-be terrorists. But it does promote interventions that are intrusive and stigmatizing, targeting those who, to echo Anderton, have broken no law—but, as U.S. President Barack Obama recently put it, are "vulnerable ... to violent extremist ideologies."[17] British Prime Minister David Cameron struck a similar note in a speech earlier this month [October 2015], promising to introduce yet more measures in the United Kingdom to tackle extremism "in all its forms," including the "non-violent," insisting that it was necessary to "stop this seed of hatred even being planted in people's minds."[18]

Who are the so-called extremists in our midst? They are everyone and no one, promiscuously crossing the gamut of social backgrounds and personality types: men, women, teenagers, children, grandparents, as well as a whole kaleidoscope of exes: ex-punk rockers, ex-medical students, ex-gangbangers, ex-engineers, ex-rappers, ex-male models. And this is just from the jihadist spectrum. Who becomes a terrorist is anyone's guess, although where you live[19] and who you are related to and know[20] are more salient factors than how you think[21] and how poor you are.[22]

The idea that there is no single, all-encompassing terrorist profile is now something of a conventional wisdom among scholars.[23] Yet the notion that terrorists, like mythical demons, take on a recognizable shape, however spectral, is strongly implicit in CVE preventive thinking. In Britain, the face of CVE is the "Prevent" strategy, a putatively "community-led" approach first launched in April 2007 and now mandated by the U.K.'s 2015 Counter-Terrorism and Security Act.[24] Its central aims are to counter "the ideological challenge of terrorism," and to offer "practical help to prevent people from being drawn into terrorism."[25] Terrorism, as Prevent constructs it, isn't a form of political activism that sentient people choose to engage in for reasons, however poorly conceived; rather, it's an ideological contagion—a "disease," as Cameron described it in February [2015][26]—that afflicts the vulnerable and "risks" their safety and well-being.[27]

The British government's radicalization "referral" program aims to stop this contagion through "early intervention" before it takes hold, though it's not fully clear what such intervention actually involves.[28] It is now a statutory obligation for specified community partners, including social workers, teachers, probation officers, and "credible community organisations," to monitor for "vulnerability indicators" that suggest people are "turn[ing] towards terrorism," and refer those who manifest these indicators to the authorities.[29] Such indicators include "spending increasing time in the company of other suspected extremists;" "changing … style of dress or personal appearance;" "loss of interest in other friends and activities not associated with the extremist ideology, group or cause;" "possession of material or symbols associated with an extremist cause;" blaming others "for all social or political ills;" and "using insulting or derogatory names or labels for another group."[30] Since ISIS's dramatic rise to prominence last year, the number of referrals to the program has skyrocketed: There were 796 referrals this summer [in 2015] alone, more than in the entire first year of the program from 2012 to 2013.[31]

Similar notions about how to detect radicalization underpin CVE programs in the United States, Canada, Australia, and France. A document the Australian government published last month [September 2015] warned that people undergoing radicalization can display "significant behavioural changes in major areas" of their lives, ranging in severity from "changes in normal behaviour" to expressions of hostility "towards people they see as the 'enemy'."[32] The Royal Canadian Mounted Police, in a 2014 handbook co-produced with the Islamic Social Services Association and the National Council of Canadian Muslims, advised concerned parents to be aware of signs that can manifest in "at-risk youth," such as "sudden onset of anti-social behaviour; spending excessive … time online, especially at night when most of the family is asleep; … excessive secrecy regarding what sites they are visiting online, where they are going, who they are meeting; … [or] external and overt expression of hyper-religiosity."

It is easy to scoff at this. Yet the emphasis on physical appearance and speech as cues of personal identity is not entirely off the mark, and finds support in a range of social-science research. The sociologist Helen Rose Ebaugh has studied how people communicate via "cuing" that they have undergone a decisive life-change.[33] Ex-nuns she observed, for example, would grow their hair long, experiment with new clothing styles, and "relearn ways of carrying their bodies so that they would not be identified as 'nunnish'."[34] Other research testifies to the centrality of the body as a vehicle for symbolic self-expression. As the sociologist Chris Shilling, one of the founding scholars of body studies and author of *The Body*,[35] told me, referring to religious individuals, "people's physical appearance serves as a canvas on which they affiliate themselves to their faith via markings that not only display their allegiance, but also prompt within them regular emotional reinforcements of this identity."

Do radicalized individuals cue their transformation toward ideological militancy in their "body canvas" and outward behavior? In *Murder in Amsterdam*, Ian Buruma recorded how Mohammed Bouyeri's adoption of jihadist ideology was preceded by a series of notable behavioral shifts. In a period of just a few months, Bouyeri, a once very secular person born to Moroccan parents in the Netherlands, radically changed his appearance, discarding his Western street clothes for a djellaba and prayer hat; growing a beard; renouncing alcohol, weed and women; and severing all ties with friends from his past.[36] Not long after this transformation, and inflamed with ideological fever and righteous fury, he murdered the film director Theo van Gogh, proclaiming at his trial that it was his religious obligation "to chop off the head of anyone who insults Allah and the prophet."[37] This was a direct reference to van Gogh's and Ayaan Hirsi Ali's *Submission*, a short film in which lines from the Quran, specifying a man's right to beat his wife, were superimposed on the naked body of a woman.

Yet the cues Bouyeri gave off are also the very same cues one might expect to see in anyone who has undergone a conversion toward non-violent or pacifistic Islamic religious conservatism, and do not necessarily indicate conversion into the Salafi-jihadist fold. The danger of CVE is that it risks conflating the two and promotes an atmosphere of mistrust. There are many cases in which ordinary Muslims have been singled out and harassed—not for anything they may have done, but because of the suspicious minds of others, who see a Muslim man reading a scholarly book on terrorism and think "terrorist,"[38] or who read support for Palestine as support for global jihadism.[39] Even converts to radical Islam—or the "non-violent extremists" whose ideology Britain's new strategy aims to counter, in addition to the violent variant—aren't necessarily appropriate targets for suspicion. As the terrorism scholar John Horgan puts it, "The overwhelming majority of people who hold radical beliefs do not engage in violence ... and ... people who engage in terrorism don't necessarily hold radical beliefs."[40]

Another major weakness of CVE lies in its naïve and simplistic view of social life, of which so much is theater, and where how people act is often at variance with their unvarnished "backstage" self. Erving Goffman, the foremost exponent of this "dramaturgical" view of social affairs, wrote that "a performer tends to conceal or underplay those activities, facts, and motives which are incompatible with an idealized version of himself,"[41] and remarked on the prevalence of "disidentifiers"- affectations or props intended to convey normalcy—among stigmatized groups.[42]

In his study of men who visited public restrooms in search of sex, Laud Humphreys described how the men, 54 percent of whom were married and living with their wives, would adopt conservative postures in public so as to detract from their then-illicit sexual liaisons with men and boys.[43] In Goffman's terminology, they were "disidentifying," much like the 9/11 hijackers, who made a point of shaving their beards[44] and visiting strip clubs prior to launching their attacks.[45] ("How conveeenient," Andrew Sullivan mordantly remarked about that stratagem.[46])

CVE seems blissfully ignorant of this theatrical dimension of everyday social life, and the lengths to which people go to conceal their innermost thoughts and feelings. "I couldn't believe it, I can't believe it ... My son ... loved music and breakdancing and football ... He wanted just to work, to have a nice cellphone, a laptop or nice clothes," said Radhia Manai, the mother of Seifeddine Rezgui, who this summer calmly slaughtered 38 people at a beach resort near the city of Sousse in Tunisia.[47] But her account could stand in for any number of recent jihadist-assassins, like 15-year-old Hassan Mahania, whose father reportedly told the BBC journalist Jeremy Bowen that "his son was a typical teenager, not political and certainly no radical."[48] Clearly, such accounts are self-exculpatory, serving to immunize the parents of terrorists against the criticism that they should have intervened to stop their children's murderous actions. But they may also be sincere and truthful.

The Atlantic, October 27, 2015

Europe's Joint-Smoking, Gay-Club Hopping Terrorists

Last month [March 2016], CNN released video footage of Brahim Abdeslam and his younger brother Salah dancing in a nightclub alongside a blond woman, with whom Brahim, the report claimed, was flirting.[49] "This was life before ISIS," the voiceover to the report says. "It's Feb. 8, 2015. Just months later, Brahim would blow himself up at a Paris cafe; Salah becomes Europe's most wanted man."

But was it life before ISIS? The automatic assumption in the report is that drinking and flirting are indicative of a secular and thoroughly unIslamized state of mind—and that wannabe jihadis don't jive or flirt. The report also assumes that something intense and convulsive happened to the Abdeslam brothers in the intervening period between Feb. 8 and Nov. 13, 2015—though it sheds no light on what that was.

Among scholars, "radicalization" is commonly understood as a gradual process in which people adopt ever more extreme postures and beliefs.[50] It is widely thought that this process begins with a dramatic event or personal crisis, paving the way for a "cognitive opening"—a receptivity to alternative views and perspectives—and a period of religious seeking, often mediated by an extremist mentor and a wider social network.[51]

"Radicalization," viewed from this perspective, is a process of self-transformation, where the transformed person comes to view themselves and the outside world in a fundamentally different light. And though scholars disagree over exactly how and where this occurs, there is a broad consensus that radical self-change lies at the heart of the process and that terrorism, though not an automatic outcome of radicalization, is inexplicable outside of it. The assumption is that while not all radicals become terrorists, all terrorists are radicals.

The Abdeslam brothers, with their sudden escalation from dancing in nightclubs to killing in them over the course of a few months, seem to challenge this picture. They also raise a deeper and more troubling question for those seeking to understand the genesis of terrorist acts: What if they were not "radicalized" and underwent no dramatic metamorphosis at all? What if their violence had only the most tenuous connection to what they believed, whatever that was? What if the story of how they came to be involved in terrorism had no real coherent narrative arc? What if the script of terrorism doesn't always feature the drama of radicalization?

According to one of the two friends who filmed the nightclub footage, the Abdeslam brothers "were nice people ... I suppose you could say they lived life to the full." The other friend, going by the name "Karim," adds: "I saw Salah joke, smoke, drink, and play cards ... If anything, he liked women. He was something of a ladies' man, and I heard he had a girlfriend at one point." The CNN report continues, "At the time, the friends said they had no idea that the two had embarked upon their journey toward radicalism ... 'They must have been changing bit by bit.'"

Or not. According to a *Sunday Times* report, Salah Abdeslam was seen in a gay bar as recently as a month before the Paris attacks. The report also quotes Karim, an apparent close friend of the brothers: "Brahim and Salah spent most of their days smoking hashish and playing on PlayStation in the bar … There was nothing to suggest they were radicalized."[52]

Referring to the secular lifestyles of the November 2015 Paris attackers, Islam expert Mathieu Guidère suggests that this behavior "may have been an example of *taqiya*, or calculated pretense, in which the warrior preparing for 'martyrdom' melts in with the enemy, adopting his way of life, to avoid detection."[53] Or it may have been no such thing, given that the Abdeslam brothers, unlike the 9/11 attackers who shaved their beards and visited strip clubs in the months prior to their mission, were not operating in enemy territory but in indifferent and supposedly jihadi-friendly Molenbeek.

Another possibility is that the Abdeslam brothers were in the process of becoming radical jihadis and that their secular habits were a hangover from the previous lifestyles that they were trying to walk away from. Or maybe they were, in fact, radicalized but living in a state of cognitive dissonance, drinking and dancing the one minute, and railing against the ways of the *kuffar* the next, much like the righteous men in Laud Humphreys's *Tearoom Trade*, who, when not publicly bemoaning the decline of family values, were out cruising for gay sex in restrooms.

But perhaps the more realistic—and in some ways more unsettling— scenario is that the Abdeslam brothers drifted in and out of jihadi activism and that this owed more to who they knew and how they lived than anything they believed.

More than half a century ago, the criminologist David Matza described, in a now classic text, how juvenile delinquents drift in and out of delinquency.[54] They are able to do this, Matza argued, because the delinquent subculture, in its embrace of excitement, its disdain for work, and its celebration of violent machismo, is actually an extension rather than a rejection of conventional society.[55] There is no ideological conversion to an alternative deviant worldview, Matza posited—just a temporary crossing over to a subterranean world that embodied, in grotesque caricature, the codes of mainstream society.

Despite its seeming exotic otherness, and for all its theological quiddities, the world of the Islamic State is not wholly disconnected from that of our own. Its ideals of heroic self-sacrifice, adventure, violence, and machismo are mirrored, albeit in a secularized and far more muted form, in our own culture; they find less constrained expression, for example, in our movies. In other words, the breach between those who join the Islamic State and "us" is not as deep as we would like to think. It is even narrower in the case of Molenbeek in Brussels, where a hybrid subculture of crime, violence, and jihadi activism has taken root.[56] The *Washington Post*'s Anthony Faiola and Souad Mekhennet describe members of this subculture as "part terrorist, part gangster":[57] liminal badasses who exist between two overlapping worlds, for whom, as terrorism expert Rik Coolsaet documents in a recent study of Belgian foreign fighters in Syria and Iraq, "joining [the Islamic State] is merely a shift to another form of deviant behavior, next to membership of street gangs, rioting, drug trafficking and juvenile delinquency."[58]

Whether terrorists like the Abdeslam brothers have been "radicalized" in the traditional sense is more than a matter of academic debate. Government programs aimed at Countering Violent Extremism (CVE) have embraced the transformational view of radicalization: Implicit in their language and rhetoric is the idea that terrorism is the end stage of a process in which people come to adopt an extremist worldview that justifies violence. CVE tries to map out this process, identifying signs of radicalization, which include changes in personal appearance and the "overt expression of hyper-religiosity," so as to intervene to obstruct its development. Yet cases like the Abdeslam brothers highlight the possibility that, when it comes to CVE, we still have very little idea of what actually constitutes best practices. As terrorism scholar John Horgan observed, "There is evidence that not all those who engage in violent behavior necessarily need to possess radical beliefs."[59] He elaborates, "A lingering question in terrorism studies is whether violent beliefs precede violent action, and it seems to be the case that while they often do, it is not always the case."

In the coming weeks and months, the world's media will continue to wonder how the "well-liked" and "ever so normal" Abdeslam brothers became ardent jihadis at war with the West, mining their pasts and our own failures and wrongdoings to explain what "drove" this transformation. Yet it is possible that no such transformation occurred. This isn't a good story, because it contains no dramatic epiphanies or conversions. But it may turn out to be true.

Foreign Policy, April 13, 2016

What ISIS Women Want

What do Western women who join Islamic State want? One prominent theory is what these women "really" want is to get laid. Another is that they don't know what they "really" want, because what they want has been decided for them by male jihadi "groomers." Both theories are meant to resolve a seeming paradox: How can any woman who enjoys democratic rights and equality before the law join or support a group which actively promotes her own oppression? But both are misconceived. Indeed, they say more about the gendered assumptions of those who proffer them than about the women they are trying to explain.

The idea that Western Islamic State "fangirls"—as they are often derogatively called—"just wanna have fun" (to paraphrase Cindy Lauper) is the thesis of, among others, Shazia Mirza, a British comedian whose latest show is called "The Kardashians Made Me Do It." The show's title references a comment made by one of the sisters of the three East London schoolgirls who absconded to Syria in February 2015. "She used to watch *Keeping Up With the Kardashians* and stuff like that, so there was nothing that indicated that she was radicalized in any way—not at home," Sahima Begum said about her missing sister, Shamima.[60] This gives Mirza's show its central theme, which is that the Western girls who join the Islamic State, also known as ISIS, share the same banal and all-too-human concerns as their non-jihadi Western peers — including, and especially, when it comes to love. Mirza's argument is that the Islamic State, for teens like Begum, is just another teenage crush. Indeed, the Islamic State, she suggests, is like a boy band—only with guns.[61]

"I'm not being frivolous," Mirza said in a recent TV interview, "but, these ISIS men, as barbaric as they are, you have to admit, they are hot. They're macho; they're hairy; they've got guns. And these girls think, 'These are a bit of all right.' What they've done is sold their mother's jewellery and bought a one-way ticket to Syria for some halal meat."[62] Or as Mirza phrased it in her 2015 Edinburgh show, referring to the three East London runaways: "They think they've gone on a Club 18–30 holiday to Ibiza … They're not religious; they're horny."[63]

This is funny—and Mirza, after all, is a comedian. But it isn't serious as a commentary on the motives of the Western women who have joined, or aspire to join, the Islamic State. Yet many news organizations have taken up the idea as though it were. Earlier this year, for example, CNN ran a news story titled "ISIS using 'jihotties' to recruit brides for fighters."[64] This was only slightly more cretinous than a BBC Newsnight report from March 2015 proclaiming, "Attractive jihadists can lure UK girls to extremism."[65]

Another way of not taking Islamic State "fangirls" seriously is to suggest that they have been "groomed" over the Internet by shadowy, charismatic men into believing that the Islamic State is the solution to all their problems. In March 2015, Hayley Richardson wrote in *Newsweek* that militant fighters "are using similar online grooming tactics to paedophiles to lure western girls to their cause."[66] Sara Khan, the founder and co-director of the anti-extremism NGO Inspire, echoed this. "Just like child abusers groom their victims online and persuade them to leave their homes and meet them," she claimed in the *Independent*, "male jihadists contact women through social media and online chatrooms, and build trust with them over time."[67]

This is a gendered reading of radicalization: Young men are not "groomed" by charismatic women who prey on their emotional weaknesses and naivety. Only women are groomed. Only women lack the necessary agency and political engagement to *want* to support or join the Islamic State. Mirza's reading of women's radicalization is similarly patronizing, but it at least puts women on an equal footing with male Islamic State jihadis, who, presumably, from within her one-dimensional worldview, also want to get laid.

The problem with the grooming narrative is that it seriously misrepresents women's radicalization as an essentially passive process and obscures, as numerous studies show,[68] the striking degree to which young women themselves are actively involved in recruiting likeminded "sisters" to the cause. It also presents an unreal picture in which women and young girls are somehow "targeted" and then seduced by online recruiters, drastically overestimating the recruiter's powers of selection and persuasion. Everything we know about radicalization suggests otherwise: that potential recruits actively seek out the message and the messenger (and that the decisive facilitator in radicalization is typically not an anonymous predatory online recruiter, but a trusted friend or family member).[69]

Over the past year, I have spent an unhealthy amount of time tracking the social media activities of Western English-speaking female Islamic State supporters as part of a wider research project on the subculture of Western jihadism. (Most of their accounts have since been shut down.) And what these women—or at least the more brazen and vocal among them—want they have made abundantly clear. Far from being slaves to their sexual desires or victims of the predatory machinations of men, many Western women join or aspire to join the Islamic State because they *want* to—because the Islamic State, unlike the secular liberal democracies in which they live, makes sense to them and reflects their fundamental moral and political convictions. What they want is to live in a properly authentic Islamic state in which Islamic law—sharia—is fully implemented. Specifically, they want to live under the "caliphate," which, they believe, it is their divine duty to support. What they do *not* want is to live in the West, for a multitude of reasons. They do not want freedom, as understood by classical liberal scholars as negative freedom—the freedom to act without restraint or interference from others.[70] And they do not want feminism. They want *submission*: to God's will and his divine law.

Consider, for example, Umm Muthanna, a 22-year-old British woman and former university student who left for Syria earlier last year. In a flurry of tweets, posted in November 2014, just months before she left Britain, Umm Muthanna recalled an incident in one of her university lectures. It provides fascinating insight into the antifeminist mindset of the Western women who leave to join the Islamic State:

Today's lecture was on Feminism … Then on came the seminar … Subhan'Allah the tutor started discussing gender differences and roles in society. Fine, I will listen and make notes but does not mean I accept your constricted ideologies. Short time after, the tutor asks a question … "Raise your hand if you are a feminist." I wanted to burst out with laughter, which my niqab helped contain. Result? … Majority of the women, 18/20 put their hands up. I sat there whilst everybody glanced at me! Haha, I felt proud, but pity for their souls … Then, here it where it gets interesting. The tutor asked, so those who are not feminists, explain why.

Everybody turned to me basically … And I said clearly, Islam has given all my rights to me as a woman and I feel liberated, I feel content and equal in society and all. I explained to them, how both men and women have rights in Islam, given us to in the Qu'raan, (at this point every-body was screwing). I explained to them not everything which a man can do, a woman can also compete with and try do. It's to do with biology. I explained how this western society has made you think in a certain way, pressurised you to feel weak and always thirsty to make money. Pressurised you to compete with men, when in reality if you knew your place as a woman, if there was Shari'ah implementation, you would not be complaining like you are now. I said all this and basically everybody tried refuting me. These feminists are deluded![71]

The big taboos for many of these women, as for all religious fundamentalists, are related to sex and gender equality. Peer inside their online lives, and it becomes clear that this is a major animating concern. They cannot abide free mixing of the sexes, which they condemn as a "disease." They cannot even abide the idea of revealing their eyes, let alone face, in their Twitter profile photos, since this would imperil their sexual modesty—and hence impugn their devotion to God. And they explicitly warn "brothers" not to "DM [direct message]" them. The Islamic State appeals to these women, not, as Mirza insists, because it has a bountiful supply of "halal meat," but because it per-fectly coheres with their militantly conservative notions of sex and gender. Hence, they support the Islamic State not despite, but *because of*, its aggressively patriarchal worldview.

Scott Atran, an anthropologist at Oxford University and France's National Center for Scientific Research, in his current research, describes these women as "postfeminist and post-adolescent."[72] He writes, "They are tired of a seem-ingly endless, genderless, culturally indistinct coming of age. The Islamic State and al-Qaeda provide clear red lines: Men are men, and women are women." Which is to say that men are warriors and women are mothers, whose primary duty, as Umm Muthanna put it in one tweet, is "to raise the next generation of lions in Islamic State." "My GOAL," she declared, "is to have lots of sons

& send them off all feesabillilah ["in the cause of Allah"] … under the Islamic State." The hashtag attached to this tweet was #RealWomanGoals. This does not mean, as Atran and other researchers have made clear, that female Islamic State members or supporters are disapproving of violence.[73] On the contrary, many seek to justify and even to encourage it. Umm Osama, for example, who is an online friend of Umm Muthanna, recently felt brave enough to issue an incitement for suicide attacks, reminding brothers of their heavenly rewards on achieving martyrdom. "To brothers," she tweeted, "when you get so excited hoping for 7ooris"—that is, wide-eyed damsels, or female companions—"remember this n say 'Mahraha adDugma' (u can do it)."

These women's greatest anxieties are related to *dunya*, or the material world, which they condemn as corrupt and polluting. This is why the niqab is so symbolically important: It acts as a protective shield against worldly poison and vice. As Andrew Sullivan perceptively observed, describing the logic of fundamentalism, "Sin begets sin. The sin of others can corrupt you as well."[74] Hence the appeal of the caliphate: a state in which sin is violently punished and constantly purged from the public body.

Yet, for all their efforts to escape the polluting stain of the material world, these women are irrevocably marked by it. They enjoy its technologies and blandishments. And, for all their efforts to Islamize their inner and outer selves, there is, as Mirza so humorously shows, an inner Kardashian in these women that coexists uneasily with their righteous selves. They record the minutiae of their daily lives, posting selfies of their latest niqab styles or photos of food they have prepared. They share their admiration for the latest "banging" *nasheed*, an a cappella hymn. They warn sisters to beware of "spies" and give shoutouts to their imprisoned sisters. One female Islamic State supporter, who uses the Twitter handle "OumDujana," even lets us inside her bedroom. It is a fascinating spectacle. In a 9-second recording she uploaded, we are shown what appear to be numerous collections of hadiths, an intricately pimped-out shrine to the Islamic State, and several boxes of Nike trainers. This woman, unlike the *Islam for Dummies* wannabe jihadis, plainly knows her religion. But she also likes her Nike trainers, though not as much as her iPhone 6.

Who is Oum Dujana? She is based in London and may have been born in Belgium or France. She is young—22, she says—and of North African heritage. Like many female Islamic State supporters, she is precocious, and her tweets show a lively intelligence and active political engagement. (Her account has since been shut down.) She appears to be intensely religious. In one tweet, she makes a reference to being under "heavy obbo," or observation, and in another refers to a police raid on her house. She also alludes to a husband in a warzone, perhaps Syria, Libya, or Iraq. Either she has tried to leave for Islamic State-controlled territory or she is married to an Islamic State fighter—or both. Regardless, she seems deeply committed to the caliphate ideal and to the Islamic State. It is impossible to know how she acquired that commitment. But infantilizing this woman as a vulnerable child or sexualizing her as a repressed Muslim is unlikely to cast much light on this.

No one is more sensitive to this disparagement than the women themselves. "Idiots that are tweeting this trend," tweeted Umm Waqqas, a Seattle-based Islamic State online recruiter who was exposed by Britain's Channel 4 News last year,[75] "should realize that NO SISTER leaves the comfort of their homes just to marry some man." She was referring to the hashtag #jihadibrides. "They cant fathom the reality," she immediately added, "that muslims from all ages are leaving to live in a REAL muslim country & to live under the shades of Sharia." Or as Oum Dujana more succinctly put it last month, "CNN said we [gonna] marry #Jihotties LOOOL."

Foreign Policy, May 17, 2016

Anjem Choudary and the Criminalization of Dissent

There is something unsettling about the conviction of Anjem Choudary,[76] and the chorus of approval that has followed it, from Muslims and non-Muslims alike.

A disciple of the Islamist cleric Omar Bakri Mohammed, who fled Britain for Lebanon in 2005, the 49-year-old former lawyer was a founding member of al-Muhajiroun, a banned Islamist group that had once called for jihad against India, Russia, and Israel and defended the 1998 U.S. Embassy bombings in Africa. For 20 years, Choudary had made a career out of Islamist activism, becoming a rent-a-quote radical the British media have been only too willing to enlist. He is a larger-than-life character, whose jihadi rhetoric and outlandish posturing make him the perfect scapegoat for assuaging fears over the real jihadis who remain hidden among us and seemingly come out of nowhere, making a mockery of our counterterrorism efforts. He is, in other words, a distraction, whose monstrous celebrity diverts us from the more unpalatable reality of the jihadi terrorism we face.

As far as we know, Choudary has not plotted to murder and maim innocent civilians; he has not tried to join the Islamic State in Syria, Iraq or any other provinces under the group's control, preferring to stay put in godless Britain, under whose generous patronage he lives; and he has not given money to the Islamic State or solicited funds on its behalf. Choudary's offense, rather, is to have pledged support for the group and encouraged others to do the same.

Choudary and his associate Mohammed Mizanur Rahman were convicted on July 28 [2016], but details of the trial, including the verdict, could not be reported until a few days ago, when the Metropolitan Police issued a statement announcing the convictions. According to the statement, Choudary and Rahman were found guilty of inviting support, between June 29, 2014, and March 6, 2015, "for a proscribed terrorist organisation, namely ISIL, also known as ISIS or the Islamic State, contrary to section 12 Terrorism Act 2000." For this, they face up to 10 years in jail and will be sentenced on Sept. 6 [2016] at the Old Bailey.[77]

The case seems to have hinged on the following evidence: On July 2, 2014, Choudary and Rahman met in a restaurant where they convened a Skype meeting with Mohammed Fachry, a convicted terrorist based in Indonesia. During this meeting, both men pledged their allegiance to the Islamic State and its leader, Abu Bakr al-Baghdadi. Fachry, with Choudary's permission, then published this oath on an Indonesian website. "The oath of allegiance was a turning point for the police," said Cmdr. Dean Haydon, head of the Metropolitan Police Service Counter Terrorism Command.[78] "At last we had the evidence that they had stepped over the line and we could prove they supported ISIS."

The police statement also notes that Choudary and Rahman "are believed to have been recruiters and radicalisers for over 20 years and have been closely associated with another proscribed organisation Al Muhajiroun [ALM]." Yet, strikingly, it does not cite or allude to any evidence supporting this claim.

Of course, there is no doubt that Choudary, over many years, disseminated speeches and wrote material that was hateful, especially toward moderate or nominal Muslims, whom he and his fellow activists in al-Muhajiroun regarded as apostates fit for slaughter. It is also clear, based on the police statement, that Choudary personally supports the Islamic State and tried to persuade others to follow him in such beliefs. But we have no evidence that Choudary went any further than that—say, by facilitating the journeys of men and women to Islamic State territory.

And despite his associations with convicted terrorists, like Michael Adebolajo, and Islamic State members, like Siddartha Dhar, we have no firm evidence that Choudary was the driving force behind their radicalization, or anyone else's for that matter. Indeed, it is not even clear that such evidence could ever be available, given the impossibility of counterfactually demonstrating that the men supposedly radicalized by Choudary would not have undergone this transformative process had they not met him. Yet none of this has prevented the British media, which loves to hate Choudary, from portraying him as the Keyser Söze of the British Islamist scene, radicalizing hundreds of men, as though these poor souls had no agency in their own life stories but were "brainwashed" by Choudary's awesome demagogic powers.[79]

Choudary, as the British journalist Andrew Anthony observed in his illuminating profile of the cleric, no doubt has a certain charm and charisma.[80] But it stretches credulity to believe that this man's sermonizing made anyone do anything they didn't already want to do, still less that they would risk everything because he told them to. It also dangerously mischaracterizes radicalization as a one-dimensional, low-budget, made-for-British-TV psychological drama of "shadowy," "charismatic" recruiters manipulating "naïve" and "vulnerable" malcontents. Whereas the little we know about radicalization[81] suggests the opposite: a convoluted and unscripted process where real people with limited knowledge, resources and power collide and make extraordinary decisions.

But even if Choudary's rhetorical powers were as formidable as his condemners suggest, this wouldn't alter or minimize the wrongheadedness of convicting him under terrorism legislation, when the behavior for which he was convicted has little or nothing to do with terrorism, as standardly defined as, in the words of the philosopher C. A. J. Coady, "the organized use of violence to attack noncombatants or innocents (in a special sense) or their property for political purposes."[82] Choudary's offense, rather, relates to a speech-act: namely, that of supporting the Islamic State and defending its legitimacy as a state. As a British citizen, this also makes Choudary a defector: someone who has gone over to the other side.

The deeper significance of Choudary's conviction is that it inaugurates a new and disturbing phase in Britain's pushback against "extremism": the criminalization of radical dissent and defection. Before Choudary's conviction, the drastic widening of the definition of terrorism to include speech-acts was an abstract worry here (the United States, for its part, began moving in this direction in 2013[83]). But now it's real.

The irony is that the thinking behind Choudary's conviction is not altogether different from that of his own. According to Choudary's worldview, a perfect Islamic society would violently punish those who rejected its foundational tenets. When asked on Fox News in 2015 about his attitudes toward apostates (i.e., those who have renounced the Islamic faith) Choudary was clear and categorical: They should be put to death.[84] This is a view that finds support across the four major schools of Islamic law, and reflects a widely held belief among classical Islamic scholars that apostasy is as grave an offense as murder, since it threatens the very unity of the Muslim community—the ummah—from within.

As the Egyptian cleric Yusuf al-Qaradawi put it: "Waging war against Allah and His Messenger by speaking openly against them is more dangerous to Islam than physically attacking its followers ... moral mischief in the land is more hazardous than physical mischief."[85] Choudary is not facing the death penalty for his sundry speech crimes, but the impetus behind his conviction is informed more by concerns over his "moral mischief" than by any physical threat he poses. The same thinking and anxieties underlie Saudi Arabia's decision, taken in 2014, to criminalize atheism as terrorism.[86] But of course atheism is no more terrorism than is defection from Western values.

Choudary is a clown with odious views. But he should not be criminalized, still less branded as a terrorist, for espousing these views. Rather, he should be subjected to trenchant criticism and ridicule. In Choudary's imagined utopia, it would be a capital offense to criticize Islam and the Prophet Mohammed. By criminalizing views that challenge its defining principles, liberal democracies risk replicating the unfreedom that Choudary so brashly and shamelessly stands for.

Foreign Policy, August 19, 2016

"The Real Housewives of ISIS" Deserves a Laugh

Crazy, blood-curdling, infidel-hating, bearded dudes are clearly very funny, as anyone who has watched the film "Four Lions" knows. Released in 2010, Chris Morris's dark satire follows five wannabe jihadists on their quest to strike a blow against the unbelievers of Britain. In the tradition of Chaplin sending up Hitler, Morris portrays these characters as more clueless idiots than fearsome fanatics, more morons than masterminds.

But what about crazy, blood-curdling, infidel-hating, burkaed-up young women recruited to the jihadi cause? Are they funny, too? The makers of a new BBC comedy show, which features a sketch in the form of a video trailer for "The Real Housewives of ISIS," obviously think so. The central conceit behind the lampoon is that the supposedly pious and puritanical Western sisters of Islamic State are just as shallow and catty and materialistic as their secular counterparts on TV in the West. Raqqa, the stronghold of the so-called "caliphate," is a world away from New York, Beverly Hills and Atlanta, where the real "Real Housewives" TV shows are set, but whatever: A girl still needs to look good.

One ISIS housewife exclaims: "It's only three days until the beheading, and I've got no idea what I'm gonna wear!" A few moments later, two of the wives are modeling the same suicide vest. "What a complete bitch, she knew I had that jacket, [she] copies everything," complains one to the camera in a "confession" shot. Coming next week: "Ali bought me a new chain, which is eight foot long. So I can almost get outside, which is great." The speaker is shown chained to her stove.

The video, which is just under two minutes long, has attracted more than 14 million views on Facebook and a raft of undeserved outrage.

As many as 850 British citizens have traveled to support or fight for jihadist groups in Syria and Iraq,[87] including at least 56 women and girls in 2015 alone.[88] Many left with great fanfare and exuberance, loudly advertising their defections on social media, as well as subsequently using Twitter and personal blogs to record their everyday activities in the newly formed caliphate.

Aqsa Mahmood (who has taken the name Umm Layth) left Scotland at 19 for Islamic State-controlled territory in Syria. On her blog she advised those thinking of following her lead: Bring good quality bras and underwear. "The shoes here are also bad quality," she added in one post.[89] "They only seem to have 3 sizes here lol so maybe bring a pair of trainers with you."

Other Western women in Islamic State have posted tweets extolling the virtues of covering, sharia punishment and Islamic schooling along with supposedly enticing pictures of pizzas, kittens and Nutella. In April 2015, just two months after arriving in Syria with two other east London schoolgirls, Amira Abase tweeted a photo of Western-style takeout: a picnic in the caliphate.

This, as "The Real Housewives of ISIS" testifies, is rich comedic terrain. But it's also elaborately booby-trapped. Can you really joke about terrorism? More to the point: Can you joke about British women and girls "groomed"—as the media narrative goes—to leave home and marry terrorists?

ISIS, incontestably, is a moral abomination. And its murderous rampage through Iraq and Syria is no laughing matter. But the men and women who actively signed up to its cause often are a joke, and the only sane response to them is derisive laughter.

However, many people have evidently taken grave offense at "The Real Housewives of ISIS." Their comments tend toward exaggerated and incoherent nonsense—about "gendered Islamophobia" and how the sketch mocks Islam, which it plainly doesn't. But the outrage nonetheless raises some important questions about what is fair game. According to the writer Will Self, true satire "afflicts the comfortable and comforts the afflicted," and when it's directed at religiously motivated extremists "it's not clear who it's afflicting, or who it's comforting."[90] A lot of the anger about "The Real Housewives of ISIS" seems to concur with this: The *real* real housewives of ISIS, and even Muslim women in general—because of the stigma they're often subjected to—simply aren't funny.

The problem with this view is that it's radically at odds with how the Western women of ISIS view themselves, which is not as oppressed victims but as spiritually redeemed martyrs to their faith. The other problem is that it infantilizes minorities by assuming that they're unable to handle the critique satire delivers. Such an assumption, as the intellectual historian Stefan Collini has rightly observed, is "ultimately corrosive of genuine respect and equality."[91]

"In a democracy," wrote the legal philosopher Ronald Dworkin, "no one, however powerful or impotent, can have a right not to be insulted or offended."[92] This applies not just to the bearded oppressors of the Islamic State but even to the women who risk everything to live under their dominion.

The Los Angeles Times, January 10, 2017

Trump's Travel Ban Will Not Help ISIS Recruitment

The conventional liberal wisdom on the Trump administration's executive order suspending immigration to the United States from seven Muslim-majority countries—also known as "the Muslim ban"—is that the ban is as counterproductive as it is illiberal.[93] The argument, roughly, is that with the order signed on Friday, the Trump administration has "played into the hands" of ISIS and other jihadist groups, giving a boon to their propaganda motif that America is at war with Islam.[94]

This argument is also widely shared among counterterrorism experts and commentators, who worry that the travel ban will imperil "the gray zone" that defines and facilitates the liberal democratic order. The "gray zone," as conceived by ISIS propagandists, is the liminal—and, as ISIS sees it, fundamentally corrupt—public space in which moderate Muslims and non-Muslims peaceably co-exist.

Trump's travel ban, his critics claim, puts that zone in grave jeopardy by creating a polarization that risks pushing more Muslims into the arms of the jihadists. The ban, Jessica Stern argued in the *Boston Globe*, is "likely to make us *less* safe."[95] Paul Pillar, a former official at the CIA's Counterterrorism Center, echoed this: "[The order] is not targeted at where the threat is, and the anti-Islam message that it sends is more likely to make America less safe."[96] According to Nada Bakos, a former CIA analyst: "All it [the ban] does is help [Islamic State] recruiting."[97]

On the crucial matter of moral principle, the conventional liberal wisdom is right: The ban is parochial and un-American and will deal a massive injustice to hundreds of genuine asylum-seekers fleeing war and genocide. But the argument that it will aid ISIS recruitment just doesn't stand up to scrutiny.

First, it contains a contemptible implication about Muslims: namely, that they're not thinking, reasoning individuals capable of agency, but mere vessels of feeling in a larger geopolitical game between America and the jihadists. From within this dehumanizing perspective, your average Muslim doesn't *do* anything, and he or she certainly doesn't make things happen. Rather, things are done or happen to them; they are "pushed" or "driven" to extremes by forces beyond their control. They are "inflamed," "provoked," "humiliated." They are, in other words, a negative emotion waiting to happen. The former Islamist and writer Maajid Nawaz calls this "the racism of lowered expectations." No doubt many Muslims oppose the ban, but the idea that some of the more "vulnerable" among them—to use the Countering Violent Extremism (CVE) buzzword—will want to wreak murderous vengeance for it against their fellow Americans is dangerous.

Second, and connectedly, it posits an overly simplistic understanding of jihadist radicalization, linking this exclusively to grievances over domestic and foreign policy. But everything we know about radicalization and terrorism suggests that it is far more complex than this and cannot be reduced to secular political grievances. Of course these grievances cannot be discounted and are, as Peter Bergen has convincingly concluded in his research on American jihadists, complexly and confusingly mixed with a range of other motives, including religious and personal ones.[98] But it is profoundly misleading to prioritize these above all others in an effort, however understandable, to amplify the idiocy of Trump's travel ban.

Third, it displays a thundering insensitivity to the ironical and contradictory aspect of the whole ban trainwreck. Trump's ban, argue his critics, has indirectly gifted ISIS propagandists.[99] The main piece of evidence cited for this claim is that a small number of anonymous ISIS fanboys have cited the ban as evidence for the "true" face of an anti-Islamic America.[100] Writing in *The Atlantic*, the analyst Charlie Winter suggests the possibility that ISIS—at some point—may incorporate the ban as a rallying-theme into its "narrative of victimhood,"[101] even though ISIS has hitherto preferred the register of victory over victimhood,[102] and in spite of the fact that the actual victims of the ban are regarded by ISIS as apostates fit for slaughter.

Far from "gifting" ISIS, what the ban has in fact given it is a poisoned chalice. In America, it has generated a raft of critical commentary from leading politicians,[103] and it has provoked a wave of vociferous protests in major cities that has brought Muslims and non-Muslims together in solidarity.[104] What the ban has done, paradoxically, is *solidify* the gray zone against which ISIS is fighting. It has revealed not a satanic American face but a pacific and liberal one. As the Lebanese satirist Karl Sharro joked on Twitter, "Trump didn't think this through. Now there are Friday protests in the US."[105] This was captioned above a news report with the headline "Detroit Protesters Laid Down Their Protest Signs So Muslims Could Pray."[106] However ISIS's leadership decides to spin these displays of solidarity, it is hard to imagine that such symbolically powerful advertisements for the "gray zone" will be greeted with hand-rubbing glee.

Aspiring jihadists, of course, are as eager to slaughter anti-Trump protesters as they are Trump supporters. But it would be a staggering assumption to suppose that Muslims generally are unable to discriminate between good and bad Americans, and that the more cognitively or emotionally impressionable members of the Muslim community will absorb ISIS's—as yet unvoiced— ban-themed propaganda pitch.

The fourth and most serious blind-spot in the conventional liberal wisdom on the travel ban is the suggestion that it will make *Americans* less safe. Rather, it risks making American *Muslims* less safe, because it will further embolden the far right in America, legitimizing their fear and loathing of the group. The recent massacre of Muslims in a mosque in Quebec could have been long in the planning, but the exact timing of it, just days after Trump's travel ban was chaotically implemented, may not have been coincidental.[107]

In a wonderfully rich and entertaining public discussion of monsters in writing, sponsored by *The New Yorker*, Martin Amis alluded to the Freudian concept of "priority magic."[108] "The big monsters," he said, "have this huge stage to be monsters in, but they create little monsters … Once the big figure, like Osama bin Laden, has done something atrocious, then all the followers feel the priority magic, feel that the ground has been cleared for moral nullity."

This may well be the real legacy of the travel ban and of Trump: that his hateful and polarizing rhetoric has cleared the path for a violent blowback aimed not at non-Muslim Americans, but at ordinary, decent Muslims who even liberal Americans can't help but implicitly demonize as terrorists-in-the-making.

The Atlantic, February 1, 2017

Terrorists Are Not Snowflakes

Something profound and seismic is happening in the way Western societies understand terrorism, and jihadi radicalization in particular.

Until now, the terms of the debate were set by two master narratives about terrorists, usefully categorized in an *Atlantic* article published just over 30 years ago by Conor Cruise O'Brien as the "hysterical stereotype" and the "sentimental stereotype."[109] The former saw terrorism as a form of pathology perpetrated by "'disgruntled abnormal[s]' given to 'mindless violence,'" whereas the latter characterized it as a form of political resistance mounted by "misguided idealist[s] … driven to violence by political or social injustice or both."

In the years since the publication of O'Brien's article, however, these two narratives have gradually lost their intellectual and cultural prominence, thanks in part to the enormous impact of Hannah Arendt's thinking on the "banality of evil"[110] and the enormity of the 9/11 attacks, which, as terrorism scholar Peter Neumann observed, made it "very difficult to talk about the 'roots of terrorism',"[111] still less to sentimentalize terrorists. In their place a very different paradigm has emerged, driven by efforts to rethink the problem of terrorism in response to the rise of al-Qaeda and, more recently, the Islamic State. At the center of this paradigm is the notion of the terrorist as an infantilized "other": a marginal person whose outstanding characteristic is vulnerability. You might call it the "snowflake theory of terrorism."

This view is clearly an advance on seeing terrorists as either crazed fanatics or social justice warriors, but its paternalistic implications are just as dangerous as those implicit in the two paradigms it displaced.

The explanatory rhetoric of the snowflake theory of terrorism could not be more different from that of the earlier two paradigms. Far from being a symptom of psychological dysfunction or political injustice, terrorism, in this new reframing, is redefined as a "risk," borne mainly by the would-be perpetrators of terrorism rather than the would-be victims of future terrorist atrocities. Far from seeing terrorists as perpetrators of violence for political ends, this theory recasts them as victims of "extreme" ideas propagated by manipulative "groomers." Nearly always, the terrorism or "risk" in question is the contaminant of jihadi-based terrorism, although the proponents of this paradigm commonly insist that it also applies to other forms of terrorism, including that of the far right.

These explanatory tropes and motifs underpin the prevailing ideology of "Countering Violent Extremism" in both Europe and North America. In Britain, for example, the 2015 Counter-Terrorism and Security Act[112] makes it perfectly clear that terrorism is a "risk" to which people can be "drawn into." It's now a legal requirement for specified authorities, including schools, colleges, universities and child care services, to conduct risk assessments to identify individuals "vulnerable to radicalization." In a 21-page document, which provides statutory guidance for the relevant authorities listed in the 2015 Act, the word "risk" appears 67 times.[113] In all cases, the risk in question relates to the "risk of individuals being drawn into terrorism." The word "vulnerable," in the context of "vulnerable to radicalization," appears 13 times.

In his remarks at the Leaders' Summit on Countering ISIL and Violent Extremism in September 2015,[114] President Barack Obama similarly used the language of safeguarding in reference to radicalization. "And finally," he said, "we recognize that our best partners in protecting vulnerable people from succumbing to violent extremist ideologies are the communities themselves— families, friends, neighbors, clerics, faith leaders who love and care for these young people."

The same tone of paternal care informs a lot of media commentary on Western members of the Islamic State, who, it is claimed, were "brainwashed" or "groomed" by recruiters into joining the group. Referring to the three East London schoolgirls who absconded to Syria in February 2015, Sara Khan, the founder and co-director of the anti-extremism NGO Inspire, wrote in *The Independent* that "they were groomed," adding, "Just like child abusers groom their victims online and persuade them to leave their homes and meet them, male jihadists contact women through social media and online chatrooms, and build trust with them over time."[115] Hayley Richardson, in *Newsweek*, similarly insisted that "ISIL are using similar online grooming tactics to pedophiles to lure Western girls to their cause."[116] In 2015, *The New York Times* ran a feature on a lonely and mentally unstable young woman from rural Washington who had been befriended online by Islamic State supporters and "flirted" with the idea of going to Syria.[117] Despite the idiosyncrasies of her case—the only Muslims she knew were those she had met online—and the fact that she had never set foot in Islamic State territory in Syria and Iraq, *The Times* asserted that her story may "provide clues about how ISIL recruits new members around the world."[118]

Or consider journalist Kurt Eichenwald's recent article for *Newsweek*, titled, "How Donald Trump Is Fueling ISIS."[119] According to Eichenwald, the president's rhetoric and policies send "a new message … that reinforces the jihadi extremists' propaganda and increases the likelihood that more Americans will die in attacks." Imagining the response of Western Muslims to Trump's use of the phrase "radical Islamic terrorism" he writes, "The emotional reaction of Muslims who are torn about whether to fight against the West would be strong." "ISIS could not have asked for more," he continued, ventriloquizing this time for the terrorist group that the world's vast majority of Muslims condemns. "If such words can anger an ally as important as the Turkish president," referring to Recep Tayyip Erdogan's rejoinder to German Chancellor Angela Merkel's use of the term "Islamist terror,"[120] "what impact does it have on ordinary Muslims being bombarded with the ISIS message that they are in a fight to save Islam?"

This image of the terrorist as an infantilized and emotionally immature "other," acutely sensitive to the slightest linguistic slur or trigger, reflects a deeper structural shift in the culture of contemporary Western societies, where, since at least the early 2000s, the language of risk and protection has come to inform and shape a growing number of social practices and organizations involving adults.[121] This language finds its most ostentatious—and, of late, infamous—expression on college campuses,[122] including the one I'm writing this from.[123]

The idea that terrorism is a "risk" to "vulnerable" Muslims has at least three unfortunate social consequences. First, as former U.S. Ambassador Alberto Fernandez recently remarked, it is profoundly demeaning. It portrays Muslims, according to Fernandez, "as if they are easily swayed yet dangerous children susceptible to becoming terrorists because of immigration policy or harsh words that supposedly hurt their feelings."[124] It has also given rise to the pernicious argument that this group should be protected from words and ideas that risk offending their presumed religious beliefs or affiliations, for fear that not doing so will "push" them toward jihadi groups. Just as the safeguarding movement on U.S. campuses presumes, in the words of Greg Lukianoff and Jonathan Haidt, "an extraordinary fragility of the collegiate psyche,"[125] so does the radicalization discourse presume an extraordinary fragility of the psyche of Western Muslims. Far from protecting Muslims, "safeguarding" exposes them to the racism of lowered expectations.

Second, it depoliticizes jihadis and their would-be emulators by denying their agency as political actors, whose embrace of jihadi rhetoric and violence is predicated on reason as much as emotion. To reframe the Islamic State as a "risk" to "vulnerable" Muslims is to deny its potent intellectual challenge, and how its dual-message of Western moral degradation and Islamic authenticity can speak to even the most resilient and precocious of Muslims.[126] Of course, stupid and naive people have joined or attempted to join the Islamic State, but many more have been highly intelligent and politically engaged, demonstrating great resilience and bravery by making it to Islamic State-controlled territory in Syria and Iraq.

Third, the recategorization of terrorism as a "risk" to impressionable Muslims inverts the perpetrator-victim relationship, whereby the former is transformed into the latter. It's like saying domestic violence is a "risk" to the person who beats his wife. But, of course, like domestic violence, terrorism is a risk primarily borne by those who are on the receiving end of it (most of whom are Muslim). It is pernicious to argue for greater protections for Muslims against inflammatory speech from a counterterrorism perspective in the same way that it would be pernicious to argue that potential wife beaters should be shielded from slights directed at them from their wives. And it should go without saying that hateful and dehumanizing rhetoric targeted at Muslims is wrong precisely because it is hateful and dehumanizing, and not because, according to some engrained, neo-orientalist expectation, Muslims will lash out violently and indiscriminately against those who espouse this rhetoric or are somehow tenuously connected to it.[127]

Terrorism is a form of political violence, and those who engage in it must be taken seriously as autonomous moral agents. No doubt the Islamic State has captivated the imaginations of many young Western Muslims, and it can hardly be disputed that the number of young people involved in Islamic State-related terrorist plots in the West has risen in the past few years. In a recent study, Robin Simcox found that from September 2014 to December 2016 there were 34 Islamic State terror plots or alleged plots in the West involving 44 preteen and teenage participants.[128]

Yet the number of young people involved in terrorism should not be exaggerated. In a 2015 report on Western defectors to the Islamic State and other Sunni jihadi groups in Syria and Iraq, Peter Bergen and his colleagues found that the average age of the 474 individuals in their dataset was 24.[129] This is young for an adult but is clearly beyond adolescence. In another study, carried out the same year, Lorenzo Vidino and Seamus Hughes reported that of the 71 individuals charged with Islamic State-related activities in the United States since March 2014, the average age was 26.[130] Moreover, the total number of teenagers involved in Islamic State-related terror plots and defections to jihadi groups in Syria and Iraq is still minuscule and does not remotely justify the reframing of terrorism as a child protection issue, still less the mass thought-policing of Muslim communities, where many young people are suspected of harboring "extreme" ideas. In Britain, of the 3,955 people referred to the government's deradicalization program in 2015, 415 were 10 years old or under, while 1,424 were between 11 and 15.[131] The ideology behind this program and the broader radicalization discourse on which it draws justify these stigmatizing interventions as "safeguarding" the very individuals they stigmatize.

Even among the small number of young people involved in terrorist plots or terrorist groups, it needs to be acknowledged that, as the sociologist Frank Furedi has observed, "it is not the 'vulnerable' but often the more idealistic and intellectually curious who are attracted to extremist ideas."[132] And this means taking them and their ideas seriously and not treating them as the whitest of "snowflakes"[133] in need of protection.

Foreign Policy, April 27, 2017

All That We'll Never Know About Manchester Bomber Salman Ramadan Abedi

The most natural questions to ask about the Manchester terrorist attack are also the most intractable: Who was the perpetrator, and what caused him to carry it out?

His name, revealed on Tuesday [May 23, 2017], is known to us: Salman Ramadan Abedi.[134] He was a British-born 22-year-old of Libyan descent from Manchester, and he was on the radar of the British security services. He attended Salford University but dropped out in the second year of a business and management degree. More details are certain to emerge over the coming days and weeks.

Often, the implicit working assumption in the "who" question is that it will help unlock the mystery of the "why" question. But this assumption rarely bears fruit. Nearly always it is frustrated by the parents, friends or acquaintances of the terrorist, whose testimony—faithfully relayed by journalists in what has become a standard ritual of reporting—attests to the all-too-human traits of the person obliterated by the "terrorist" label: to his ordinariness, to his decency, to his banal enthusiasms and affinities. (Abedi was a Manchester United supporter.)

Whenever a terrorist atrocity occurs, we expect a monster, someone roughly equivalent to the monstrosity perpetrated. But nearly always our expectation is defeated and we are confronted with the glaring discrepancy between the act and the person who authored it. Because the actions are so monstrous, we so badly want the actors to be monsters, but they rarely are.

According to a *Guardian* news report, Abedi was "a slightly withdrawn, devout young man, always respectful to his elders."[135] This is disconcerting: First, because it eliminates the distance between the perpetrator and us, raising all kinds of uncomfortable questions. If Abedi—this ordinary, respectful person—could do what he did, then who else among the vast community of ordinary souls is capable of such a monstrosity (my neighbor, my brother, my son, *me*)? Second, it complicates the "why" question. If the perpetrator was indeed a monster, then the mystery of the "why" is dissolved and the explanation revealed: It was his monstrousness that caused him to act so monstrously. But what if the perpetrator is not a monster?

In the absence of monstrousness, the natural inclination is to search for motives or reasons to understand the atrocity. But this too is fraught with difficulty. A motive or reason is an inner subjective state that explains what caused someone to act. Accordingly, motives are difficult to recover, because they can't readily be empirically verified. You can't see a motive, and often the rationale for an action isn't always clear even to the person who performs it.

At best, one can only intuit or surmise a motive, based on a searching examination of a person's interests, beliefs and the wider context in which he acted. But even here the project of explanation is massively complicated and constricted by several factors.

For example, even in cases where people have carefully and fully explained their actions, either before or after carrying them out, what is presented is often less a guide to their inner subjectivity and drives than a self-serving catalog of justifications or excuses for doing what they did. So instead of providing a neutral account of a person's actions, author-verified "explanations" serve to explain only why they were right or justified in acting, rather than explaining why they acted.

New York University law professor Stephen Holmes puts it in this way: "Sometimes people do what they do for the reasons they profess. But private motivations cannot always be inferred from public justifications."[136] In other words, people are prone to lie about their motives, either to others or to themselves, so as to preserve their moral self-image.

A second and related complicating factor is the way commentators explain jihadist atrocities by identifying the reason or cause that most readily coheres with their own politics and wider philosophical view of the world. For left-leaning intellectuals, the primary reason or cause is secular, anti-Western political grievance. For sociologists, it is any number of social ills, including alienation, anomie, racism, anti-imperialist war and Islamophobia—but almost never religious imperatives. For some right-leaning politicians and commentators, it is the theological edicts of Islam itself. Invariably, the reason or cause identified turns out to be the very thing to which that explicator is diametrically opposed.

Who was Salman Ramadan Abedi and what caused him to murder and maim so many young people at Manchester Arena on Monday night? No matter how hard we look and probe, we may never know who Abedi "really" was, for the simple reason that he is or was, like everyone else on the planet, more or less unknowable at the level of the core self. This is made all the more difficult by the monstrosity of his deed, for which every significant experience or gesture in his tangled life-history is set to become pregnant with a retrospective meaning, as if it somehow anticipated what transpired Monday night.

And however much we learn about Abedi's radicalization and beliefs, or about any possible psychic wounds he encountered in his short life, there remains an inordinate causal abyss between all this convoluted human entanglement—into which so many like Abedi are immersed—and the singular act of murdering innocent teenagers at a pop concert. No amount of expertise or knowing is likely to fully bridge that gap and make the inexplicable explicable.

Los Angeles Times, May 24, 2017

Can Ex-Militants, and Their Redemption Stories, Stop Anyone from Joining Islamic State?

It seems like common sense—enlist disillusioned extremists as credible voices against terrorism and put them to work persuading others to rethink their flirtation with political violence.

Richard Barrett, a former counter-terrorism chief in Britain, told *The Observer*: "Many of the people who have been most successful in undermining the terrorist narrative are themselves ex-extremists."[137] And in a recent report summarizing the stories of 58 Islamic State defectors, Peter Neumann concluded that their narratives "can be important in helping to prevent young people from being radicalized and recruited."[138]

Yet the case for enlisting ex-militants to prevent the radicalization of others remains contentious; there is little or no empirical data to back it up. Neither

Barrett in *The Observer* nor Neumann in his report offered any evidence—not even anecdotal—for the effectiveness of former Islamic State members as agents against future radicalization.

A burst of tweets last year from Georgia State University professor John Horgan in reaction to a news-story about Harry Sarfo, a reformed Islamic State recruit from Germany,[139] made the problem explicit. "We all kinda say 'their stories might prevent others …' but we should (from a research standpoint) be getting clearer traction on this."[140] And in a follow-up tweet: "Can we find evidence that defector narratives dissuade initial involvement of potential recruits?"[141]

Although there is a small body of research on how to best frame and disseminate "counter-narratives" against terrorist propaganda (spearheaded by Horgan and Kurt Braddock[142]), it doesn't speak to the empirical issue of how effective these messages are with their intended audience. The one study that has tried to figure it out captured likes, shares and comments related to three different counter-narrative campaigns on social media, but that doesn't tell us anything about who was liking, sharing and commenting, or whether minds were changed.[143]

A close examination of the stories told by reformed militants reveals that, in common with other kinds of "defector narratives" (from ex-cons, former cultists or reformed addicts),[144] they are often exercises in self-justification. Because the ex-militant is in need of exoneration and self-forgiveness, he must come up with a suitably absolving explanation for why he joined the now-reviled group in the first place. This usually takes the form of a "brainwashing" tale in which he is more sinned against than sinning.

For example, many repentant female Islamic State supporters claim they were forced into traveling to Syria, or they insist—ludicrously, given the incessant news coverage of Islamic State atrocities—they were "lured" by promises of a paradise on Earth for Muslims, with bountiful markets, pristine hospitals and parks, and righteous justice. One French returnee conceded her own guilt but also blamed "those who manipulated me, exploited my naivety, my weakness, my insecurity."[145]

Stories of evil manipulation and exploitation may be psychologically useful for former extremists, but there's little evidence that the radicalized (or those leaning in that direction) are buying them. As one British female Islamic State recruit witheringly put it in a tweet: "We're not stupid young brainwashed females we've come here to syria for ALLAH alone."

Nor do these retrospective atrocity tales do much to explain to the general public how normal people come to embrace violent extremism. The stories don't "tell it like it is," just how *bad* it is. They also tend to minimize the glamor and attractiveness of violent causes for young recruits. To the extent that studies tell us how radicalization works, far from being a pathological or passive process, it is the culmination of an active search for meaning and fulfilment,[146] often undertaken with friends or kin.

Another argument used to justify belief in the preventive power of counter-messages is that former militants have the requisite street cred to be taken seriously by young Muslims. Only most don't, because once, say, a member of Islamic State or al-Qaeda repents and rejects his former views, he relinquishes credibility with those who see truth in extremism. Worse, if the ex-militant is working with the secular liberal or moderate establishment, he's considered a sell-out.

Maajid Nawaz, who co-founded the Quilliam Foundation in London, the world's first counter-extremism think tank, is an obvious case in point. For all his bona fides as a former member of the transnational Islamist group Hizb ut-Tahrir, an association that earned him jail time in an Egyptian prison, Nawaz is regarded with suspicion among even moderate British Muslims,[147] while those at the extreme end of the spectrum regard him with contempt as a traitor or "apostate."

And yet, the ex-extremist, and his redemption narrative, finds eager supporters. This may have more to do with society's need for catharsis than with any benefit he brings to fighting political violence. Like the one-time criminal who has found the right path after a lifetime of doing wrong, these repentant "formers" make the rest of us feel good. Their change of heart validates and reinforces our better angels. That's especially satisfying in times of uncertainty, when we feel insecure about who we are and where we are going.

Los Angeles Times, September 5, 2017

The Myth of the ISIS Patsy

When ISIS announced the formation of the caliphate in June 2014, the group's contingent of foreign recruits could barely contain their excitement, rushing to social media to celebrate the passing of this historic moment. And in the frenzied and bloody months which followed many of them defended and glorified ISIS's most heinous actions and practices, including sexual enslavement and staged mass beheadings, in brazen tweet after tweet. To anyone who would listen, they were telling their stories: of the munificence, justice and divine glory of ISIS rule.

Now that ISIS's territorial dominion is all but over, some of the captured, surrendered or defected among its depleted ranks are telling a very different story—that of the innocent patsy who was misled into signing up for a cause that was ultimately betrayed by ISIS.

In outline, the story goes like this: When Recruit X left home and joined ISIS, he was expecting to join a community of Muslims united by a profound sense of justice and religious rectitude. But within weeks or months of arriving in ISIS-controlled territory these expectations were dashed and what he instead found, to his shock and horror, was a society mired in brutality and injustice, ruled by capricious human beings who were cynically manipulating Holy Scripture for their own political ends.

In this version of events, mirrored in Peter Kominksy's recent TV drama "The State,"[148] Recruit X is transformed from an aggressor and potential threat into a victim, more sinned against than sinning. He was duped, lied to, misled. His only crime was the sin of naivety: The naivety of the idealist who dreamed of a better world. He is someone whose essential decency and moral conscience was wickedly manipulated by shadowy propagandists who sold him the lie of the caliphate dream. Stupid and naïve he may have been, but evil or dangerous he is not.

If you think this summary is a caricature, check out Rukmini Callimachi's 2016 "jailhouse" interview with Harry Sarfo, a former ISIS recruit from Germany. "I thought to myself I'd go down there (to Syria) and live under sharia," he told Callimachi, who then interjected: "And how quickly after you got to Syria did you realize that you'd made a mistake?" "After one week," Sarfo answered, with a grin on his face. "What happened after one week?" Callimachi inquired, laughing. "After one week I realized this is all bollocks, I can't tell you."[149]

The interview then switches to B-roll footage of the detention facility in which Sarfo is housed, over which Callimachi ventriloquizes: "He witnessed teenage recruits being beaten senseless for not being able to keep up, a gay man being thrown from a building, but the dark memory of a beheading has lingered the longest." Asking him whether he turned away or felt "sick to your stomach" at seeing the beheading in question, Sarfo duly responded to Callimachi's prompt: "I was shaking, cause I was shocked … everybody screaming 'Allahu Akbar' and you're thinking to yourself there's nothing holy about this." Referring to Sarfo's escape from ISIS, Callimachi describes this as "a dash for freedom," but the last words of the interview are Sarfo's: "What they're (ISIS) doing has nothing to do with Islam and the principles of Islam."

Quite what Sarfo himself was doing in joining and leaving ISIS, despite Callimachi's explanatory efforts, is still anyone's guess, although it has now transpired that despite his claims to the contrary Sarfo violently participated in a staged mass beheading video.[150]

While Sarfo's account is obviously self-serving, it lacks the sheer preposterousness of other accounts given by some ISIS recruits, like the recently captured ISIS fighters in Kirkuk who, if they are to be believed, were all just farmers or cooks.[151] Or the ISIS fighter who said he was "brainwashed" into raping and killing Yezidis.[152] Or the ISIS returnee from Kosovo—a "mild-mannered college graduate," no less—who claims: "I was not part of ISIS. I met them accidentally."[153]

Yet Sarfo's account still strains credulity, because it asks us to believe the impossible—namely, that he was blissfully ignorant of ISIS's demonic savagery until it was too late. Unfortunately for Sarfo, not only was ISIS a demonically savage group from the off; it also made a concerted point of publicly advertising that savagery as part of a strategy of violent coercion and intimidation.[154]

In fact, no sentient adult who owned a TV or had access to an internet connection in the summer of 2014, when ISIS started slaughtering Yezidis and beheading Western journalists in High Definition videos, could reasonably claim that they didn't know of ISIS's demonic savagery. Everybody knew. And no one was more knowledgeable than those who joined ISIS, many of whom gleefully celebrated and circulated every new ISIS snuff movie well before they left to join the group. They knew, and they justified and exalted in what they knew. As Graeme Wood recently observed, referring to the "ludicrous claims" of some ISIS returnees: "The claim of ignorance of ISIS's true nature is impossible to credit, since press coverage of ISIS's atrocities has barely ceased during the last three years, and ISIS itself boasts of its crimes in its propaganda."[155]

When Nazi war criminals were tried at Nuremberg for their role in the Holocaust, the common refrain among the accused was that they were "simply" following orders, and that they felt powerless to resist the authority of their superiors. The same excuse was used by the killers and rapists of Charlie Company, who slaughtered and raped their way through the hamlet of My Lai in 1968. Lieutenant William L. Calley, who led the rampage, notoriously wrote in his autobiographical account of the massacre, "Body Count," that "personally, I didn't kill any Vietnamese that day: I mean personally. I represented the United States of America. My country."[156]

For the self-styled ISIS patsy, however, this particular rhetorical trope seemingly holds little appeal. Perhaps this is because they intuit just how degraded and dishonorable it has become in the wider culture. So instead they enlist a narrative that is more in keeping with the infantilizing ethos of the societies to which they want to return, where even the most political and hardnosed of acts—terrorism—has undergone redefinition as a "risk" not only to its victims but to would-be terrorists, whose multiple "vulnerabilities" make them ideal recruits for terrorist propagandists and demagogues.

For many ISIS defectors or captives, it is likely that the real source of disillusionment was not that ISIS was brutal beyond belief, but that its caliphate project simply failed. What is distinctly less likely is that they will ever come clean and acknowledge this.

The New York Daily News, October 23, 2017

What We Talk About When We Talk About Violent Extremism

Violent extremists demand a response. But what is it to be?

Historically, the responses have differed along political lines. The right, broadly conceived, has tended to condemn violent extremists, attributing to their monstrous deeds a monstrousness of moral character. By contrast, the left, broadly conceived, has sought to "understand" them, attributing to their monstrous deeds a monstrousness of moral circumstance. For the former, the violent extremist is a terrible person, and any attempt to explain their actions or how they became terrible is a form of excuse-making that diminishes the moral odiousness of who they are and what they have done. For the latter, the violent extremist is an ordinary human being, whose actions are unintelligible unless contextualized against the background of their individual life story and the wider structural circumstances in which they acted.

These lines were not always so neatly drawn, but in an age of ISIS-inspired terrorism and the rise of white nationalism in America, they have become increasingly blurred. Arguably, they have switched places.

Consider, for example, President Trump's refusal to unequivocally condemn the menace of the alt-right,[157] compared to his razor-sharp readiness to condemn and amplify the menace of what he calls "radical Islamic terrorism."[158] Or consider the razor-sharp readiness of liberal-leftists to condemn and amplify the menace of what they call "neo-Nazis,"[159] compared their reluctance to apply the same clear-eyed and unequivocal approach to the menace of jihadist terrorism.[160]

This blurring of lines was particularly evident in the controversy sparked last November [2017] by Richard Fausset's *New York Times* profile of Tony Hovater, a white nationalist from Huber Heights, Ohio. Titled "A Voice of Hate in America's Heartland," Fausset's article sought to contrast the sheer extremity and odiousness of Hovater's political beliefs with the sheer ordinariness and inoffensiveness of his everyday life.[161] "Most Americans," Fausset wrote, "would be disgusted and baffled by his casually approving remarks about Hitler, disdain for democracy and belief that the races are better off separate," adding: "But his tattoos are innocuous pop-culture references: a slice of cherry pie adorns one arm, a homage to the TV show 'Twin Peaks.'"

The effect was jarring, and many *New York Times* readers were disgusted and baffled by Fausset's humanizing portrayal of Hovater as "the Nazi sympathizer next door, polite and low-key."

Although Fausset didn't mention Hannah Arendt, the great German-American political theorist who died in 1975, his entire piece is infused with her notion of the "banality of evil": a reference not to the evil that people do, but to the human authors of evil, who, like Adolf Eichmann, the Nazi bureaucrat who sent hundreds of thousands of Jews to their death in the Holocaust and who Arendt had in mind when she coined the phrase, were often bland non-entities: in her words, "neither perverted nor sadistic ... but terribly and terrifyingly normal."[162]

Just as Arendt was assailed by many critics for "normalizing" Eichmann, so too was Fausset for "normalizing" Hovater. But Fausset's fiercest critics came not from the right, but from the liberal-left. According to *The New York Times's* national editor Mark Lacey:

> Whatever our goal, a lot of readers found the story offensive, with many seizing on the idea we were normalizing neo-Nazi views and behavior. "How to normalize Nazis 101!" one reader wrote on Twitter. "I'm both shocked and disgusted by this article," wrote another. "Attempting to 'normalize' white supremacist groups—should Never have been printed!"[163]

This seems to point to a new consensus among progressives on "othering": Don't "other" the "True Other"—i.e. those who belong to a minority status-group and who, by virtue of that status, face discrimination and oppression; no, "other" instead the alt-right "Other," whose privileged status and unearned disproportionate power makes them worthy of contempt and vilification. Or conversely: Do "normalize" the "True Other," and attend to their legitimate grievances, but don't "normalize" the alt-right "Other," whose grievances are non-existent or illegitimate.

As well as shining a light on the politicized nature of our current discourse on violent extremism, the controversy surrounding Fausset's article also raises two large questions: Is it right to normalize violent extremists, and how should journalists cover them in their reportage?

On the first question, the answer should be patently clear. Of course it is right to normalize violent extremists, for the simple reason that they are, as decades of research on mass violence, genocide and terrorism shows, for the most part psychologically normal individuals. Or as Shane Bauer, a senior reporter at *Mother Jones*, more tersely put it, commenting of the Fausset story: "People mad about this article want to believe that Nazis are monsters we cannot relate to. White supremacists are normal ass white people and it's been that way in America since 1776. We will continue to be in trouble till we understand that."[164]

And of course acknowledging the normality of violent extremists doesn't preclude condemning them: Indeed it is because they're psychologically normal individuals, with agency, that one ought to condemn them.

It should also be made clear, if it isn't already, that normalizing violent extremists is not the same thing as normalizing their ideas or actions: that you can be a sane and devoted father (or mother) and at the same time espouse and act on utterly reprehensible beliefs.

The second question about how to report on violent extremists is much harder to answer. One view, prominently aired during the Fausset controversy, is that whatever form that coverage should take it should not be over-done, since publicity is exactly what violent extremists want. For example, Luke O'Brien, who wrote *The Atlantic's* December cover story on the alt-right dema-gogue Andrew Anglin,[165] warned reporters against giving extremists "a plat-form for irrational, hateful views." "[They] are propagandists," he told the *Columbia Journalism Review*. "They are liars. They are dangerous people. They are political extremists who have a very clear-cut agenda, and part of that involves manipulating the media."[166]

Ijeoma Oluo, who was quoted in the same article, was even more forthright, insisting that reporters should stop focusing on extremists and start addressing those who are on the receiving end of their hate: "When your only goal is to understand the dehumanizing, and not understanding the impact that this is having on the people who are being dehumanized, you're continuing that cycle of dehumanization." This echoed Soledad O'Brien's take on the Fausset article: "Would be interesting," she tweeted, "if instead of normalizing nazis, if the @nyt actually assessed them through the eyes of those they hate: blacks and jews."[167]

While these comments reflect serious concerns about how much exposure the media should give to violent extremists, they evade the thornier issue of how to write about dangerous people with dangerous ideas.

One thing the Fausset controversy reveals is that while it's important to capture the normality of violent extremists, it is equally important not to over-state their ordinariness. The core problem with Fausset's article wasn't that it normalized Hovater; it was that his normality *was* the story. It was that Fausset couldn't really see beyond the banality of Hovater—the plain T-shirt-wearing, 29-year-old welder with "Midwestern manners [that] would please anyone's mother," who listens to National Public Radio, likes *Seinfeld* and owns four cats.

But who did Fausset think Hovater was before meeting him? A howling loon who cooked children instead of pasta? Hovater, it turns out, is just an ordinary man, engaged to be married to a no less ordinary woman—a "small-town girl who had fallen away from the Catholic Church ('It was just really boring'), and once considered herself liberal." But of course he is an ordinary man. Of course he watches TV and drives a motor vehicle. Of course he is human. We all know this. What we instead needed from Fausset is a picture of who Hovater is, beneath the banal exterior, and how he became that.

By Fausset's own admission, he failed to provide this: "There is a hole at the heart of my story about Tony Hovater, the white nationalist and Nazi sympathizer," Fausset wrote in a short follow-up piece to his article, explaining why he wrote it and what he was trying to do.[168] That hole was the mystery of Hovater's radical turn toward white nationalism, despite Hovater's own best efforts to explain it. But what Fausset did have was an embarrassment of, as he put it, "quotidian details, though to be honest, I'm not even sure what these add up to." A more knowing and self-critical writer would probably know what these details added up to: a skewed profile.

The controversy over Fausset's article points to three core challenges.

The first is how to walk the tightrope between recognizing the fundamental humanity and ordinariness of violent extremists without over-emphasizing these traits so that we lose sight of the moral insanity of what they believe in and are trying to make happen. It is about being respectful, but not too respectful. As the *LA Times* contributor Jamil Smith incisively put it: "[T]he @nytimes erred, I think, by covering the banality of evil by displaying all the banality, and not nearly enough evil."[169]

The second challenge, connectedly, is how to walk the tightrope between recognizing the moral depravity of what violent extremists think and do without over-emphasizing these things so that we lose sight of their fundamental humanity and ordinariness. It is about registering disapproval, without being too disapproving.

And the third challenge is related to how much credence should be given to the testimony of violent extremists, especially when so much of it is engineered, whether consciously or otherwise, to excuse, rationalize or justify their beliefs and actions. Too often, the avowed motives of violent extremists are uncritically accepted by journalists and commentators as their true motives, instead of rhetorical accounts designed to make them appear sympathetic and essentially decent.

There are many other challenges too, and while there has never been a more propitious time to write about violent extremists, the moral risks involved have never been higher.

The New York Daily News, January 12, 2018

NOTES

Preface

1 Alberto M. Fernandez, "Here to Stay and Growing: Combating ISIS Propaganda Networks," The Brookings Project on U.S. Relations with the Islamic World U.S.-Islamic World Forum Papers, October 2015, https://www.brookings.edu/wp-content/uploads/2016/07/IS-Propaganda_Web_English_v2-1.pdf, 9 (accessed June 28, 2018).
2 Olivia Becker, "ISIS Has a Really Slick and Sophisticated Media Department," *Vice*, July 12, 2014, available at: https://news.vice.com/article/isis-has-a-really-slick-and-sophisticated-media-department (accessed June 28, 2018).
3 Quoted in Haroon Siddique, "Jihadi Recruitment Video for Islamist Terror Group Isis Features Three Britons," *The Guardian*, June 21, 2014, available at: https://www.theguardian.com/world/2014/jun/20/jihadi-recruitment-video-islamist-terror-group-isis-features-britons (accessed June 28, 2018).
4 See Rod Nordland, "Captured ISIS Fighters' Refrain: 'I Was Only a Cook'," *The New York Times*, October 1, 2017, https://www.nytimes.com/2017/10/01/world/middleeast/iraq-islamic-state-kurdistan.html (accessed June 28, 2018).
5 Scott Atran, "The Devoted Actor: Unconditional Commitment and Intractable Conflict across Cultures," *Current Anthropology*, 57/13 (June 2016), 192.
6 Ibid., 197.
7 Kevin McDonald, *Radicalization* (Cambridge: Polity Press, 2018).

Chapter 1 ISIS and the Theatre of Horror

1 Michael Burleigh, *Blood and Rage: A Cultural History of Terrorism* (London: Harper Perennial, 2008), 503.
2 See Mark Hosenball and Tabassum Zakaria, "Pornography found in bin Laden Hideout," *Reuters*, May 13, 2011, available at: https://www.reuters.com/article/us-binladen-porn/exclusive-pornography-found-in-bin-laden-hideout-officials-idUSTRE74C4RK20110513 (accessed June 28, 2018).
3 Quoted in Asra Q. Nomani, "Osama bin Laden's Porn and Muslim Hypocrisy on Sex," *The Daily Beast*, May 14, 2011, available at: https://www.thedailybeast.com/osama-bin-ladens-porn-and-muslim-hypocrisy-on-sex (accessed June 28, 2018).
4 Martin Amis, "A Rough Trade," *The Guardian*, March 17, 2001, available at: https://www.theguardian.com/books/2001/mar/17/society.martinamis1 (accessed June 28, 2018).

5 Ann Marie Oliver and Paul F. Steinberg, *The Road to Martyrs' Square: A Journey into the World of the Suicide Bomber* (New York: Oxford University Press, 2005), 72–73.

6 See Arab Salem et al., "Multimedia Content Coding and Analysis: Unraveling the Content of Jihadi Extremist Groups' Videos," *Studies in Conflict & Terrorism*, 31 (7) (2008), 613.

7 See Dexter Filkins, "The Death of Steven Sotloff," *The New Yorker*, September 2, 2014, available at: https://www.newyorker.com/news/news-desk/death-steven-sotloff (accessed June 28, 2018).

8 See Scott Shane and Ben Hubbard, "ISIS Displaying a Deft Command of Varied Media," *The New York Times*, August 30, 2014, available at: https://www.nytimes.com/2014/08/31/world/middleeast/isis-displaying-a-deft-command-of-varied-media.html (accessed June 28, 2018).

9 See Bruce Wallace, "ISIS has Mastered High-end Video Production in its New Propaganda Wing," *PRI*, September 11, 2014, available at: https://www.pri.org/stories/2014-09-11/isis-has-mastered-high-end-video-production-its-new-propaganda-wing (accessed June 28, 2018).

10 Quoted in "New ISIS Video Purports to Show Beheading of Another U.S. Journalist," *CBS*, September 2, 2014, available at: https://washington.cbslocal.com/2014/09/02/new-isis-video-purports-to-show-beheading-of-another-us-journalist/ (accessed June 28, 2018).

11 Mark Juergensmeyer, *Terror in the Mind of God: The Global Rise of Religious Violence* (Berkeley: University of California Press, 2001), xi; see also 124–28. In subsequent articles I sought to qualify this, arguing that ISIS videos served both expressive and instrumental purposes—that they were animated by both a need to (de)humiliate and a desire to electrify supporters and intimidate enemies.

12 See "British Hip Hop Jihadist Abdel-Majed Abdel Bary Poses in Syria with Severed Head," *Huffington Post*, August 14, 2014, available at: https://www.huffingtonpost.co.uk/2014/08/14/british-hip-hop-jihadist-abdel-majed-abdel-bary-syria-severed-head_n_5677555.html?guccounter=1 (accessed June 28, 2018).

13 Mia Bloom, "Even al-Qaeda Denounced Beheading Videos. Why the Islamic State brought them Back," *The Washington Post*, August 22, 2014, available at: https://www.washingtonpost.com/posteverything/wp/2014/08/22/even-al-qaeda-denounced-beheading-videos-why-the-islamic-state-brought-them-back/?utm_term=.05e224f5d29a (accessed June 28, 2018).

14 Walter Laqueur, "Anarchism and Al Qaeda," *Middle East Strategy at Harvard*, December 23, 2007, available at: https://historynewsnetwork.org/article/45933 (accessed June 28, 2018).

15 Brian M. Jenkins, "International Terrorism: A New Kind of Warfare," RAND Corporation, 1974, available at: https://www.rand.org/content/dam/rand/pubs/papers/2008/P5261.pdf, 4 (accessed June 25, 2018).

16 This is a reference to the staged beheading of British aid worker Alan Henning (see Ian Cobain et al., "Isis Video Shows Murder of British Hostage Alan Henning," *The Guardian*, October 4, 2014, available at: https://www.theguardian.com/uk-news/2014/oct/03/alan-henning-isis-syria-video-murder (accessed June 26, 2018). Henning was the fourth Western hostage killed by ISIS, following the filmed beheadings of James Foley, Steven Sotloff and David Haines. In what became a convention in the ISIS execution videos of Western hostages Henning was shown at the end of the Haines beheading video, kneeling before "Jihadi John" in an orange

jump-suit (see Raya Jalabi, "David Haines Video has Marked Similarities to Sotloff and Foley Killings," *The Guardian*, September 14, 2014, available at: https://www.theguardian.com/world/2014/sep/14/david-haines-video-similarities-sotloff-foley-killings (accessed June 26, 2018).

17 See "Islamic State Murders US Journalist Steven Sotloff," *Channel 4 News*, September 2, 2014, available at: https://www.channel4.com/news/is-video-shows-beheading-of-steven-sotloff (accessed June 26, 2018).

18 See David Brown, "Briton Seen Holding Up Severed Head," *The Times*, August 14, 2014, available at: https://www.thetimes.co.uk/article/briton-seen-holding-up-severed-head-vh3stmn7v3s (accessed June 26, 2018).

19 Christopher Browning, *Ordinary Men: Reserve Police Battalion 101 and the Final Solution in Poland* (New York: HarperCollins, 1992).

20 Daniel Goldhagen, *Hitler's Willing Executioners: Ordinary Germans and the Final Solution* (New York: Knopf, 1996).

21 Primo Levi, *The Drowned and The Saved* (London: Abacus Books, 1989), 83.

22 Joanna Bourke, *An Intimate History of Killing: Face-to-Face Killing in Twentieth Century Warfare* (New York: Basic Books, 1999).

23 Albert Bandura, "Mechanisms of Moral Disengagement," in W. Reich, ed., *Origins of Terrorism: Psychologies, Ideologies, Theologies, States of Mind*, (Washington, DC: The Woodrow Wilson Centre Press, 1990), 182.

24 See "Reddit: Shiraz Maher Conducts Reddit AMA at /r/SyrianCivilWar," ICSR, December 3, 2013, available at: http://icsr.info/2013/12/reddit-shiraz-maher-conducts-reddit-ama-rsyriancivilwar/ (accessed June 26, 2018).

25 Wrongly, as it turned out: ISIS's beheader-in-chief was in fact Mohammed Emwazi.

26 See Becker, "ISIS Has a Really Slick and Sophisticated Media Department."

27 Thomas Harris, *Silence of The Lambs* (London: Arrow, 1989), 24.

28 Philip Roth, *The Human Stain* (London: Jonathan Cape, 2000), 242.

29 See Alice Speri, "New Islamic State Video Shows Hostage John Cantlie Allegedly Reporting from the Ground in Kobane," *Vice*, October 27, 2014, available at: https://news.vice.com/article/new-islamic-state-video-shows-hostage-john-cantlie-allegedly-reporting-from-the-ground-in-kobane (accessed June 28, 2018).

30 See Shiv Malik, "Isis Video Appears to Show Hostage Peter Kassig Has Been Killed," *The Guardian*, November 16, 2014, available at: https://www.theguardian.com/world/2014/nov/16/isis-beheads-peter-kassig-reports (accessed June 28, 2018).

31 David Bromwich, "The Meaning of Shock and Awe," *Huffington Post*, March 9, 2013, available at: https://www.huffingtonpost.com/david-bromwich/the-meaning-of-shock-and-_b_2844688.html (accessed June 28, 2018).

32 Quoted in Bourke, *An Intimate History of Killing*, 209.

33 See http://avalon.law.yale.edu/20th_century/mp10.asp (accessed June 28, 2018).

34 See Greg Botelho and Kevin Conlon, "Last Crewman of U.S. Plane that Dropped A-bomb on Hiroshima Dies at 93," *CNN*, July 31, 2014, available at:https://edition.cnn.com/2014/07/29/us/enola-gay-crew-member-dies/ (accessed June 28, 2018).

35 See Bourke, *An Intimate History of Killing*, 247.

36 Randall Collins, *Violence: A Micro-Sociological Theory* (Princeton: Princeton University Press, 2008), 24.

37 Ibid.

38 Ibid., 78.

39   See John Whiteclay Chambers II, "S. L. A. Marshall's Men Against Fire: New Evidence Regarding Fire Ratios," *Parameters*, Autumn 2003.

40   Ibid., 74.

41   Dave Grossman, *On Killing: The Psychological Cost of Learning to Kill in War and Society* (New York: Back Bay Books, 1995), 4.

42   Ibid., 102.

43   Zygmunt Bauman, *Modernity and the Holocaust* (Cambridge: Polity, 1999), 155.

44   See Aaron Zelin, "The Massacre Strategy: Why ISIS Brags about its Brutal Sectarian Murders," *Politico Magazine*, June 17, 2014, available at: https://www.politico.com/magazine/story/2014/06/the-massacre-strategy-107954 (accessed June 28, 2018).

45   Abu Bakr Naji, *The Management of Savagery*, translated by William McCants, May 23, 2006, available at: https://azelin.files.wordpress.com/2010/08/abu-bakr-naji-the-management-of-savagery-the-most-critical-stage-through-which-the-umma-will-pass.pdf, 74 (accessed June 28, 2018).

46   Nina Rastogi, "Decapitation and the Muslim World: Is There Any Special Significance to Beheading in Islam?," *Slate*, February 20, 2009, available at: http://www.slate.com/articles/news_and_politics/explainer/2009/02/decapitation_and_the_muslim_world.html?via=gdpr-consent (accessed June 28, 2018).

47   See Michael Walzer, *Just and Unjust Wars* (New York: Basic Books, 1977), 254.

48   Thomas Nagel, "War and Massacre," *Philosophy & Public Affairs*, 1 (2) (1972), 127.

49   Quoted in Vanessa Altin, "Inside Kobane: Drug-crazed ISIS Savages Rape, Slaughter and Behead Children," *The Mirror*, October 11, 2014, available at: https://www.mirror.co.uk/news/world-news/inside-kobane-drug-crazed-isis-savages-4423619 (accessed June 28, 2018).

50   See Martin Chulov, "Latest Islamic State Horror Masks a Week of Defeats," *The Observer*, November 16, 2014, available at: https://www.theguardian.com/world/2014/nov/16/islamic-state-video-week-defeats?CMP=share_btn_tw (accessed June 28, 2018).

51   See Michael Martinez, "ISIS Video Claims to Show Boy Executing Two Men Accused of being Russian Spies," *CNN*, January 15, 2015, available at: https://edition.cnn.com/2015/01/14/middleeast/isis-video-boy-execution-russian-spies/index.html (accessed June 30, 2018).

52   See Tom Wyke and Darren Boyle, "ISIS Release Shocking New Video of Child SOLDIERS from Kazakhstan Being Trained with AK47s," *Mail Online*, November 22, 2014, available at: http://www.dailymail.co.uk/news/article-2845531/ISIS-release-shocking-new-video-child-soldiers-Kazakhstan-trained-AK47s.html (accessed June 30, 2018).

53   See Jon Boone, "Agony and Anger as Pakistan Buries Dead after School Attack," *The Guardian*, December 17, 2014, https://www.theguardian.com/world/2014/dec/17/agony-anger-pakistan-buries-dead-school-attack (accessed June 30, 2018).

54   Kathy Gilsinan, "Terrorist Attacks on Schools Have Soared in the Past 10," *The Atlantic*, December 17, 2014, available at: https://www.theatlantic.com/international/archive/2014/12/terrorist-attacks-on-schools-have-soared-in-the-past-10-years/383825/ (accessed June 30, 2018).

55   See Monica Mark, "Boko Haram's 'DEADLIEST Massacre': 2,000 Feared Dead in Nigeria," *The Guardian*, January 10, 2015, available at: https://www.theguardian.com/world/2015/jan/09/boko-haram-deadliest-massacre-baga-nigeria (accessed June 30, 2018).

56 See Adam Nossiter, "In Nigeria, New Boko Haram Suicide Bomber Tactic: 'It's a Little Girl'," *The New York Times*, January 10, 2015, available at: https://www.nytimes.com/2015/01/11/world/africa/suicide-bomber-hits-maiduguri-nigeria-market.html?ref=world (accessed June 30, 2018).

57 See "UN Commission of Inquiry: Syrian Victims Reveal ISIS's Calculated use of Brutality and Indoctrination," https://www.ohchr.org/EN/NewsEvents/Pages/DisplayNews.aspx?NewsID=15295 (accessed June 30, 2018).

58 See Arango, "A Boy in ISIS."

59 Alistair Dawber et al., "Isis Video Shows Death of Jordanian Hostage Muath al-Kasaesbeh," *The Independent*, February 3, 2015, available at: https://www.independent.co.uk/news/world/middle-east/isis-video-purports-to-show-jordanian-pilot-hostage-moaz-al-kasasbeh-being-burned-to-death-10021462.html (accessed June 30, 2018).

60 David C. Rapoport, "Fear and Trembling: Terrorism in Three Religious Traditions," *The American Political Science Review*, 78 (3) (1984), 660.

61 Conor Cruise O'Brien, "Thinking about Terrorism," *The Atlantic*, June (1986). available at: https://www.theatlantic.com/magazine/archive/1986/06/thinking-about-terrorism/305045/ (accessed June 25, 2018).

62 Quoted in "Jordan pilot hostage Moaz al-Kasasbeh 'burned alive'," *BBC News*, February 3, 2015, available at: https://www.bbc.co.uk/news/world-middle-east-31121160 (accessed June 30, 2018).

63 See Matt Schiavenza, "Nigeria's Horror in Paris's Shadow: Why a 10-year-old suicide Bomber Isn't Front-page News," *The Atlantic*, January 11, 2015, available at: https://www.theatlantic.com/international/archive/2015/01/boko-harams-quiet-destruction-of-northeast-nigeria/384416/ (accessed June 30, 2018).

64 Frantz Fanon, *The Wretched of the Earth* (New York: Grove Press, 1966), 122.

65 See Jethro Mullen et al., "Jordanian Pilot's Father: 'Annihilate' ISIS," *CNN*, February 5, 2015, available at: https://edition.cnn.com/2015/02/04/world/isis-jordan-reaction/ (accessed June 30, 2018).

66 David Ensor, "Al Qaeda Letter called 'chilling'."

67 David Carr, "With Videos of Killings, ISIS Sends Medieval Message by Modern Method," *The New York Times*, September 7, 2014, available at: https://www.nytimes.com/2014/09/08/business/media/with-videos-of-killings-isis-hones-social-media-as-a-weapon.html (accessed June 30, 2018).

68 Brian Knowlton, "Digital War Takes Shape on Websites Over ISIS," *The New York Times*, September 26, 2014, available at: https://www.nytimes.com/2014/09/27/world/middleeast/us-vividly-rebuts-isis-propaganda-on-arab-social-media.html (accessed June 30, 2018).

69 See esp. J. M. Berger, "How ISIS Games Twitter," *The Atlantic*, June 16, 2014, available at: https://www.theatlantic.com/international/archive/2014/06/isis-iraq-twitter-social-media-strategy/372856/ (accessed June 30, 2018).

70 See Peter R. Neumann, "Foreign Fighter Total in Syria/Iraq now Exceeds 20,000; Surpasses Afghanistan Conflict in the 1980s," ICSR, January 26, 2015, available at: http://icsr.info/2015/01/foreign-fighter-total-syriairaq-now-exceeds-20000-surpasses-afghanistan-conflict-1980s/ (accessed June 22, 2018).

71 Ray Monk, *Ludwig Wittgenstein: The Duty of Genius* (New York: Free Press, 1990), 112.

72 Scott Atran, *Talking to the Enemy: Violent Extremism, Sacred Values, and What it Means to Be Human* (London: Allen Lane, 2010), 290.

73 See esp. Kathy Gilsinan, "Is ISIS's Social-Media Power Exaggerated?" *The Atlantic*, February 23, 2015, available at: https://www.theatlantic.com/international/archive/2015/02/is-isiss-social-media-power-exaggerated/385726/ (accessed June 30, 2018).

74 See https://twitter.com/TAPAlerts/status/505937525312356352 (accessed June 30, 2018).

75 See Taylor Luck, "Have US Laws Created an Online Haven for Islamic State Propaganda?," *The Christian Science Monitor*, August 25, 2015, available at: https://m.csmonitor.com/World/Middle-East/2015/0825/Have-US-laws-created-an-online-haven-for-Islamic-State-propaganda (accessed June 30, 2018).

76 J. M. Berger and Jonathon Morgan, "The ISIS Twitter Census: Defining and Describing the Population of ISIS Supporters on Twitter," The Brookings Project on U.S. Relations with the Islamic World, March 2015, available at: https://www.brookings.edu/wp-content/uploads/2016/06/isis_twitter_census_berger_morgan.pdf (accessed June 30, 2018).

77 Gilsinan, "Is ISIS's Social-Media Power Exaggerated?"

78 J. M. Berger, "Taming ISIS on Twitter: More than a Game of Whack-a-Mole," CNN, April 2, 2015, available at: https://edition.cnn.com/2015/03/13/opinions/isis-twitter-crackdown/ (accessed June 30, 2018).

79 Jessica Stern and J. M. Berger, "A 6-Point Plan to Defeat ISIS in the Propaganda War," *Time*, March 30, 2015, available at: http://time.com/3751659/a-6-point-plan-to-defeat-isis-in-the-propaganda-war/ (accessed June 30, 2018).

80 Berger, "Taming ISIS on Twitter."

81 See Brian Ross et al., "Twitter Escalates Its Own ISIS Battle: 2,000 Accounts Suspended Last Week," *ABC News*, March 2, 2015, available at: https://abcnews.go.com/International/twitter-escalates-isis-skirmish-2000-accounts-suspended-week/story?id=29335434 (accessed June 30, 2018).

82 See Alex Hern, "Isis Threatens Twitter Employees over Blocked Accounts," *The Guardian*, March 2, 2015, available at: https://www.theguardian.com/technology/2015/mar/02/isis-threatens-twitter-employees-over-blocked-accounts-jack-dorsey (accessed June 30, 2018).

83 Rita Katz, "The State Department's Twitter War with ISIS Is Embarrassing," *Time*, September 16, 2014), available at: http://time.com/3387065/isis-twitter-war-state-department/ (accessed June 30, 2018).

84 See Aisha Gani and Ewen MacAskill, "Suspected UK extremist and English-speaking Boy Warn of Attacks in Isis Video," *The Guardian*, January 4, 2016, available at: https://www.theguardian.com/world/2016/jan/03/islamic-state-hostage-video-shows-young-boy-and-jihadi-warning-of-attacks (accessed June 30, 2018).

85 See Taylor Berman, "Graphic Execution Video Shows ISIS Drowning, Immolating Prisoners," *Gawker*, June 23, 2015, available at: http://gawker.com/graphic-execution-video-shows-isis-drowning-immolating-1713379881 (accessed June 30, 2018).

86 See Nicole Rojas, "Islamic State Execution: New Video Shows Isis Crushing Prisoner under Tank," *International Business Times*, October 26, 2015, available at: https://www.ibtimes.co.uk/islamic-state-execution-new-video-shows-isis-crushing-prisoner-under-tank-1525630 (accessed June 30, 2018).

87 See Adam Withnall, "Isis Video Showing Libyan 'Spy' Dragged to Death behind a Speeding Truck Betrays Disturbing New Trend," *The Independent*, October 20, 2015,

available at: https://www.independent.co.uk/news/world/middle-east/isis-video-showing-libyan-spy-dragged-to-death-behind-a-speeding-truck-betrays-disturbing-new-trend-a6701521.html (accessed June 30, 2018).

88 See Shiraz Maher, "Burning the Earth: Isis and the Threat to Britain," *The New Statesman*, November 16, 2015, available at: https://www.newstatesman.com/politics/uk/2015/11/burning-earth-isis-and-threat-britain (accessed June 30, 2018).

89 See Lizzie Dearden, "Isis Video: Full Transcript of 'A Message to David Cameron'," *The Independent*, January 5, 2016, available at: https://www.independent.co.uk/news/uk/home-news/isis-video-full-transcript-of-a-message-to-david-cameron-siddhartha-dhar-isa-dare-a6797671.html (accessed June 30, 2018).

90 See Aisha Gani, "London Man says Child in Isis Video is his Grandson," *The Guardian*, January 5, 2016, available at: https://www.theguardian.com/world/2016/jan/04/child-isis-video-son-london-woman-grandfather-lewisham-channel-four (accessed June 30, 2018).

91 See Lin Jenkins, "Isis Video Shows Killing of Syrian Troops at Palmyra Amphitheatre," *The Observer*, July 4, 2015, available at: https://www.theguardian.com/world/2015/jul/04/isis-video-killing-palmyra-amphitheatre (accessed June 30, 2018).

92 See John Horgan and Mia Bloom, "This Is How the Islamic State Manufactures Child Militants," *Vice*, July 8, 2015, available at: https://news.vice.com/article/this-is-how-the-islamic-state-manufactures-child-militants (accessed June 30, 2018).

93 See Max Abrahms, "Why Groups Use Terrorism: A Reassessment of the Conventional Wisdom," April 22, 2015, available at: http://politicalviolenceataglance.org/2015/04/22/why-groups-use-terrorism-a-reassessment-of-the-conventional-wisdom/ (accessed June 30, 2018).

94 Giorgio, *Memoirs of an Italian Terrorist*, trans. Antony Shugaar (New York: Carroll & Graf Publishers, 2003), 64.

95 See Alex Perry, "Once Upon a Jihad," available at: http://reprints.longform.org/perry-once-upon-a-jihad (accessed June 30, 2018).

96 Alissa J. Rubin and Lilia Blaise, "Killing Twice for ISIS and Saying So Live on Facebook," *The New York Times*, June 14, 2016, available at: https://www.nytimes.com/2016/06/15/world/europe/france-stabbing-police-magnanville-isis.html (accessed June 30, 2018).

97 See Lizzie Dearden, "France Police Stabbing: Facebook Live Video Shows Isis Supporter Who Killed Officer and Wife Calling for More Attacks," *The Independent*, June 14, 2016, available at: https://www.independent.co.uk/news/world/europe/video-shows-isis-supporter-who-stabbed-french-police-officer-and-wife-to-death-paris-magnanville-a7081816.html (accessed June 30, 2018).

98 See Matt Vasilogambros, "Was Orlando the Deadliest Mass Shooting in U.S. History?," *The Atlantic*, June 15, 2016, available at: https://www.theatlantic.com/news/archive/2016/06/orlando-deadliest-mass-shooting/487058/ (accessed June 30, 2018). This, alas, must now be revised: on October 1, 2017 Stephen Paddock gunned down on a crowd of concertgoers from his Las Vegas hotel room, killing 58 and injuring almost 500 (see "Deadliest Mass Shootings in Modern US History," *CNN*, May 23, 2018, available at: https://edition.cnn.com/2013/09/16/us/20-deadliest-mass-shootings-in-u-s-history-fast-facts/index.html (accessed June 30, 2018).

99   See Caitlin Dewey and Sarah Parnass, "For the First Time an Alleged Terrorist has Broadcast a Confession in Real Time on Facebook Live," *The Washington Post*, June 14, 2016, available at: https://www.washingtonpost.com/news/the-intersect/wp/2016/06/14/for-the-first-time-an-alleged-terrorist-has-broadcast-a-confession-in-real-time-on-facebook-live/ (accessed June 30, 2018).

100   Jason Burke, "How the Changing Media is Changing Terrorism," *The Guardian*, February 25, 2016, available at: https://www.theguardian.com/world/2016/feb/25/how-changing-media-changing-terrorism (accessed June 30, 2018).

101   See Jason Burke, "Theatre of Terror," *The Observer*, November 21, 2004, available at: https://www.theguardian.com/theobserver/2004/nov/21/features.review7 (accessed June 30, 2018).

102   See "Who was French Police Killer Larossi Abballa?," *BBC News*, June 14, 2016, available at: https://www.bbc.co.uk/news/world-europe-36526067 (accessed June 30, 2018).

103   Frances Larson, *Severed: A History of Heads Lost and Heads Found* (New York: Liveright, 2014), 69.

104   Susan Sontag, *Regarding the Pain of Others* (New York: Farrar, Straus and Giroux, 2003), 41.

105   Karen Halttunen, "Humanitarianism and the Pornography of Pain in Anglo-American Culture," *The American Historical Review*, 100 (2) 1995), 309.

106   Gray, *The Warriors*, 29.

107   Jenkins, "International Terrorism," 4.

108   Ibid., 7.

109   Ibid., 12.

110   See, for example, "A Glimpse of Omar Mateen's Past, from School Reports to Job Dismissal," *The New York Times*, June 18, 2016, available at: https://www.nytimes.com/interactive/2016/06/18/us/omar-mateen-documents.html?_r=0 (accessed June 30, 2018).

111   Adriana Cavarero, *Horrorism: Naming Contemporary Violence*, trans. William McCuaig (New York: Columbia University Press, 2009), 8.

112   See Tim Lister, "Terror Export Fears as ISIS 'Caliphate' Shrinks," *CNN*, July 11, 2016, available at: https://edition.cnn.com/2016/07/11/middleeast/isis-territory-analysis-lister/ (accessed June 30, 2018).

113   Karen J. Renner, *Evil Children in the Popular Imagination* (New York: Palgrave, 2016), 1.

114   Quoted in Kimiko de Freytas-Tamura, "Teenage Girl Leaves for ISIS, and Others Follow," *The New York Times*, February 24, 2015, available at: https://www.nytimes.com/2015/02/25/world/from-studious-teenager-to-isis-recruiter.html (accessed June 21, 2018).

115   Quoted in Greenwood et al., "Police Spoke to Schoolgirl Jihadi Brides in December.."

116   Quoted in Laura Smith Spark, "UK Girls' List for Syria Trip: Makeup, Bras, Epilator," *CNN*, March 10, 2015, available at: https://edition.cnn.com/2015/03/10/europe/uk-missing-girls-syria/index.html (accessed June 30, 2018).

117   See esp. Maura Conway, "Determining the Role of the Internet in Violent Extremism and Terrorism: Six Suggestions for Progressing Research," *Studies in Conflict & Terrorism*, 40(1) (2017).

118   See Simon Cottee and Jack Cunliffe, "Watching ISIS: How Young Adults Engage with Official English-language ISIS Videos," *Studies in Conflict & Terrorism* (2018).

119 See Cori E. Dauber and Mark Robinson, "ISIS and the Hollywood Visual Style," *Jihadology*, July 6, 2015, available at: https://jihadology.net/2015/07/06/guest-post-isis-and-the-hollywood-visual-style/ (accessed June 30, 2018).

120 Martyn Frampton et al., *The New Netwar: Countering Extremism Online*, Policy Exchange, 2017, available at: https://policyexchange.org.uk/wp-content/uploads/2017/09/The-New-Netwar-2.pdf, 15 (accessed June 30, 2018).

121 William Ian Miller, *The Anatomy of Disgust* (Cambridge, Mass: Harvard University Press, 1997), 112.

122 See "New video message from The Islamic State: 'The Failed Confrontation—Wilāyat Saynā'," *Jihadology*, March 23, 2018, available at: https://jihadology.net/category/the-islamic-state/wilayat-sina-sinai/ (accessed June 30, 2018).

123 See "New Video Message from The Islamic State: 'Inside the Caliphate #7', *Jihadology*, February 7, 2018, available at: https://jihadology.net/2018/02/07/new-video-message-from-the-islamic-state-inside-the-caliphate-7/ (accessed June 30, 2018).

124 See "Europol Internet Referral Unit One year On," July 22, 2016, available at: https://www.europol.europa.eu/newsroom/news/europol-internet-referral-unit-one-year (accessed June 30, 2018).

125 See Ellie Hall, "Telegram App Shuts Down 78 ISIS-Related Channels," *Buzzfeed News*, November 18, 2015, available at: https://www.buzzfeed.com/ellievhall/telegram-app-shuts-down-78-isis-related-channels?utm_term=.jbryWerKD#.xulMnE3e4 (accessed June 30, 2018).

126 Cottee and Cunliffe, "Watching ISIS."

Chapter 2 The Meaning and Appeal of Jihadist Violence

1 Martin Amis, *The Second Plane: September 11: Terror and Boredom* (London: Knopf Jonathan Cape, 2008).

2 Bernard-Henri Levy, *Who Killed Daniel Pearl?* (London: Duckworth, 2003), 82.

3 Cesare Lombroso, *L'uomo Delinquente* (Milan: Hoepli, 1876).

4 See Souad Mekhennet and Adam Goldman, "'Jihadi John': Islamic State Killer is Identified as Londoner Mohammed Emwazi," *The Washington Post*, February 26, 2015, available at: https://www.washingtonpost.com/world/national-security/jihadi-john-the-islamic-state-killer-behind-the-mask-is-a-young-londoner/2015/02/25/d6dbab16-bc43-11e4-bdfa-b8e8f594e6ee_story.html?noredirect=on&utm_term=.17a8d512e5a6 (accessed June 21, 2018).

5 Cesare Lombroso, *Comptes-Rendus du VI-e Congrès International D'Anthropologie Criminelle* (Hachette BNF, 1906), XXXI.

6 Leon Radzinowicz, *Ideology and Crime* (London: Heinemann, 1966), 48.

7 See Heather Saul, "'Jihadi John': Mohammed Emwazi was 'Extremely Kind, Gentle, Beautiful Young Man', says Cage Director," *The Independent*, February 26, 2015, available at: https://www.independent.co.uk/news/uk/home-news/jihadi-john-mohammed-emwazi-was-an-extremely-kind-gentle-beautiful-young-man-says-cage-director-10073338.html (accessed June 21, 2018).

8 According to one news report on Emwazi, "a school picture captured what appeared to be an angelic smile" (Brian Ross, Rhonda Schwartz and Rym Momtaz, "Officials: Mom Knew Her Son Mohammed Emwazi Was 'Jihadi John'," *ABC News*,

March 2, 2015, available at: https://abcnews.go.com/International/officials-mom-knew-son-jihadi-john/story?id=29321335 (accessed June 21, 2018).

9 Harold Garfinkel, "Conditions of Successful Degradation Ceremonies," *American Journal of Sociology*, 61 (1956), 420–24.

10 When "Jihadi John's" identity was revealed by Souad Mekhennet and Adam Goldman in late February, 2015, a photo surfaced of Emwazi wearing an oversized baseball cap, making him look ridiculous (see: http://www.channel4.com/media/images/Channel4/c4-news/2015/March/03/03_emwazi_student_w-(None)_LRG.jpg (accessed June 21, 2018)).

11 Lewis A. Coser, *The Functions of Social Conflict* (London: Routledge and Kegan Paul, 1956), 69.

12 Mary Douglas, *Purity and Danger* (London: Routledge, 1966), 49.

13 According to CAGE, Emwazi was radicalized by his oppressive treatment at the hands of the British security services.

14 Christopher Hitchens, "Guilty Bystanders," *Slate*, January 22, 2007, available at: http://www.slate.com/articles/news_and_politics/fighting_words/2007/01/guilty_bystanders.html?via=gdpr-consent (accessed June 21, 2018).

15 "Video: 'Jihadi John' Unmasked," *CNN*, March 6, 2015, available at: https://edition.cnn.com/videos/world/2015/03/06/emwazi-amateur-video-basketball.cnn (accessed June 21, 2018).

16 Elie Wiesel, *One Generation After* (New York: Random House, 1970), 4.

17 Hannah Arendt, *Eichmann in Jerusalem: A Report on the Banality of Evil* (New York: Viking Press, 1963).

18 Quoted in "My Sister was into Any Normal Teenage Things," *CBS News*, March 11, 2015, available at: https://www.cbsnews.com/news/families-of-uk-teenage-girls-apparent-isis-recruits-testify-hearing/ (accessed June 21, 2018).

19 See de Freytas-Tamura, "Teenage Girl Leaves for ISIS, and Others Follow."

20 See "Video: 'Jihadi John' Unmasked," *CNN*.

21 See "The Bombers," *BBC News*, http://news.bbc.co.uk/1/shared/spl/hi/uk/05/london_blasts/investigation/html/bombers.stm (accessed June 21, 2018).

22 According to a report in the *Daily Mail* the girls had been "ruthlessly groomed online" and were "brainwashed in their bedrooms" (Chris Greenwood et al., "Police Spoke to Schoolgirl Jihadi Brides in December—But there was 'No Evidence' they had been Radicalised, Insists Headteacher," *The Daily Mail*, February 22, 2015, http://www.dailymail.co.uk/news/article-2964421/Brainwashed-bedrooms-British-schoolgirl-jihadi-brides-fled-Syria-join-ISIS-following-70-extremists-Twitter-accounts-internet-giant-refused-axe.html (accessed June 21, 2018)).

23 J. Glenn Gray, *The Warriors: Reflections on Men in Battle* (Lincoln: University of Nebraska Press, 1959), 215.

24 Philip Caputo, *A Rumor of War* (London: Pimlico, 1977), 5.

25 This debate was sparked by Graeme Wood's March 2015 *Atlantic* article "What ISIS Really Wants," *The Atlantic*, March 2015, available at: https://www.theatlantic.com/magazine/archive/2015/03/what-isis-really-wants/384980/ (accessed June 21, 2018).

26 See Bruce Hoffman, "Foreword," in Andrew Silke, ed., *Research on Terrorism: Trends, Achievements, and Failures* (Oxon: Routledge, 2004), xviii.

27 See Randy Borum, *Psychology of Terrorism* (Tampa: University of South Florida, 2004), 32; and Andrew Silke, "Cheshire-Cat Logic: The Recurring Theme of Terrorist Abnormality in Psychological Research," *Psychology, Crime & Law*, 4(1) (1998), 51–69.

28 See esp. Arne Johan Vetlesen, *Evil and Human Agency: Understanding Collective Evildoing* (Cambridge: Cambridge University Press, 2005); C. Fred Alford, *What Evil Means to Us* (Ithaca, NY: Cornell University Press, 1997).

29 Bandura, "Mechanisms of Moral Disengagement," 182.

30 See, for example, Noam Chomsky, *Power and Terror: Post-9/11 Talks and Interviews* (New York: Seven Stories Press, 2003); Tariq Ali, *The Clash of Fundamentalisms: Crusades, Jihads and Modernity* Paperback (London: Verso, 2003); and Tariq Ali, *Bush in Babylon: The Recolinisation of Iraq* (London: Verso, 2004).

31 See Erin Marie Saltman and Melanie Smith, "'Till Martyrdom Do Us Part': Gender and the ISIS Phenomenon," Institute for Strategic Dialogue, 2015, available at: https://www.isdglobal.org/wp-content/uploads/2016/02/Till_Martyrdom_Do_Us_Part_Gender_and_the_ISIS_Phenomenon.pdf (accessed June 21, 2018).

32 Jack Katz, *Seductions of Crime: Moral and Sensual Attractions in Doing Evil* (New York: Basic Books, 1988), 3–4.

33 David Aaronovitch, "Violence in Search of a Cause: What a Famous Book Tells Us About Terrorism," *The Times*, August 29, 2006, available at: https://www.thetimes.co.uk/article/violence-in-search-of-a-cause-what-a-famous-book-tells-us-about-terrorism-kccr6vdpcrp (accessed June 21, 2018).

34 Philip Roth, *American Pastoral* (London: Vintage, 1998), 81.

35 See, for example, Bruce Lawrence (ed.), *Messages to the World: The Statements of Osama bin Laden* (London: Verso, 2005).

36 Stephen Holmes, "Al-Qaeda, September 11, 2001," in D. Gambetta, ed., *Making Sense of Suicide Missions* (Oxford: Oxford University Press, 2005), 132–33.

37 See, classically, Marvin B. Scott and Stanford M. Lyman, "Accounts," *American Sociological Review* 33(1) (1968), 46–62.

38 John Horgan, "Don't Ask Why People Join the Islamic State—Ask How," *Vice*, September 10, 2014, available at: https://news.vice.com/article/dont-ask-why-people-join-the-islamic-state-ask-how (accessed June 21, 2018).

39 Paul Hollander, *Political Pilgrims: Western Intellectuals in Search of the Good Society*, 4th edn. (New Brunswick, Transaction Publishers, 1997).

40 See Neumann, "Foreign Fighter Total in Syria/Iraq now Exceeds 20,000." By December 2015, that figure rose to around 5,000, according to The Soufan Group (2015), "Foreign Fighters: An Updated Assessment of the Flow of Foreign Fighters into Syria and Iraq," December 2, 2015, available at: http://soufangroup.com/wp-content/uploads/2015/12/TSG_ForeignFightersUpdate3.pdf, 12 (accessed June 22, 2018). For a note of skepticism about these estimates, see Hassan Hassan, "ISIL and the Numbers Game: What Exactly is the Size of its Army?," *The National*, October 25, 2017, available at: https://www.thenational.ae/opinion/comment/isil-and-the-numbers-game-what-exactly-is-the-size-of-its-army-1.670132 (accessed June 22, 2018).

41 See Saltman and Smith, "'Till Martyrdom Do Us Part'," 4.

42 See Mark Townsend et al., "What Happened to the British Medics Who Went to Work for Isis?," *The Observer*, July 12, 2015, available at: https://www.theguardian.com/world/2015/jul/12/british-medics-isis-turkey-islamic-state (accessed June 22, 2018).

43 Beren Cross, "Abdel-Majed Abdel Bary: British Jihadist 'Deserts Isis in Syria and goes on the Run in Turkey'," *The Independent*, July 12, 2015, available at: https://www.independent.co.uk/news/uk/home-news/abdel-majed-abdel-bary-british-jihadist-deserted-isis-in-syria-and-is-on-the-run-in-turkey-10384099.html (accessed June 22, 2018). Bary's whereabouts, as I write, is still unknown.

44   See Lizzie Dearden, "Isis Recruiting Violent Criminals and Gang Members across Europe in Dangerous New 'Crime-Terror Nexus'," *The Independent*, October 10, 2016, available at: https://www.independent.co.uk/news/world/europe/isis-recruiting-violent-criminals-gang-members-drugs-europe-new-crime-terror-nexus-report-drugs-a7352271.html (accessed June 22, 2018).

45   See Sally Chidzoy and David Keller, "Luton Family of 12 'may have gone to Syria'," *BBC News*, July 1, 2015, available at: https://www.bbc.co.uk/news/uk-england-beds-bucks-herts-33347117 (accessed June 22, 2018).

46   Ashley Fantz and Atika Shubert, "From Scottish Teen to ISIS Bride and Recruiter: The Aqsa Mahmood Story," *CNN*, February 24, 2015, available at: https://edition.cnn.com/2015/02/23/world/scottish-teen-isis-recruiter/ (accessed June 22, 2018).

47   Robert Conquest, *Reflections on a Ravaged Century* (London: John Murray, 1999), 125.

48   Karl Mannheim, *Ideology and Utopia, Volume 1* (London: Routledge, 1998), 184.

49   Chidzoy and Keller, "Luton Family of 12 'may have gone to Syria'."

50   Vikram Dodd and Nadia Khomami, "Luton Family of 12 Feared to have gone to Syria," *The Guardian*, July 1, 2015, available at: https://www.theguardian.com/world/2015/jul/01/luton-family-of-12-feared-gone-syria(accessed June 22, 2018).

51   See "ITV News Exclusive: 'My Dad doesn't want to be in Syria with Islamic State'," *ITV News*, July 9, 2015, available at: http://www.itv.com/news/2015-07-09/itv-news-exclusive-my-dad-doesnt-want-to-be-in-syria-with-islamic-state-luton/ (accessed June 22, 2018).

52   See "Missing UK Family 'Safer than Ever with Islamic State'," *BBC News*, July 4, 2015, available at: https://www.bbc.co.uk/news/uk-33393628 (accessed June 22, 2018).

53   See Jay Akbar, " 'All 12 of us are in the Islamic State': Luton Family Confirm they ARE in Syria and Encourage Other Britons to Join them," *Mail Online*, July 4, 2015, available at: http://www.dailymail.co.uk/news/article-3149190/All-12-Islamic-State-Luton-family-release-statement-confirming-Syria.html (accessed June 22, 2018).

54   Quoted in "Missing UK Family 'Safer than Ever with Islamic State'."

55   Saltman and Smith, " 'Till Martyrdom Do Us Part'."

56   See Anita Peresin and Alberto Cervone, "The Western Muhajirat of ISIS," *Studies in Conflict & Terrorism*, 38 (7) (2015), 495–509.

57   See "Extremism: PM Speech," July 20, 2015, available at: https://www.gov.uk/government/speeches/extremism-pm-speech (accessed June 22, 2018).

58   See, for example, "United, We can Protect Our Young People from Extremists," *The Guardian*, July 8, 2015, available at: https://www.theguardian.com/uk-news/2015/jul/08/united-we-can-protect-our-young-people-from-extremists (accessed June 22, 2018); Part 5 of Counter-Terrorism and Security Act 2015, available at: http://www.legislation.gov.uk/ukpga/2015/6/part/5/enacted (accessed June 22, 2018); and Jake Burman, "Teachers Warned to Look Out for Future Terrorists amid ISIS 'Child Grooming' Fears," *The Express*, June 30, 2015, available at: https://www.express.co.uk/news/uk/587732/David-Cameron-ISIS-terror-extremism-primary-secondary-schools-Tunisia (accessed June 22, 2018).

59   See, for example, "PREVENT will have a Chilling Effect on Open Debate, Free Speech and Political Dissent," *The Independent*, July 10, 2015, available at: https://www.independent.co.uk/voices/letters/prevent-will-have-a-chilling-effect-on-open-debate-free-speech-and-political-dissent-10381491.html (accessed June 22, 2018); "Jihadi

John: 'Radicalised' by Britain," February 26, 2015, CAGE, available at: https://www.cage.ngo/jihadi-john-radicalised-britain(accessed June 22, 2018); and Michaela Whitton, "Prevent or Pursuit? The Government's New Deradicalization Strategy," *New Internationalist*, July 14, 2015, available at: https://newint.org/features/web-exclusive/2015/07/14/prevent-terrorism-programme/ (accessed June 22, 2018).

60 Christina Nemr, "Countering Islamic State Recruitment: You're Doing it Totally Wrong," *War on the Rocks*, July 14, 2015, available at: https://warontherocks.com/2015/07/countering-islamic-state-recruitment-youre-doing-it-totally-wrong/ (accessed June 22, 2018).

61 See Matt Chorley, "'Disease' of Islamic Extremism will Hang Over my Generation, says Cameron as he describes Watching Hostage Videos," *Mail Online*, February 5, 2015, available at: http://www.dailymail.co.uk/news/article-2940979/The-disease-Islamic-extremism-hang-generation-Cameron-admits-insists-Britain-doing-defeat-ISIS-monstrosity.html (accessed June 22, 2018).

62 See esp. Scott Atran, "ISIS is a Revolution," *Aeon*, December 15, 2015, available at: https://aeon.co/essays/why-isis-has-the-potential-to-be-a-world-altering-revolution (accessed June 22, 2018).

63 See Jytte Klausen, "Tweeting the Jihad: Social Media Networks of Western Foreign Fighters in Syria and Iraq," *Studies in Conflict & Terrorism*, 38 (1) (2015), 15–16.

64 "Jihadi-cool," July 16, 2015, available at: https://bintchaos.wordpress.com/2015/07/16/jihadi-cool/ (accessed June 22, 2018).

65 See, illuminatingly, Bryan Schatz, "Inside the World of ISIS Propaganda Music," *Mother Jones*, February 9, 2015, available at: https://www.motherjones.com/politics/2015/02/isis-islamic-state-baghdadi-music-jihad-nasheeds/ (accessed June 22, 2018).

66 "Jedi Knights, Browncoats, Fremen and Mujahideen," May 25, 2015, available at: https://bintchaos.wordpress.com/tag/dune/ (accessed June 22, 2018).

67 "Gene Flow, Memetic Fitness, the Islamic State and Warrior Demes," March 28, 2015, available at: https://bintchaos.wordpress.com/2015/03/28/gene-flow-and-meme-flow-the-islamic-state-and-warrior-demes/ (accessed June 22, 2018).

68 See "Why It's So Hard to Stop ISIS Propaganda," this volume.

69 "The Wretched Hive: Brookings," March 23, 2015, available at: https://bintchaos.wordpress.com/2015/03/23/the-wretched-hive-brookings/ (accessed June 22, 2018).

70 "Embracing Apocalypse I: The Islamic State and the Prophetic Methodology," June 13, 2015, available at: https://bintchaos.wordpress.com/2015/06/13/embracing-apocalypse-the-islamic-state-and-the-prophetic-methodology/ (accessed June 22, 2018).

71 See https://twitter.com/tomwyke/status/600073855865069568 (accessed June 22, 2018).

72 Barry McCarthy, "Warrior Values: A Socio-Historical Survey," in John Archer, ed., *Male Violence* (London: Routledge, 1994), 112.

73 Richard E. Nisbett and Dov Cohen, *Culture of Honor: The Psychology of Violence in the South* (Boulder, CO: Westview Press, 1996), 93.

74 Thomas Hegghammer, "The Soft Power of Militant Jihad," *The New York Times*, December 18, 2015, available at: https://www.nytimes.com/2015/12/20/opinion/sunday/militant-jihads-softer-side.html (accessed June 22, 2018).

75 See "Why It's So Hard to Stop ISIS Propaganda," this volume.

76 See, classically, Jean-Francois Lyotard, *The Postmodern Condition: A Report on Knowledge* (Minnesota: University of Minnesota Press, 1984).

77   See "Archive Footage Shows Paris Attacks Mastermind Abdelhamid Abaaoud in Syria," *The Telegraph*, November 19, 2015, available at: https://www.telegraph.co.uk/news/worldnews/europe/france/12005519/Archive-footage-shows-Paris-attacks-mastermind-Abdelhamid-Abaaoud-in-Syria.html (accessed June 22, 2018).

78   Andrew Higgins, "Belgium Confronts the Jihadist Danger Within," *The New York Times*, January 24, 2015, available at: https://www.nytimes.com/2015/01/25/world/europe/belgium-confronts-the-jihadist-danger-within.html?_r=1 (accessed June 22, 2018).

79   See esp. Mark S. Hamm, *The Spectacular Few: Prisoner Radicalization and the Evolving Terrorist Threat* (New York: New York University Press, 2013).

80   See Natalia Drozdiak and Matthew Dalton, "Two Suspects Sold Bar in Brussels Not Long Before Paris Attacks," *The Wall Street Journal*, November 18, 2015, available at: https://www.wsj.com/articles/two-suspects-sold-bar-in-brussels-not-long-before-paris-attacks-1447863006 (accessed June 22, 2018).

81   Salah Abdeslam was arrested on March 18, 2016, after a shootout with Belgian police, for which he received a 20-year prison sentence (see Erin McLaughlin and Hilary Clarke, "Saleh Abdeslam Jailed for 20 Years over Police Shootout," *CNN*, April 23, 2018, available at: https://edition.cnn.com/2018/04/23/europe/paris-suspect-saleh-abdeslam-jailed-belgium–intl/index.html (accessed June 22, 2018)). He has yet to face trial for his involvement in the 2015 Paris attacks.

82   See Matthew Campbell et al., "Gay Sex, Drugs, then Suicidal Slaughter," *The Sunday Times*, November 22, 2015, available at: https://www.thetimes.co.uk/article/gay-sex-drugs-then-suicidal-slaughter-8mx82kjmbqq (accessed June 22, 2018). Actually, in this respect, Salah Abdeslam may well exactly have been your typical finger-waving ideological fanatic: see "Osama bin Laden's Secret Masturbation Fatwa," this volume.

83   Anthony Faiola and Souad Mekhennet, "The Islamic State Creates a New Type of Jihadist: Part Terrorist, Part Gangster," *The Washington Post*, December 20, 2015, available at: https://www.washingtonpost.com/world/europe/the-islamic-state-creates-a-new-type-of-jihadist-part-terrorist-part-gangster/2015/12/20/1a3d65da-9bae-11e5-aca6-1ae3be6f06d2_story.html?utm_term=.aa707a27b194 (accessed June 22, 2018).

84   See Mia Bloom, "Cubs of the Caliphate," *Foreign Affairs*, July 21, 2015, available at: https://www.foreignaffairs.com/articles/2015-07-21/cubs-caliphate (accessed June 22, 2018).

85   See Mary Anne Weaver, "The Short, Violent Life of Abu Musab al-Zarqawi," *The Atlantic*, July/August 2006, available at: https://www.theatlantic.com/magazine/archive/2006/07/the-short-violent-life-of-abu-musab-al-zarqawi/304983/ (accessed June 22, 2018).

86   Dominic Casciani, "Who is Siddhartha Dhar?," *BBC News*, January 4, 2016, available at: https://www.bbc.co.uk/news/uk-35225636 (accessed June 22, 2018).

87   Mat Heywood et al., "Who is Abu Rumaysah, Alleged to be the Masked Man in the Latest Isis Film?," *The Guardian*, January 5, 2016, available at: https://www.theguardian.com/uk-news/video/2016/jan/05/who-is-abu-rumaysah-alleged-to-be-the-masked-man-in-the-latest-isis-film-video (accessed June 22, 2018).

88   See Cahal Milmo, "Isis Video: 'New Jihadi John' Suspect Siddhartha Dhar is a 'Former Bouncy Castle Salesman from East London'," *The Independent*, January 4, 2016, available at: https://www.independent.co.uk/news/uk/home-news/isis-video-new-jihadi-john-suspect-is-a-former-bouncy-castle-salesman-from-east-london-a6796591.html (accessed June 22, 2018).

89   Bakker, "Jihadi Terrorists in Europe and Global Salafi Jihadis."

90 Robin Simcox, "'We Will Conquer Your Rome': A Study of Islamic State Terror Plots in the West," *HJS*, 2015, available at: http://henryjacksonsociety.org/wp-content/uploads/2015/09/ISIS-brochure-Web.pdf (accessed June 22, 2018), 3.

91 Scott Kleinman and Scott Flower, "From Convert to Extremist: New Muslims and Terrorism," *The Conversation*, May 24, 2013, available at: https://theconversation.com/from-convert-to-extremist-new-muslims-and-terrorism-14643 (accessed June 22, 2018).

92 Eric Hoffer, *The True Believer: Thoughts on the Nature of Mass Movements* (New York: Harper & Row, 1951).

93 Ibid.

94 Quintan Wiktorowicz, *Radical Islam Rising: Muslim Extremism in the West* (Lanham MD: Rowman and Littlefield, 2005), 51–60.

95 See Marion van San, "Lost Souls Searching for Answers? Belgian and Dutch Converts Joining the Islamic State," *Perspectives on Terrorism*, 9 (5) (2015), available at: http://www.terrorismanalysts.com/pt/index.php/pot/article/view/460/html (accessed June 22, 2018); and Ben McPartland, "Converts from all Corners of France Lured into Jihad," *TheLocal.com*, November 20, 2014, available at: https://www.thelocal.fr/20141120/jihad-french-nationals-is-isis (accessed June 22, 2018).

96 See esp. Kate Zebiri, *British Muslim Converts: Choosing Alternative Lives* (Oxford: Oneworld Publications, 2008).

97 Lewis A. Coser, "The Alien as a Servant of Power: Court Jews and Christian Renegades," *American Sociological Review*, 37 (5) (1972), 580.

98 Olivier Roy, "France's Oedipal Islamist Complex," *Foreign Policy*, January 7, 2016, available at: http://foreignpolicy.com/2016/01/07/frances-oedipal-islamist-complex-charlie-hebdo-islamic-state-isis/ (accessed June 22, 2018).

99 Marc Sageman, *Leaderless Jihad: Terror Networks in the Twenty-First Century* (Philadelphia: University of Pennsylvania Press, 2008).

100 Atran, *Talking to the Enemy*.

101 Hoffer, *The True Believer*.

102 Diego Gambetta, ed., *Making Sense of Suicide Missions* (New York: Oxford University Press, 2005), 273.

103 This article was written just days after the coordinated suicide bombings at Brussels airport and a metro station in the city on March 22, 2016, which killed 32 people.

104 Uri Friedman, "The 'Strategic Logic' of Suicide Bombing," *The Atlantic*, March 23, 2016, available at: https://www.theatlantic.com/international/archive/2016/03/brussels-attacks-terrorism-isis/474858/ (accessed June 22, 2018).

105 Robert A. Pape, *Dying to Win: The Strategic Logic of Suicide Terrorism* (New York: Random House, 2005), 23.

106 Ibid., 92.

107 Friedman, "The 'Strategic Logic' of Suicide Bombing."

108 See "Islamic State Commander Omar Shishani Dead, says Pentagon," *BBC News*, March 14, 2016, available at: https://www.bbc.co.uk/news/world-middle-east-35808738 (accessed June 22, 2018).

109 See David A. Graham, "What's the Matter With Belgium?," *The Atlantic*, November 17, 2015, available at: https://www.theatlantic.com/international/archive/2015/11/belgium-radical-islam-jihad-molenbeek-isis/416235/ (accessed June 22, 2018).

110 Jeremy Waldron, "Terrorism and the Uses of Terror," *The Journal of Ethics* 8 (1) (2004), 27.

111   Clint Watts, "A Wounded Islamic State Is a Dangerous Islamic State," *Foreign Policy*, March 23, 2016, available at: http://foreignpolicy.com/2016/03/23/a-wounded-islamic-state-is-a-dangerous-islamic-state-brussels-attacks/ (accessed June 22, 2018).

112   Juergensmeyer, *Terror in the Mind of God*, 124.

113   Fanon, *The Wretched of the Earth*, 94, 122.

114   Quoted in William Saletan, "Preaching to the Choir," *Slate*, May 15, 2015, available at: http://www.slate.com/articles/news_and_politics/foreigners/2015/05/abu_bakr_al_baghdadi_sounds_a_lot_like_a_republican_presidential_candidate.html (accessed June 22, 2018).

115   See Issue 7 of *Dabiq*, available at: https://azelin.files.wordpress.com/2015/02/the-islamic-state-e2809cdc481biq-magazine-722.pdf, 54–66 (accessed June 22, 2018).

116   See Jessica Stern, "ISIS Targets 'Gray Zone' of Moderate Islam," *The Boston Globe*, March 23, 2016, available at: https://www.bostonglobe.com/opinion/2016/03/23/isis-targets-grayzone-moderate-islam/p9Uiv35DEnHSt7Fzk9SL1K/story.html?utm_content=buffer29ebd&utm_medium=social&utm_source=twitter.com&utm_campaign=buffer (accessed June 22, 2018).

117   See Max Abrahms, "Why People Keep Saying, 'That's What the Terrorists Want'," November 20, 2015, available at: https://hbr.org/2015/11/why-people-keep-saying-thats-what-the-terrorists-want (accessed June 22, 2018). Funnily enough, Abrahms's 2008 journal article for *International Security* was titled "What Terrorists Really Want" (32(4), 78–105).

118   Mia Bloom, *Dying to Kill: The Allure of Suicide Terror* (New York: Columbia University Press, 2005).

119   See "CCTV Shows Paris Bomber Detonating Suicide Belt," *Sky News*, April 26, 2016, available   at: https://news.sky.com/story/cctv-shows-paris-bomber-detonating-suicide-belt-10258608 (accessed June 23, 2018).

120   This is a reference to the red-colored soft drink—and to the utterly preposterous rumor, which circulated in early 2016, that ISIS used it to fake blood in its gory execution videos (see "The 'Vimto Caliphate'—Islamic State Group Mocked Over Fake Blood Claims," *BBC News*, February 24, 2016, available at: https://www.bbc.co.uk/news/blogs-trending-35640385 (accessed June 23, 2018).

121   See "What It's Really Like to Fight for the Islamic State," *Vice News*, April 27, 2016, available   at: https://news.vice.com/video/what-its-really-like-to-fight-for-the-islamic-state (accessed June 23, 2018).

122   See Nour Malas "Military Setbacks, Financial Strains Pressure Islamic State in Home Territory," *The Wall Street Journal*, March 22, 2016, https://www.wsj.com/articles/military-setbacks-financial-strains-pressure-islamic-state-in-home-territory-1458680727 (accessed June 23, 2018).

123   See Gordon Rayner and Camilla Turner, "Suicide Bomber 'Blew Himself Up Because of Stress', says Ibrahim Abdeslam's Family," *The Telegraph*, November 16, 2015, available at: https://www.telegraph.co.uk/news/worldnews/islamic-state/11998297/Suicide-bomber-blew-himself-up-because-of-stress-says-Ibrahim-Abdeslams-family.html (accessed June 23, 2018).

124   See Hannah Roberts, "The Pot-smoking Paris Suicide Bomber: Ex-wife Reveals 'Blood Brother' Terrorist was a Jobless Layabout Who Spent his Time taking Drugs and Sleeping … and Never went to the Mosque," *Mail Online*, November 17, 2015, available at: http://www.dailymail.co.uk/news/article-3322385/Ex-wife-Comptoir-Voltaire-caf-bomber-reveals-jobless-layabout-spent-day-bed-smoking-pot-French-say-blew-mistake-fiddling-suicide-vest.html (accessed June 23, 2018).

125 Atika Shubert, "UK Schoolgirl's Interests went from Chelsea FC to ISIS," *CNN*, May 28, 2015, available at: https://edition.cnn.com/videos/world/2015/05/28/uk-isis-schoolgirls-shubert-pkg.cnn (accessed June 23, 2018).

126 Holmes, "Al-Qaeda, September 11, 2001," 137.

127 Diego Gambetta, "Can We Make Sense of Suicide Missions," in D. Gambetta, ed., *Making Sense of Suicide Missions*, 295.

128 Ibid., 296.

129 Adam Lankford, "Could Suicide Terrorists Actually Be Suicidal?," *Studies in Conflict & Terrorism*, 34 (4) (2011), 337.

130 See Ariel Merari, *Driven to Death: Psychological and Social Aspects of Suicide Terrorism* (Oxford: Oxford University Press, 2010).

131 Merari et al., "Personality Characteristics of 'Self Martyrs'/'Suicide Bombers' and Organizers of Suicide Attacks," *Terrorism and Political Violence*, 22 (1) (2009), 96, 95.

132 See Robert J. Brym and Bader Araj, "Are Suicide Bombers Suicidal?," *Studies in Conflict & Terrorism*, 35 (6) (2012).

133 See esp. Atran, *Talking to the Enemy*.

134 Rex Hudson, "The Sociology and Psychology of Terrorism: Who becomes a Terrorist and Why?," Library of Congress, September 1999, available at: https://www.loc.gov/rr/frd/pdf-files/Soc_Psych_of_Terrorism.pdf, 60 (accessed June 23, 2018).

135 See "Brussels Attacks: Molenbeek's Gangster Jihadists," *BBC News*, March 24, 2016, available at: https://www.bbc.co.uk/news/magazine-35890960 (accessed June 23, 2018).

136 Wood, "What ISIS Really Wants."

137 See, for example, Caner K. Dagli, "The Phony Islam of ISIS," *The Atlantic*, February 27, 2015, available at: https://www.theatlantic.com/international/archive/2015/02/what-muslims-really-want-isis-atlantic/386156/ (accessed June 22, 2018).

138 See Jay Michaelson "If Omar Mateen Was Gay, It Makes the LGBT Nightclub Attack More Homophobic," *The Daily Beast*, June 15, 2016, available at: https://www.thedailybeast.com/if-omar-mateen-was-gay-it-makes-the-lgbt-nightlub-attack-more-homophobic (accessed June 22, 2018).

139 See Peter Bergen, "Why It's So Hard to Track a 'Lone Wolf'," *Spiegel Online*, June 17, 2016, available at: http://www.spiegel.de/international/world/the-danger-of-lone-wolf-terrorists-like-omar-mateen-a-1098263.html (accessed June 22, 2018).

140 See Adam Withnall, "Isis Official Calls for 'Lone Wolf' Attacks in US and Europe during Ramadan," *The Independent*, May 22, 2016, available at: https://www.independent.co.uk/news/world/middle-east/isis-official-calls-for-lone-wolf-attacks-in-us-and-europe-during-ramadan-a7042296.html (accessed June 22, 2018).

141 Cited in Quentin Skinner, *Visions of Politics: Volume 1: Regarding Method* (Cambridge: Cambridge University Press, 2002), 145.

142 See Leon Wieseltier, "Reason and the Republic of Opinion," *The New Republic*, November 12, 2014, available at: https://newrepublic.com/article/120197/defense-reason-new-republics-100-year-anniversary (accessed June 22, 2018).

143 Cited in Skinner, *Visions of Politics*, 145.

144 Goldhagen, *Hitler's Willing Executioners*.

145 Browning, *Ordinary Men*.

146 Nick Zangwill, "Perpetrator Motivation: Some Reflections on the Browning/Goldhagen Debate," in Eve Garrard and Geoffrey Scarre, eds., *Moral Philosophy and the Holocaust* (Aldershot: Ashgate, 2003), 92.

147 Cited in Mehdi Hasan, "How Islamic is Islamic State?," *New Statesman*, March 10, 2015, available at: https://www.newstatesman.com/world-affairs/2015/03/mehdi-hasan-how-islamic-islamic-state (accessed June 22, 2018).

148 Kathy Gilsinan, "Could ISIS Exist Without Islam?," *The Atlantic*, July 3, 2015, available at: https://www.theatlantic.com/international/archive/2015/07/isis-islam/397661/ (accessed June 23, 2018).

149 Hasan, "How Islamic is Islamic State?"

150 Ishaan Tharoor, "Belgium's Big Problem with Radical Islam," *The Washington Post*, March 22, 2016, available at: https://www.washingtonpost.com/news/worldviews/wp/2016/03/22/belgiums-big-problem-with-radical-islam/ (accessed June 23, 2018).

151 Sam Harris, "Holy Terror: Religion Isn't the Solution—It's the Problem," *Los Angeles Times*, August 15, 2004, available at: http://articles.latimes.com/2004/aug/15/opinion/op-harris15/2 (accessed June 23, 2018).

152 Ayaan Hirsi Ali, "Islam Is a Religion of Violence," *Foreign Policy*, November 9, 2015, available at: http://foreignpolicy.com/2015/11/09/islam-is-a-religion-of-violence-ayaan-hirsi-ali-debate-islamic-state/ (accessed June 23, 2018).

153 Peter Bergen, "Why Do Terrorists Commit Terrorism?," *The New York Times*, June 14, 2016, available at: https://www.nytimes.com/2016/06/15/opinion/why-do-terrorists-commit-terrorism.html (accessed June 23, 2018).

154 Skinner, *Visions of Politics*, 156.

155 Ibid.

156 See https://azelin.files.wordpress.com/2016/07/the-islamic-state-e2809cdacc84biq-magazine-1522.pdf (accessed June 23, 2018).

157 Kareem Shaheen, "Airstrikes Have become Routine for People in Raqqa, Says Activist," *The Guardian*, December 2, 2015, available at: https://www.theguardian.com/world/2015/dec/02/airstrikes-routine-people-raqqa-syria-says-activist (accessed June 23, 2018).

158 See "Man Detained for Smuggling Daesh Recruits in Southern Turkey, 9 others Deported," August 1, 2016, available at: https://www.dailysabah.com/war-on-terror/2016/08/01/man-detained-for-smuggling-daesh-recruits-in-southern-turkey-9-others-deported (accessed June 23, 2018).

159 John McCoy and Andy Knight, "Homegrown Violent Extremism in Trinidad and Tobago: Local Patterns, Global Trends," *Studies in Conflict & Terrorism*, 40/4 (2017).

160 See Gail Alexander, "Serious threat to T&T," *Trinidad and Tobago Guardian*, April 16, 2016, available at: http://www.guardian.co.tt/news/2016-04-15/serious-threat-tt (accessed June 23, 2018).

161 Martin Amis, *Visiting Mrs Nabokov and Other Excursions* (New York: Random House, 1993), 71.

162 Ibid., 72.

163 https://www.osac.gov/Pages/ContentReportDetails.aspx?cid=19522 (accessed June 23, 2018).

164 See "Trinidad Declares State of Emergency in Crime Hot-spots," *BBC News*, August 23, 2011, available at: https://www.bbc.co.uk/news/world-latin-america-14627050 (accessed June 23, 2018).

165 See esp. Ramesh Deosaran, *A Society under Siege* (St. Augustine: University of the West Indies Press, 1997).

166   Quoted in Martine Powers, "Caribbean Nationals Join Forces with ISIS," *Miami Herald*, October 15, 2014, available at: http://www.miamiherald.com/news/nation-world/world/americas/article2838599.html (accessed June 23, 2018).

167   Daurius Figueira, *Salafi Jihadi Discourse of Sunni Islam in the 21st century: The discourse of Abu Muhammad al-Maqdisi and Anwar al-Awlaki* (iUniverse, 2011).

168   Cynthia Mahabir, "Allah's Outlaws: The Jamaat al Muslimeen of Trinidad and Tobago," *British Journal of Criminology*, 53 (2012), 59–73.

169   Chris Zambelis, "Jamaat al-Muslimeen: The Growth and Decline of Islamist Militancy in Trinidad and Tobago," *Terrorism Monitor*, 7 (23), July 30, 2009, available at: https://jamestown.org/program/jamaat-al-muslimeen-the-growth-and-decline-of-islamist-militancy-in-trinidad-and-tobago/ (accessed June 23, 2018).

170   Danny Gold, "The Islamic Leader Who Tried to Overthrow Trinidad Has Mellowed… a Little," *Vice*, May 30, 2014, available at: https://news.vice.com/article/the-islamic-leader-who-tried-to-overthrow-trinidad-has-mellowed-a-little (accessed June 23, 2018).

171   See 'I'M NO ISIS POINT MAN', *Trinidad and Tobago Sunday Express*, October 18, 2014, available at: http://web.trinidadexpress.com/news/IM-NO-ISIS–POINT-MAN-279688692.html (accessed June 23, 2018).

172   In early 2018 the government of T&T introduced numerous amendments to its terrorism legislation, but these have yet to be passed: see Gail Alexander, "Proposed Anti-terrorism Laws on Hold," *Trinidad and Tobago Guardian*, April 11, 2018, available at: http://www.guardian.co.tt/news/2018-04-10/proposed-anti-terrorism-laws-hold (accessed June 23, 2018).

173   Mark Fraser, "Why My Son Fights with ISIS," *Trinidad and Tobago Daily Express*, October 10, 2014, available at: https://www.trinidadexpress.com/news/local/why-my-son-fights-with-isis/article_606e2327-546e-5658-ac31-35b0e1db43fa.html (accessed June 23, 2018).

174   See "Isis Lures British Girls with Flights and Marriage Offer," *The Times*, December 19, 2014, available at: https://www.thetimes.co.uk/article/isis-lures-british-girls-with-flights-and-marriage-offer-zpzl7shwbtc (accessed June 23, 2018).

175   See Colleen Curry, "A British Mother Reportedly Left Welfare Behind and Is Now Helping Recruit for the Islamic State," *Vice*, December 22, 2014, available at: https://news.vice.com/article/a-british-mother-reportedly-left-welfare-behind-and-is-now-helping-recruit-for-the-islamic-state (accessed June 23, 2018).

176   Jason Burke "Isis sends Female Supporters to Serve as Frontline Suicide Bombers," *The Observer*, November 12, 2016, available at: https://www.theguardian.com/world/2016/nov/12/isis-women-frontline-suicide-bombers   (accessed   June 23, 2018). This proved to be one of the great myths about ISIS—that in mid-2017 it had lifted the ban on using women as combatants. But it never did, and even when the group was at its most desperate in late 2017 the waves of female combatants making it to the frontlines never in fact materialized (see esp. Simon Cottee and Mia Bloom, "The Myth of the ISIS Female Suicide Bomber," *The Atlantic*, September 8, 2017, available at: https://www.theatlantic.com/international/archive/2017/09/isis-female-suicide-bomber/539172/ (accessed June 23, 2018)).

177   Omar Wahid, "Gun-toting Jihadi 'Bride-Maker' Who Grooms British Girls for ISIS Fighters in Syria is Student from London Whose Father is a Successful Businessman,"

The Mail on Sunday, July 3, 2016, available at: http://www.dailymail.co.uk/news/article-3671824/Unmasked-Gun-toting-Jihadi-bride-maker-grooms-British-girls-ISIS-fighters-Syria-student-London-father-successful-businessman.html (accessed June 23, 2018)).

178 See "Daesh isis fanboy @umm_muthanna raw tweet dump," December 7, 2014, https://pastebin.com/9RdGupP6 (accessed June 23, 2018)).

179 Hoffer, *The True Believer.*

180 See de Freytas-Tamura, "Teenage Girl Leaves for ISIS, and Others Follow."

181 See https://www.dni.gov/index.php/features/bin-laden-s-bookshelf?start=1 (accessed June 24, 2018).

182 https://www.dni.gov/files/documents/ubl2017/english/Letter%20to%20Abu%20Muhammad%20Salah.pdf (accessed June 24, 2018).

183 See Peter Bergen, "Bin Laden: Seized Documents Show Delusional Leader and Micromanager," *CNN*, May 3, 2012, available at: https://edition.cnn.com/2012/04/30/opinion/bergen-bin-laden-document-trove/ (accessed June 24, 2018).

184 Richard Dawkins, "Religion's Misguided Missiles," *The Guardian*, September 15, 2001, available at: https://www.theguardian.com/world/2001/sep/15/september11.politicsphilosophyandsociety1 (accessed June 24, 2018).

185 Christopher Hitchens, *God is Not Great: How Religion Poisons Everything* (New York: Twelve, 2007), 78.

186 Sayyid Qutb, "The America I Have Seen," in *The Scale of Human Values* (1951), available at: https://archive.org/stream/SayyidQutb/The%20America%20I%20have%20seen_djvu.txt (accessed June 24, 2018).

187 Martin Amis, "The Age of Horrorism (Part One)," *The Guardian*, September 10, 2006, available at: https://www.theguardian.com/world/2006/sep/10/september11.politicsphilosophyandsociety (accessed June 24, 2018).

188 See https://www.pbs.org/wgbh/pages/frontline/shows/network/personal/attawill.html (accessed June 24, 2018).

189 Roy, "France's Oedipal Islamist Complex."

190 Scott Sayare, "The Untold Story of the Bastille Day Attacker," *GQ*, January 24, 2017, available at: https://www.gq.com/story/nice-france-bastille-day-attack-untold-story (accessed June 24, 2018).

191 Mia Bloom, *Bombshell: Women and Terrorism* (Philadelphia: University of Pennsylvania Press, 2011), 63.

192 See Deeyah Khan, "For Isis Women, It's not about 'Jihadi Brides': It's about Escape," *The Observer*, June 21, 2015, available at: https://www.theguardian.com/world/2015/jun/21/isis-women-its-not-about-jihadi-brides-its-about-escape (accessed June 24, 2018).

193 See "London Attack: What We Know," *The Atlantic*, March 27, 2017, available at: https://www.theatlantic.com/liveblogs/2017/03/british-parliament-shots-fired/520395/ (accessed June 24, 2018).

194 See "Islamic State Claims it was behind Westminster Terror Attack," *Sky News*, March 24, 2017, https://news.sky.com/story/seven-arrested-in-raids-in-birmingham-and-london-linked-to-westminster-attack-10811141 (accessed June 24, 2018).

195 Quoted in Aaron Zelin, "ISIS Is Dead, Long Live the Islamic State," *Foreign Policy*, June 30, 2014, available at: http://foreignpolicy.com/2014/06/30/isis-is-dead-long-live-the-islamic-state/ (accessed June 24, 2018).

196 Sarah Almukhtar et al., "ISIS Has Lost Many of the Key Places It Once Controlled," *The New York Times*, October 13, 2016, available at: https://www.nytimes.com/interactive/2016/06/18/world/middleeast/isis-control-places-cities.html (accessed June 23, 2018).

197 Stefan Heibner et al., "Caliphate in Decline: An Estimate of Islamic State's Financial Fortunes," ICSR, 2017, available at: http://icsr.info/wp-content/uploads/2017/02/ICSR-Report-Caliphate-in-Decline-An-Estimate-of-Islamic-States-Financial-Fortunes.pdf (accessed June 24, 2018), 3.

198 Griff Witte et al., "Flow of Foreign Fighters Plummets as Islamic State Loses its Edge," *The Washington Post*, September 9, 2016, available at: https://www.washingtonpost.com/world/europe/flow-of-foreign-fighters-plummets-as-isis-loses-its-edge/2016/09/09/ed3e0dda-751b-11e6-9781-49e591781754_story.html (accessed June 23, 2018).

199 Zachary Cohen and Ryan Browne, "ISIS Terrorizes Europe but Loses Ground at Home," *CNN*, March 29, 2016, available at: https://edition.cnn.com/2016/03/28/politics/isis-losses-iraq-syria-brussels/ (accessed June 23, 2018).

200 See Eric Schmitt and Anne Barnard, "Senior ISIS Strategist and Spokesman Is Reported Killed in Syria," *The New York Times*, August 30, 2016, available at: https://www.nytimes.com/2016/08/31/world/middleeast/al-adnani-islamic-state-isis-syria.html (accessed June 23, 2018).

201 See Paul Torpey et al., "The Battle for Mosul in Maps," *The Guardian*, June 26, 2017, available at: https://www.theguardian.com/world/2016/nov/04/battle-for-mosul-maps-visual-guide-fighting-iraq-isis (accessed June 24, 2018).

202 See Jon Lee Anderson, "Inside the Surge," *The New Yorker*, November 19, 2007, available at: https://www.newyorker.com/magazine/2007/11/19/inside-the-surge (accessed June 24, 2018).

203 See Bruce Hoffman, "The Battle Against ISIS: The Trump Administration's 30-day Review," *The Cipher Brief*, February 26, 2017, available at: https://www.thecipherbrief.com/column/expert-view/the-battle-against-isis-the-trump-administrations-30-day-review-2 (accessed June 24, 2018).

204 Hassan Hassan, "The Islamic State After Mosul," *The New York Times*, October 24, 2016, available at: https://www.nytimes.com/2016/10/24/opinion/the-islamic-state-after-mosul.html (accessed June 24, 2018).

205 See Rukmini Callimachi, "Not 'Lone Wolves' After All: How ISIS Guides World's Terror Plots from Afar," *The New York Times*, February 4, 2017 available at: https://www.nytimes.com/2017/02/04/world/asia/isis-messaging-app-terror-plot.html (accessed June 24, 2018).

206 Hoffman, "The Battle Against ISIS."

207 Mara Revkin, "Does ISIS Need Territory to Survive?," *The New York Times*, October 21, 2016, available at: https://www.nytimes.com/roomfordebate/2016/10/21/does-isis-need-territory-to-survive (accessed June 24, 2018).

208 Charlie Winter, "Media Jihad: The Islamic State's Doctrine for Information Warfare," ICSR, 2017, available at: http://icsr.info/wp-content/uploads/2017/02/Media-jihad_web.pdf (accessed June 24, 2018), 19.

209 Quoted in Robin Wright, "After the Islamic State," *The New Yorker*, December 12, 2016, available at: https://www.newyorker.com/magazine/2016/12/12/after-the-islamic-state (accessed June 24, 2018).

210   See John Horgan, *Walking Away from Terrorism: Accounts of Disengagement from Radical and Extremist Movements* (New York: Routledge, 2009).

211   John Horgan, "Deradicalization or Disengagement?," *Perspectives on Terrorism*, 2 (4) (2008), available at: http://www.terrorismanalysts.com/pt/index.php/pot/article/view/32/html (accessed June 24, 2018).

212   Revkin, "Does ISIS Need Territory to Survive?."

213   Peter R. Neumann, "Victims, Perpetrators, Assets: The Narratives of Islamic State Defectors," ICSR, 2015, available at: http://icsr.info/wp-content/uploads/2015/09/ICSR-Report-Victims-Perpetrators-Assets-The-Narratives-of-Islamic-State-Defectors.pdf (accessed June 24, 2018), 10.

214   Amarnath Amarasingam, "Three Kinds of People Return Home After Joining the Islamic State—And They Must All Be Treated Differently," *Vice*, December 3, 2015, available at: https://news.vice.com/article/three-kinds-of-people-return-home-after-joining-the-islamic-state-and-they-must-all-be-treated-differently (accessed June 24, 2018).

215   See "Half of Returning Jihadists Still Devoted to Cause: Report," *TheLocal.com*, November 28, 2016, available at: https://www.thelocal.de/20161128/one-in-four-jihadists-cooperated-with-authorities-upon-return-to-germany (accessed June 24, 2018).

216   Paul Hollander, *The End of Commitment: Intellectuals, Revolutionaries, and Political Morality* (Chicago: Ivan R. Dee, 2006), 242

217   See https://socialistregister.com/index.php/srv/article/view/5351/2252#.WLhSBfnyvIU (accessed June 24, 2018).

218   Eric Hobsbawm, *Interesting Times: A Twentieth-Century Life* (New York: Pantheon, 2002), 56.

219   Stephen Spender *in* Richard Crossman (ed), *The God That Failed* (New York: Columbia University Press, 2001), 251.

220   Martin Amis, "Fear and Loathing," *The Guardian*, September 18, 2001, available at: https://www.theguardian.com/world/2001/sep/18/september11.politicsphilosophyandsociety (accessed July 25, 2018).

221   See esp. Andrew Anthony, "A History of Television, the Technology that Seduced the World—and Me," *The Observer*, September 7, 2013, available at: https://www.theguardian.com/tv-and-radio/2013/sep/07/history-television-seduced-the-world (accessed July 25, 2018).

222   Lars Svendsen, *A Philosophy of Fear* (London: Reaktion Books, 2008), 86.

223   Collins, *Violence*, 10.

224   Martin Amis, "Blown Away," *The New Yorker*, May 30, 1994, available at: https://www.newyorker.com/magazine/1994/05/30/blown-away-3 (accessed July 25, 2018).

225   See Mark Juergensmeyer, "Religious Terrorism as Performance Violence," in Michael Jerryson, Mark Juergensmeyer and Margo Kitts, eds., *The Oxford Handbook of Religion and Violence* (Oxford: Oxford University Press, 2013).

226   Waldron, "Terrorism and the Uses of Terror," 9.

227   Jenkins, "International Terrorism."

228   See Steven Brill, "Is America Any Safer?," *The Atlantic*, September 2016, available at: https://www.theatlantic.com/magazine/archive/2016/09/are-we-any-safer/492761/ (accessed June 25, 2018).

229 See Colin P. Clarke and Louis Klarevas, "London and the Mainstreaming of Vehicular Terrorism," *The Atlantic*, June 4, 2017, available at: https://www.theatlantic.com/international/archive/2017/06/london-bridge-terrorism-attack/529116/ (accessed June 25, 2018).

230 See esp. Olivier Roy, *Jihad and Death: The Global Appeal of Islamic State* (London: Hurst & Co., 2017).

231 See Marc Sageman, "The Next Generation of Terror," *Foreign Policy*, October 8, 2009, available at: http://foreignpolicy.com/2009/10/08/the-next-generation-of-terror/ (accessed June 25, 2018).

232 See "Who is Richard Reid?," *BBC News*, December 28, 2001, http://news.bbc.co.uk/1/hi/uk/1731568.stm (accessed June 25, 2018).

233 See Hans Magnus Enzensberger, "The Radical Loser," *signandsight.com*, December 1, 2005, available at: http://www.signandsight.com/features/493.html (accessed June 25, 2018).

234 Yara Bayoumy, "Isis Urges more Attacks on Western 'Disbelievers'," *The Independent*, September 22, 2014, available at: https://www.independent.co.uk/news/world/middle-east/isis-urges-more-attacks-on-western-disbelievers-9749512.html (accessed June 25, 2018).

235 Al-Adnani was killed in an airstrike in August 2016: see Robin Wright, "Abu Muhammad al-Adnani, the Voice of ISIS, Is Dead," *The New Yorker*, August 30, 2016, available at: https://www.newyorker.com/news/news-desk/abu-muhammad-al-adnani-the-voice-of-isis-is-dead (accessed June 25, 2018).

236 See Shirin Jaafari, "ISIS has Detailed Instructions for Carrying Out Truck Attacks. They're Pretty Horrifying," PRI, April 12, 2017, available at: https://www.pri.org/stories/2017-04-12/isis-has-detailed-instructions-carrying-out-truck-attacks-theyre-pretty (accessed June 25, 2018).

237 See Sam Kriss, "The Script We All Follow After a Terror Attack," *Vice*, March 23, 2017, available at: https://www.vice.com/en_uk/article/z4k5dy/the-script-we-all-follow-after-a-terror-attack (accessed June 25, 2018).

238 See Alia E. Dastagir, "When Terrorism's Greatest Threat Isn't the Terrorist," *USA Today*, July 4, 2016, available at: https://eu.usatoday.com/story/news/2016/06/30/when-terrorisms-greatest-threat-isnt-terrorist/86573940/ (accessed June 25, 2018).

239 See, for example, Victoria Finan, "French Government 'Suppressed Gruesome Torture' of Bataclan Victims as Official Inquiry is told some were Castrated and had their Eyes Gouged out by the ISIS Killers," *Mail Online*, July 15, 2016, available at: http://www.dailymail.co.uk/news/article-3692359/French-government-suppressed-gruesome-torture-Bataclan-victims-official-inquiry-told-castrated-eyes-gouged-ISIS-killers.html (accessed June 25, 2018).

240 See, for example, Stephen Wright et al., "The Toyboy Terrorist: Bastille Day Killer's Main Lover was 73-year-old Man," *The Daily Mail*, July 19, 2016, available at: http://www.dailymail.co.uk/news/article-3696622/Trucker-terror-killer-gay-lover-73.html (accessed June 25, 2018).

241 Arendt, *Eichmann in Jerusalem*, 276.

242 See Roger Berkowitz, "Misreading 'Eichmann in Jerusalem'," *The New York Times*, July 7, 2013, available at: https://opinionator.blogs.nytimes.com/2013/07/07/misreading-hannah-arendts-eichmann-in-jerusalem/ (accessed June 25, 2018).

243   See Jon Henley, "Champs Élysées: Driver Dead as Car Carrying Firearms Rams Police Van," *The Guardian*, June 19, 2017, available at: https://www.theguardian. com/world/2017/jun/19/champs-elysees-sealed-off-car-hits-police-van-paris (accessed June 25, 2018).

244   Christopher Dickey and Nadette de Visser, "There Are So Many Attacks It's a Terror Blur," *The Daily Beast*, June 23, 2017, available at: https://www.thedailybeast. com/there-are-so-many-attacks-its-a-terror-blur-but-those-who-keep-track-are-very-worried (accessed June 25, 2018).

245   Wiesel, *One Generation After*, 4.

246   Thomas Hegghammer *Jihadi Culture: The Art and Social Practices of Militant Islamists* (Cambridge: Cambridge University Press, 2017).

247   Wiesel, *One Generation After*, 5.

248   See Hegghammer, "The Soft Power of Militant Jihad."

249   Hegghammer, *Jihadi Culture*, 17.

250   Ibid., 171.

251   Graeme Wood, "What We Still Don't Know About the Islamic State's Foreign Fighters," *The Atlantic*, August 19, 2017, available at: https://www.theatlantic.com/international/ archive/2017/08/isis-foreign-fighters/537279/ (accessed June 25, 2018).

252   Andrew Anthony, "The Art of Making a Jihadist," *The Observer*, July 23, 2017, available at: https://www.theguardian.com/world/2017/jul/23/the-culture-that-makes-a-jihadi-thomas-hegghammer-interview-poetry-militancy (accessed June 25, 2018).

253   The *New York Times* journalist Tim Arango alludes to homosexual sex in an ISIS training camp here: Tim Arango, "A Boy in ISIS. A Suicide Vest. A Hope to Live," *The New York Times*, December 26, 2014, available at: https://www.nytimes.com/ 2014/12/27/world/middleeast/syria-isis-recruits-teenagers-as-suicide-bombers. html?_r=1 (accessed June 25, 2018).

254   See Joakim Medin, "Video Shows Cocaine Allegedly Found at Home of Islamic State Leader," *Vice*, January 6, 2015, available at: https://news.vice.com/article/ exclusive-video-shows-cocaine-allegedly-found-at-home-of-islamic-state-leader (accessed June 25, 2018).

255   Stanley Cohen, *Folk Devils and Moral Panics*, 2nd edn (Oxford: Martin Robertson, 1980).

256   Claude Levi-Strauss, *Tristes Tropiques* (London: Penguin, [1955] 2011), 383.

257   Cohen, *Folk Devils and Moral Panics*.

258   Howard S. Becker, "Whose Side are We On?," *Social Problems*, 14 (3) (1967), 239–47.

259   Alvin W. Gouldner, "The Sociologist as Partisan: Sociology and the Welfare State," *The American Sociologist*, 3 (2) (1968).

260   See "What We Talk About When We Talk About Violent Extremism," this volume.

Chapter 3 How Not To Think About ISIS

1   Lawrence Wright, *The Looming Tower: Al-Qaeda's Road to 9–11* (London: Allen Lane, 2006).

2   See, for example, Paul Bentley, "Revealed: How British Jihadi Brides are being Groomed by ISIS using a Phone Messaging App after Brainwashing them on Twitter," *The Daily Mail*, February 24, 2015, available at: http://www.dailymail. co.uk/news/article-2966116/How-British-jihadi-brides-groomed-ISIS-using-phone-messaging-app-brainwashing-Twitter.html (accessed June 26, 2018).

3   See "David Cameron: Syria-bound Schoolgirls 'Deeply Concerning'," *The Telegraph*, February 21, 2015, available at: https://www.telegraph.co.uk/news/uknews/crime/11426836/David-Cameron-Syria-bound-schoolgirls-deeply-concerning.html (accessed June 26, 2018).

4   Greenwood et al., "Police Spoke to Schoolgirl Jihadi Brides in December."

5   Loulla-Mae Eleftheriou-Smith, "Aqsa Mahmood: Parents of 'Bedroom Radical' Fighting in Syria Plead for Return of Daughter," *The Independent*, September 4, 2014, available at: https://www.independent.co.uk/news/uk/home-news/iraq-syria-crisis-parents-of-isis-bedroom-radical-plead-for-daughter-to-come-home-9711447.html (accessed June 26, 2018).

6   Humaira Patel, "Without More Support, Muslim Girls may well be Tempted by Isis's HR Department," *The Guardian*, February 24, 2015, available at: http://www.theguardian.com/commentisfree/2015/feb/24/muslim-girls-isis-teenage-east-london (accessed June 26, 2018).

7   See Marisa L. Porges, "The Saudi Deradicalization Experiment," *Council on Foreign Relations*, Expert Brief, January 22, 2010, available at: https://www.cfr.org/expert-brief/saudi-deradicalization-experiment (accessed June 26, 2018).

8   Jessica Stern, "Mind Over Martyr: How to Deradicalize Islamist Extremists," *Foreign Affairs*, January/February 2010 Issue, available at: https://www.foreignaffairs.com/articles/saudi-arabia/2009-12-21/mind-over-martyr?cid=rss-essays-mind_over_martyr-000000 (accessed June 26, 2018).

9   Anson Shupe et al., "Deprogramming: The New Exorcism," in James T. Richardson, ed., *Conversion Careers: In and Out of the New Religions* (Beverley Hills, Calif: Sage, 1978).

10 David G. Bromley, "The Social Construction of Contested Exit Roles: Defectors, Whistleblowers, and Apostates," in Bromley, ed., *The Politics of Religious Apostasy: The Role of Apostates in the Transformation of Religious Movements* (Westport, Conn.: Praeger, 1998), 37.

11 See Martha Crenshaw, "The Causes of Terrorism," *Comparative Politics*, 13 (4) (1981), 390.

12 See Bruce Hoffman, "Today's Highly Educated Terrorists," *The National Interest*, September 15, 2010, available at: http://nationalinterest.org/blog/bruce-hoffman/todays-highly-educated-terrorists-4080 (accessed June 26, 2018).

13 See Sara Reardon, "Looking for the Roots of Terrorism," *Nature*, January 15, 2015, available at: https://www.nature.com/news/looking-for-the-roots-of-terrorism-1.16732 (accessed June 26, 2018).

14 Lawrence W. Sherman and Heather Strang, *Restorative Justice: The Evidence*, The Smith Institute 2007, available at: http://www.iirp.edu/pdf/RJ_full_report.pdf (accessed June 26, 2018).

15 Peter Bradshaw, "Minority Report," *The Guardian*, June 28, 2002, available at: https://www.theguardian.com/film/2002/jun/28/culture.reviews (accessed June 26, 2018).

16 See "Countering Violent Extremism: A Guide for Practitioners and Analysts," https://s3.amazonaws.com/s3.documentcloud.org/documents/1657824/cve-guide.pdf (accessed June 26, 2018).

17 See "Remarks by President Obama at the Leaders' Summit on Countering ISIL and Violent Extremism," September 29, 2015, available at: https://obamawhitehouse.archives.gov/the-press-office/2015/09/29/remarks-president-obama-leaders-summit-countering-isil-and-violent (accessed June 26, 2018).

18 Daniel Boffey, "David Cameron Announces Funding for Anti-extremism Strategy," *The Guardian*, October 18, 2015, available at: https://www.theguardian.com/politics/2015/oct/18/cameron-funding-anti-extremism-social-media (accessed June 26, 2018).

19 See Scott Atran, "Who Becomes a Terrorist Today?," *Perspectives on Terrorism*, 2 (5) (2008), available at: http://www.terrorismanalysts.com/pt/index.php/pot/article/view/35/html (accessed June 26, 2018).

20 See Marc Sageman, *Understanding Terror Networks* (Philadelphia: University of Pennsylvania Press, 2004).

21 See James Khalil, "Radical Beliefs and Violent Actions Are Not Synonymous," *Studies in Conflict & Terrorism*, 37 (2), 2014.

22 See Alan B. Krueger and Jitka Maleckova, "Does Poverty Cause Terrorism?," *The New Republic*, June 24, 2002, available at: https://newrepublic.com/article/91841/does-poverty-cause-terrorism (accessed June 26, 2018).

23 See John Horgan, *The Psychology of Terrorism* (New York: Routledge, 2005); and John Horgan, "From Profiles to Pathways and Roots to Routes: Perspectives from Psychology on Radicalization into Terrorism," *Annals of the American Academy of Political and Social Science*, 618 (July 2008), 80–94.

24 "Counter-Terrorism and Security Act 2015, Chapter 6," available at: http://www.legislation.gov.uk/ukpga/2015/6/pdfs/ukpga_20150006_en.pdf (accessed June 26, 2018).

25 "2010 to 2015 Government Policy: Counter-Terrorism," May 8, 2015, available at: https://www.gov.uk/government/publications/2010-to-2015-government-policy-counter-terrorism/2010-to-2015-government-policy-counter-terrorism (accessed June 26, 2018).

26 Chorley, "'Disease' of Islamic Extremism will Hang Over My Generation, says Cameron as he describes Watching Hostage Videos."

27 See esp. "Channel: Vulnerability Assessment Framework," October 2012, available at: http://course.ncalt.com/Channel_General_Awareness/01/resources/docs/vul-assessment.pdf (accessed June 26, 2018).

28 See William Sheridan Combes, "Assessing Two Countering Violent Extremism Programs: Saudi Arabia's Prac and the United Kingdom's Prevent Strategy," *Small Wars Journal*, 2013, available at: http://smallwarsjournal.com/jrnl/art/assessing-two-countering-violent-extremism-programs-saudi-arabia%E2%80%99s-prac-and-the-united-king (accessed June 26, 2018).

29 See "Channel: Protecting Vulnerable People from Being Drawn into Terrorism: A Guide for Local Partnerships," October 2012, available at: http://www.npcc.police.uk/documents/TAM/2012/201210TAMChannelGuidance.pdf (accessed June 26, 2018).

30 Ibid., 12.

31 See "Deradicalisation Programme Referrals on Rise," *BBC News*, October 8, 2015, available at: https://www.bbc.co.uk/news/uk-34469331 (accessed June 26, 2018).

32 "Preventing Violent Extremism and Radicalisation in Australia," Commonwealth of Australia, 2015, available at: https://www.livingsafetogether.gov.au/informationadvice/Documents/preventing-violent-extremism-and-radicalisation-in-australia.pdf, 8 (accessed June 26, 2018).

33 Helen Rose Ebaugh, *Becoming an Ex: The Process of Role Exit* (Chicago: The University of Chicago Press, 1988).

34 Ibid., 152.

35 Chris Shilling, *The Body: A Very Short Introduction* (Oxford: Oxford University Press, 2016).

36 Buruma, *Murder in Amsterdam: The Death of Theo van Gogh and the Limits of Tolerance* (London: Atlantic Books, 2006), 208–9.

37 Quoted in "Van Gogh Killer Jailed for Life," *BBC News*, July 26, 2006, available at: http://news.bbc.co.uk/1/hi/world/europe/4716909.stm (accessed June 26, 2018).

38 See Randeep Ramesh and Josh Halliday, "Student Accused of being a Terrorist for Reading Book on Terrorism," *The Guardian*, September 24, 2015, available at: https://www.theguardian.com/education/2015/sep/24/student-accused-being-terrorist-reading-book-terrorism (accessed June 26, 2018).

39 See Simon Hooper, "Stifling Freedom of Expression in UK Schools," aljazeera.com, July 23, 2015, available at: https://www.aljazeera.com/indepth/features/2015/07/stifling-freedom-expression-uk-schools-150721080612049.html (accessed June 26, 2018).

40 Quoted in John Knefel, "Everything You've Been Told About Radicalization Is Wrong," *Rolling Stone*, May 6, 2013, available at: https://www.rollingstone.com/politics/news/everything-youve-been-told-about-radicalization-is-wrong-20130506 (accessed June 26, 2018).

41 Erving Goffman, *The Presentation of Self in Everyday Life* (London: Penguin, 1959), 56.

42 Erving Goffman, *Stigma: Notes on the Management of Spoiled Identity* (London: Penguin, 1963), 60.

43 Laud Humphreys, *Tearoom Trade: Impersonal Sex in Public Places* (New Jersey: Transaction, 1970), 105.

44 See Mike Boettcher, "Video Shows Inside Look at al Qaeda Cell, Authorities Say," *CNN*, May 7, 2003, available at: http://edition.cnn.com/2003/US/05/07/hamburg.wedding/ (accessed June 26, 2018).

45 See Toby Harnden, "Seedy Secrets of Hijackers Who Broke Muslim Laws," *The Telegraph*, October 6, 2001, available at: https://www.telegraph.co.uk/news/1358665/Seedy-secrets-of-hijackers-who-broke-Muslim-laws.html (accessed June 26, 2018).

46 Andrew Sullivan, "The Murderer of Van Gogh," *The Dish*, November 5, 2004, available at: http://dish.andrewsullivan.com/2004/11/05/the-murderer-of-van-gogh/ (accessed June 26, 2018).

47 Christina Lamb, " 'My Son, the Killer, couldn't Hurt a Mouse'," *The Sunday Times*, July 5, 2015, available at: https://www.thetimes.co.uk/article/my-son-the-killer-couldnt-hurt-a-mouse-x8fl259nwp2 (accessed June 26, 2018).

48 Jeremy Bowen, "Jerusalem Knife Attacks: Fear and Loathing in Holy City," *BBC News*, October 15, 2015, available at: https://www.bbc.co.uk/news/world-middle-east-34543808 (accessed June 26, 2018).

49 Nina dos Santos, "Inside the Paris Attackers' Inner Circle," *CNN*, March 29, 2016, available at: https://edition.cnn.com/2016/03/28/europe/paris-attacker-inner-circle/index.html (accessed June 26, 2018).

50 Clark McCauley and Sophia Moskalenko, "Mechanisms of Political Radicalization: Pathways Toward Terrorism," *Terrorism and Political Violence*, 20 (3) (2008), 19–20; and Peter R. Neumann, "The Trouble with Radicalization," *International Affairs*, 89(4) (July 2013), 874.

51 See, in particular, Wiktorowicz, *Radical Islam Rising*.

52   Campbell et al., "Gay Sex, Drugs, then Suicidal Slaughter."

53   Ibid.

54   David Matza, *Delinquency and Drift* (New York: Wiley, 1964).

55   This theme is richly explored and developed in David Matza and Gresham M. Sykes, "Juvenile Delinquency and Subterranean Values', *American Sociological Review*, 26 (5) (1961), 712–19.

56   See Lorenzo Vidino, "Current Trends in Jihadi Networks in Europe," *The Jamestown Terrorism Monitor*, 5 (20), 2007, available at: https://jamestown.org/program/current-trends-in-jihadi-networks-in-europe/ (accessed June 26, 2018). In this article, Vidino writes that "Europe today is witnessing the growth of a disturbing new subculture that mixes violent urban behaviors, nihilism and Islamic fundamentalism."

57   Faiola and Mekhennet, "The Islamic State Creates a New Type of Jihadist."

58   Rik Coolsaet, "Facing the Fourth Foreign Fighters Wave," *Egmont*, March, 2016, available at: https://biblio.ugent.be/publication/7125403/file/7125408.pdf, 3 (accessed June 26, 2018).

59   John Horgan, "Discussion Point: The End of Radicalization?," START, September 28, 2012, available at: http://www.start.umd.edu/news/discussion-point-end-radicalization (accessed June 26, 2018).

60   Quoted in "My Sister was into Any Normal Teenage Things," *CBS News*.

61   See Shazia Mirza, "From Playground to Warzone," *The Financial Times*, February 12, 2016, available at: https://www.ft.com/content/88edf7c6-d040-11e5-831d-09f7778e7377 (accessed June 27, 2018).

62   See Emma Powell, "Loose Women Viewers Slam Comedian Shazia Mirza Over 'Hot' Terrorist Joke," *The Independent*, April 20, 2016, available at: https://www.standard.co.uk/showbiz/celebrity-news/loose-women-viewers-slam-comedian-shazia-mirza-over-hot-terrorist-joke-a3229896.html (accessed June 27, 2018).

63   Quoted in Dominic Cavendish, "Edinburgh 2015: Shazia Mirza," *The Telegraph*, August 12, 2015, available at: https://www.telegraph.co.uk/comedy/what-to-see/edinburgh-2015-shazia-mirza-stand-review/ (accessed June 27, 2018).

64   See   https://edition.cnn.com/videos/world/2016/01/20/jihotties-isis-recruiting-brides-todd-dnt-tsr.cnn (accessed June 22, 2018).

65   See "Attractive Jihadists can Lure UK Girls to Extremism," *BBC News*, March 3, 2015, available at: https://www.bbc.co.uk/news/uk-31704408 (accessed June 27, 2018).

66   Hayley Richardson, "ISIS 'Using Paedophile Grooming Tactics' to Lure Young Jihadi Brides," *Newsweek*, March 16, 2015, available at: http://www.newsweek.com/isis-using-paedophile-grooming-tactics-lure-young-jihadi-brides-314140 (accessed June 27, 2018).

67   Sara Khan, "The Jihadi Girls Who went to Syria weren't Just Radicalised by Isis — They were Groomed," *The Independent*, February 25, 2015, available at: https://www.independent.co.uk/voices/comment/the-jihadi-girls-who-went-to-syria-werent-just-radicalised-by-isis-they-were-groomed-10069109.html (accessed June 27, 2018).

68   See esp. Peresin and Cervone, "The Western Muhajirat of ISIS"; and Saltman and Smith, "'Till Martyrdom Do Us Part'."

69   See esp. Sageman, *Leaderless Jihad*.

70   See, classically, Isaiah Berlin, "Two Concepts of Liberty," in I. Berlin, *Four Essays on Liberty* (Oxford: Oxford University Press, 1969).

71   See "Daesh isis fanboy @umm_muthanna raw tweet dump."

72 See Scott Atran and Nafees Hamid, "Comment Devient-on Djihadiste?, *Idées*, April 7, 2016, available at: http://www.telerama.fr/monde/comment-devient-on-djihadiste-1-2-par-scott-atran-anthropologue,140496.php (accessed June 27, 2018).

73 See Carolyn Hoyle et al., "Becoming Mulan? Female Western Migrants to ISIS," Institute for Strategic Dialogue, 2015, available at: http://www.isdglobal.org/wp-content/uploads/2016/02/ISDJ2969_Becoming_Mulan_01.15_WEB.pdf, 28–29 (accessed June 27, 2018).

74 Andrew Sullivan, "This Is a Religious War," *The New York Times*, October 7, 2001, available at: https://www.nytimes.com/2001/10/07/magazine/this-is-a-religious-war.html?pagewanted=all (accessed June 27, 2018).

75 See "Senior Female ISIS Agent Unmasked and Traced to Seattle," *Channel 4 News*, April 28, 2015, available at: https://www.channel4.com/news/female-isis-women-girl-umm-waqqas-unmasked-seattle (accessed June 27, 2018).

76 See "Radical Cleric Anjem Choudary guilty of Inviting IS Support," *BBC News*, August 16, 2016, https://www.bbc.co.uk/news/uk-37098751 (accessed June 27, 2018).

77 Choudary was given a sentence of five and a half years imprisonment (see Vikram Dodd, "Anjem Choudary Jailed for Five-and-a-half Years for Urging Support of Isis," *The Guardian*, September 6, 2016, available at: https://www.theguardian.com/uk-news/2016/sep/06/anjem-choudary-jailed-for-five-years-and-six-months-for-urging-support-of-isis (accessed June 27, 2018)).

78 Quoted in Jamie Grierson et al., "Anjem Choudary Convicted of Supporting Islamic State," *The Guardian*, August 16, 2016, available at: https://www.theguardian.com/uk-news/2016/aug/16/anjem-choudary-convicted-of-supporting-islamic-state(accessed June 27, 2018).

79 See, for example, Martin Evans et al., "Radical Preacher Anjem Choudary behind Bars as Police Reveal his Links to 500 Isil Jihadists," *The Telegraph*, August 17, 2016, available at: https://www.telegraph.co.uk/news/2016/08/16/radical-preacher-anjem-choudary-behind-bars-after-drumming-up-su/ (accessed June 27, 2018).

80 Andrew Anthony, "Anjem Choudary: The British Extremist Who Backs the Caliphate," *The Observer*, September 7, 2014, available at: https://www.theguardian.com/world/2014/sep/07/anjem-choudary-islamic-state-isis (accessed June 27, 2018).

81 See Matt Apuzzo, "Who Will Become a Terrorist? Research Yields Few Clues," *The New York Times*, March 27, 2016, available at: https://www.nytimes.com/2016/03/28/world/europe/mystery-about-who-will-become-a-terrorist-defies-clear-answers.html?_r=0 (accessed June 27, 2018).

82 C. A. J. Coady, "Terrorism, Morality, and Supreme Emergency," *Ethics*, 114 (2004), 772.

83 See Gary Schmitt, "Terrorism and the First Amendment," *The Weekly Standard*, January 23, 2012, available at: https://www.weeklystandard.com/terrorism-and-the-first-amendment/article/616735 (accessed June 27, 2018).

84 See "Radical Imam Anjem Choudary on Charlie Hebdo Attack," January 8, 2015, *Fox News*, available at: http://www.foxnews.com/transcript/2015/01/08/radical-imam-anjem-choudary-charlie-hebdo-attack.html (accessed June 27, 2018).

85 Yusuf Al-Qaradawi, "Apostasy: Major and Minor," in Patrick Sookhdeo, ed., *Freedom to Believe: Challenging Islam's Apostasy Law* (McClean, Virginia: Isaac Publishing, 2009), 113.

86 See Adam Withnall, "Saudi Arabia Declares all Atheists are Terrorists in New Law to Crack Down on Political Dissidents," *The Independent*, April 1, 2014, available at: https://www.independent.co.uk/news/world/middle-east/saudi-arabia-declares-all-atheists-are-terrorists-in-new-law-to-crack-down-on-political-dissidents-9228389. html (accessed June 27, 2018).

87 See "Who are Britain's Jihadists?," *BBC News*, October 12, 2017, https://www.bbc. co.uk/news/uk-32026985 (accessed June 27, 2018).

88 See Mark Tran, "More than 55 UK Females went to Syria in 2015, Data Shows," *The Guardian*, January 12, 2016, available at: https://www.theguardian.com/uk-news/ 2016/jan/12/more-than-55-uk-females-went-to-syria-in-2015-data-shows (accessed June 27, 2018).

89 Quoted in Janet Reitman, "The Children of ISIS," *Rolling Stone*, March 25, 2015, available at: https://www.rollingstone.com/culture/features/teenage-jihad-inside-the-world-of-american-kids-seduced-by-isis-20150325 (accessed June 27, 2018).

90 Will Self, "The Charlie Hebdo Attack and the Awkward Truths About Our Fetish for 'Free Speech'," *Vice*, January 9, 2015, available at: https://www.vice.com/en_ uk/article/kwpvax/will-self-charlie-hebdo-attack-the-west-satire-france-terror-105 (accessed June 27, 2018).

91 Stefan Collini, *"That's Offensive! Criticism, Identity, Respect* (Calcutta: Seagull Books, 2011).

92 Ronald Dworkin, "The Right to Ridicule," *The New York Review of Books*, March 23, 2006, available at: http://www.nybooks.com/articles/2006/03/23/the-right-to-ridicule/ (accessed June 27, 2018).

93 The "travel ban"—Executive Order 13769—was signed by President Trump on January 27, 2017 (see, helpfully, Saba Hamedy, "Everything you Need to know about the Travel Ban: A Timeline," *CNN*, June 26, 2018, available at: https://edition.cnn. com/2018/06/26/politics/timeline-travel-ban/index.html (accessed June 27, 2018)).

94 See Maria Abi-Habib, "Online Islamists Cast U.S. Bans as War on Islam," *The Wall Street Journal*, January 30, 2017, available at: https://www.wsj.com/articles/online-islamists-cast-u-s-bans-as-war-on-islam-1485811365?mod=e2tw (accessed June 27, 2018).

95 Jessica Stern, "Trump's Executive Order will Make us Less Safe," *The Boston Globe*, January 30, 2017, available at https://www.bostonglobe.com/opinion/2017/01/ 30/trump-executive-order-will-make-less-safe/BPSK9KWyU3NwHtZg6l2jiK/story. html (accessed June 27, 2018).

96 Quoted in Greg Miller and Missy Ryan, "Officials Worry that U.S. Counterterrorism Defenses will be Weakened by Trump Actions," *The Washington Post*, January 29, 2017, available at: https://www.washingtonpost.com/world/national-security/officials-worry-that-us-counterterrorism-defenses-will-be-weakened-by-trump-actions/2017/ 01/29/1f045074-e644-11e6-b82f-687d6e6a3e7c_story.html?noredirect=on&utm_ term=.9cedeeb3734b (accessed June 27, 2018).

97 Quoted in Greg Jaffe, "Trump Redefines the Enemy and 15 Years of Counterterrorism Policy," *The Washington Post*, January 28, 2017 available at: https://www.washingtonpost.com/world/national-security/trump-redefines-the-enemy-and-15-years-of-counterterrorism-policy/2017/01/28/ff1093cc-e58f-11e6-ba11-63c4b4fb5a63_story.html?utm_term=.d8967aae242d (accessed June 27, 2018).

98   Bergen, "Why Do Terrorists Commit Terrorism?"

99   See Joby Warrick, "Jihadist Groups Hail Trump's Travel Ban as a Victory," *The Washington Post*, January 29, 2017, available at: https://www.washingtonpost.com/world/national-security/jihadist-groups-hail-trumps-travel-ban-as-a-victory/2017/01/29/50908986-e66d-11e6-b82f-687d6e6a3e7c_story.html?utm_term=.3694979a1bba (accessed June 27, 2018).

100 See Alex Kassirer, "Jihadists React to President Trump's Executive Order," *Flashpoint*, January 31, 2017, available at: https://www.flashpoint-intel.com/blog/terrorism/blog-jihadists-react-executive-order/ (accessed June 27, 2018).

101 Charlie Winter, "Trump's Immigration Order Is a Propaganda Victory for ISIS," *The Atlantic*, January 30, 2017, available at: https://www.theatlantic.com/international/archive/2017/01/trump-executive-order-isis-propaganda/514968/ (accessed June 27, 2018).

102 See esp. Fernandez, "Here to Stay and Growing."

103 See Alan Yuhas, "Trump Defends Travel Ban and Lashes Out at GOP Critics McCain and Graham," *The Guardian*, January 30, 2017, available at: https://www.theguardian.com/us-news/2017/jan/29/trump-muslim-country-travel-ban-john-mccain (accessed June 27, 2018).

104 See Gisela Crespo, "Two Children, Two Faiths, One Message," *CNN*, February 1, 2017, available at: https://edition.cnn.com/2017/01/31/us/muslim-jewish-children-at-protest-irpt-trnd/index.html (accessed June 27, 2018); and https://www.nytimes.com/video/us/politics/100000004900820/protests-against-travel-ban-sweep-country.html (accessed June 27, 2018).

105 See https://twitter.com/KarlreMarks/status/826454647669927937 (accessed June 27, 2018).

106 Ryan Beckler, "Detroit Protesters Laid Down Their Protest Signs So Muslims Could Pray," *Vocativ*, January 30, 2017, available at: http://www.vocativ.com/397811/detroit-protest-signs-muslim-prayer/ (accessed June 27, 2018).

107 See Ian Austen and Craig S. Smith, "Quebec Mosque Attack Forces Canadians to Confront a Strain of Intolerance," *The New York Times*, January 30, 2017, available at: https://www.nytimes.com/2017/01/30/world/canada/quebec-mosque-shooting.html (accessed June 27, 2018).

108 See https://video.newyorker.com/watch/martin-amis-and-ian-buruma-on-monsters (accessed June 27, 2018).

109 O'Brien, "Thinking about Terrorism."

110 For an excellent synopsis of this much misunderstood concept, see Norman Geras, "Hannah Arendt: The Banality of Evil," normblog, January 27, 2008, available at: http://normblog.typepad.com/normblog/2008/01/hannah-arendt-t.html (accessed June 27, 2018).

111 Peter R. Neumann, Introduction to "Perspectives on Radicalisation and Political Violence," Papers from the First International Conference on Radicalisation and Political Violence London, January 17–18, 2008, available at: http://icsr.info/wp-content/uploads/2012/10/1234516938ICSRPerspectivesonRadicalisation.pdf, 4 (accessed June 27, 2018).

112 "Counter-Terrorism and Security Act 2015, Chapter 6," available at: http://www.legislation.gov.uk/ukpga/2015/6/pdfs/ukpga_20150006_en.pdf (accessed June 26, 2018).

113   "Revised Prevent Duty Guidance: for England and Wales," July 16, 2015, available at: https://assets.publishing.service.gov.uk/government/uploads/system/uploads/attachment_data/file/445977/3799_Revised_Prevent_Duty_Guidance__England_Wales_V2-Interactive.pdf (accessed June 27, 2018).

114   See https://www.dni.gov/index.php/features/bin-laden-s-bookshelf?start=1 (accessed June 24, 2018).

115   Khan, "The Jihadi Girls Who went to Syria Weren't Just Radicalised by Isis — They were Groomed."

116   Richardson, "ISIS 'Using Paedophile Grooming Tactics' to Lure Young Jihadi Brides."

117   Rukmini Callimachi, "ISIS and the Lonely Young American," *The New York Times*, June 27, 2015, available at: https://www.nytimes.com/2015/06/28/world/americas/isis-online-recruiting-american.html (accessed June 27, 2018).

118   Poh Si Teng and Ben Laffin, "Flirting with the Islamic State," *The New York Times*, June 27, 2015, available at: https://www.nytimes.com/video/world/100000003749550/flirting-with-the-islamic-state.html (accessed June 27, 2018).

119   Eichenwald, "How Donald Trump Is Fueling ISIS."

120   See "Erdogan Rebukes Merkel Over 'Islamist Terror' Comment," *The Nation*, February 3, 2017 available at: https://nation.com.pk/03-Feb-2017/erdogan-rebukes-merkel-over-islamist-terror-comment (accessed June 27, 2018).

121   See esp. Frank Furedi, *Culture of Fear Revisited* (London: Continuum, 2006).

122   See esp. Frank Furedi, *What's Happened to The University? A Sociological Exploration of Its Infantilisation* (New York: Routledge, 2017).

123   This was Wellesley College, Massachusetts.

124   Alberto M. Fernandez, "The Western Plot to Treat Muslims as Dangerous Children," MEMRI Daily Brief 121, March 8, 2017, available at: https://www.memri.org/reports/western-plot-treat-muslims-dangerous-children (accessed June 27, 2018).

125   Greg Lukianoff and Jonathan Haidt, "The Coddling of the American Mind," *The Atlantic*, September 2015, available at: https://www.theatlantic.com/magazine/archive/2015/09/the-coddling-of-the-american-mind/399356/ (accessed June 27, 2018).

126   See Atran, "ISIS is a Revolution."

127   See Özlem Sensoy, "Angry Muslim Men: Neo-orientalism and the Pop Culture Curriculum," *Critical Education*, 7 (16) 2016, available at: http://ices.library.ubc.ca/index.php/criticaled/article/viewFile/186189/185397 (accessed June 27, 2018).

128   Robin Simcox, "The Islamic State's Western Teenage Plotters," *CTC Sentinel*, 10 (2), February 2017, available at: https://ctc.usma.edu/the-islamic-states-western-teenage-plotters/ (accessed June 27, 2018).

129   Peter Bergen et al., *ISIS in the West: The New Faces of Extremism*, November 2015, New America, available at: https://static.newamerica.org/attachments/11813-isis-in-the-west-2/ISP-Isis-In-The-West-v2.b4f2e9e3a7c94b9e9bd2a293bae2e759.pdf, 3 (accessed June 27, 2018).

130   Lorenzo Vidino and Seamus Hughes, *ISIS in America: From Retweets to Raqqa*, December 2015, Program on Extremism, available at: https://cchs.gwu.edu/sites/g/files/zaxdzs2371/f/downloads/ISIS%20in%20America%20-%20Full%20Report.pdf, 5 (accessed June 27, 2018).

131 Josh Halliday, "Almost 4,000 People Referred to UK Deradicalisation Scheme Last Year," *The Guardian*, March 20, 2016, available at: https://www.theguardian.com/uk-news/2016/mar/20/almost-4000-people-were-referred-to-uk-deradicalisation-scheme-channel-last-year (accessed June 27, 2018).

132 Frank Furedi, "Are 'Terrorist Groomers' Warping Our Kids?," *Spiked*, November 6, 2007, available at: http://www.spiked-online.com/newsite/article/4050#.WzOomadKjIU (accessed June 27, 2018).

133 On the meaning and provenance of this term, see Rebecca Nicholson, "'Poor Little Snowflake'—The Defining Insult of 2016," *The Guardian*, November 28, 2016, available at: https://www.theguardian.com/science/2016/nov/28/snowflake-insult-disdain-young-people (accessed June 27, 2018).

134 See Laura Smith-Spark et al., "Salman Abedi: Bomber in Ariana Grande Concert Attack," *CNN*, May 24, 2017, available at: https://edition.cnn.com/2017/05/23/europe/manchester-bombing-salman-abedi/index.html (accessed June 27, 2018).

135 Ian Cobain et al., "Salman Ramadan Abedi Named by Police as Manchester Arena Attacker," *The Guardian*, May 23, 2017, available at: https://www.theguardian.com/uk-news/2017/may/23/manchester-arena-attacker-named-salman-abedi-suicide-attack-ariana-grande (accessed June 27, 2018).

136 Holmes, "Al-Qaeda, September 11, 2001."

137 Quoted in Mark Townsend et al., "Isis Fighters must be Allowed Back into UK, says ex-MI6 Chief," *The Observer*, September 7, 2014, available at: https://www.theguardian.com/world/2014/sep/06/richard-barrett-mi6-isis-counter-terrorism (accessed June 27, 2018).

138 Neumann, "Victims, Perpetrators, Assets," 6.

139 Rukmini Callimachi, "How a Secretive Branch of ISIS Built a Global Network of Killers," *The New York Times*, August 3, 2016, available at: https://www.nytimes.com/2016/08/04/world/middleeast/isis-german-recruit-interview.html?_r=0&mtrref=undefined&gwh=9C75A871C8E24F1E35E0E3677AD66395&gwt=pay (accessed July 28, 2018).

140 See https://twitter.com/Drjohnhorgan/status/761658253344464896 (accessed July 28, 2018).

141 See https://twitter.com/Drjohnhorgan/status/761659128913731584 (accessed July 28, 2018).

142 See John Horgan and Kurt Braddock, "Towards a Guide for Constructing and Disseminating Counternarratives to Reduce Support for Terrorism," *Studies in Conflict & Terrorism*, 39 (5) (2016), 381–404.

143 See Tanya Silverman et al., "The Impact of Counter-Narratives," Institute for Strategic Dialogue, 2016, available at: https://www.isdglobal.org/wp-content/uploads/2016/08/Impact-of-Counter-Narratives_ONLINE_1.pdf (accessed July 28, 2018).

144 See Simon Cottee, *The Apostates: When Muslims Leave Islam* (London: Hurst & Co, 2015).

145 Quoted in Kim Willsher, "'I went to Join Isis in Syria, taking My Four-year-old. It was a Journey into Hell'," *The Observer*, January 9, 2016, available at: https://www.theguardian.com/world/2016/jan/09/sophie-kasiki-isis-raqqa-child-radicalised (accessed July 28, 2018).

146 See esp. Lorne L. Dawson and Amarnath Amarasingam, "Talking to Foreign Fighters: Insights into the Motivations for Hijrah to Syria and Iraq," *Studies in Conflict & Terrorism*, 40 (3) (2017).

147 See, for example, Nawaz Hanif, "Maajid Nawaz's with-us or against-us Mindset is Out of Touch with Reality," *The Guardian*, January 31, 2014, available at: https://www.theguardian.com/commentisfree/2014/jan/31/maajid-nawaz-lib-dem-quilliam-jesus-muhammad-islam (accessed July 28, 2018).

148 This four-part drama, which aired on Channel 4 on August 20, 2017, followed the experiences of four young men and women who leave Britain to join the Islamic State in Syria.

149 See Andrew Glazer, "Exporting Terror: ISIS Defector Reveals Secrets," *The New York Times*, available at: https://www.nytimes.com/video/world/middleeast/100000004566132/exporting-terror.html (accessed July 28, 2018).

150 See Greg Miller and Souad Mekhennet, "Militant Who Denounced Islamic State Faces Murder, War Crimes Charges in Germany," *The Washington Post*, January 3, 2017, available at: https://www.washingtonpost.com/world/national-security/militant-who-denounced-islamic-state-faces-murder-war-crimes-charges-in-germany/2017/01/03/02f5cee6-d1ca-11e6-9cb0-54ab630851e8_story.html?noredirect=on&utm_term=.b20030abbdd5 (accessed July 28, 2018); and Rick Gladstone, "German ISIS Member Who Denied Killing Is Charged in Murders," *The New York Times*, January 3, 2017, available at: https://www.nytimes.com/2017/01/03/world/europe/harry-sarfo-isis-germany.html (accessed July 28, 2018).

151 See Nordland, "Captured ISIS Fighters' Refrain."

152 See Josie Ensor, "'I got Four Yazidi Virgins as Part of My Isil Salary and had Sex with a Different One Every Night'," *The Telegraph*, July 31, 2017, available at: https://www.telegraph.co.uk/news/2017/07/31/quivering-isil-suspects-face-investigations-court-mosul-atrocities/ (accessed July 28, 2018).

153 Quoted in Alexander Smith and Vladimir Banic, "What Should the West do with Fighters Returning from Syria and Iraq?," *NBC News*, October 12, 2017, available at: https://www.nbcnews.com/storyline/isis-uncovered/what-should-west-do-fighters-returning-syria-iraq-n800261 (accessed July 28, 2018).

154 See Hassan Hassan, "Isis has Reached New Depths of Depravity. But there is a Brutal Logic Behind it," *The Observer*, February 8, 2015, available at: https://www.theguardian.com/world/2015/feb/08/isis-islamic-state-ideology-sharia-syria-iraq-jordan-pilot (accessed July 28, 2018).

155 Wood, "What We Still Don't Know About the Islamic State's Foreign Fighters."

156 William Calley, *Body Count: Lieutenant Calley's Story, as told to John Sack* (London: Hutchinson and Co., 1971), 106.

157 See Ben Jacobs and Warren Murray, "Donald Trump under Fire after Failing to Denounce Virginia White Supremacists," *The Guardian*, August 13, 2017, available at: https://www.theguardian.com/us-news/2017/aug/12/charlottesville-protest-trump-condemns-violence-many-sides (accessed July 28, 2018).

158 See Zack Beauchamp, "Trump Loves saying 'Radical Islamic Terrorism.' He has a Tough Time with 'White Supremacy.'," vox.com, August 14, 2017, available at: https://www.vox.com/world/2017/8/14/16143634/trump-charlottesville-white-supremacy-terrorism-islamism (accessed July 28, 2018).

159 See, for example, https://twitter.com/mehdirhasan/status/896465670069735427 (accessed July 28, 2018).

160 See, for example, Mehdi Hasan, "You Shouldn't Blame Islam for Terrorism. Religion Isn't a Crucial Factor in Attacks," *The Intercept*, March 29, 2017, available at: https://theintercept.com/2017/03/29/you-shouldnt-blame-islam-for-terrorism-religion-isnt-a-crucial-factor-in-attacks/ (accessed July 28, 2018).

161 Richard Fausset, "A Voice of Hate in America's Heartland," *The New York Times*, November 25, 2017, available at: https://www.nytimes.com/2017/11/25/us/ohio-hovater-white-nationalist.html (accessed July 28, 2018).

162 Arendt, *Eichmann in Jerusalem*, 276.

163 Marc Lacey, "Readers Accuse Us of Normalizing a Nazi Sympathizer; We Respond," *The New York Times*, November 26, 2017, available at: https://www.nytimes.com/2017/11/26/reader-center/readers-accuse-us-of-normalizing-a-nazi-sympathizer-we-respond.html (accessed July 28, 2018).

164 See https://twitter.com/shane_bauer/status/934531130954539009 (accessed July 28, 2018).

165 Luke O'Brien, "The Making of an American Nazi," *The Atlantic*, December 2017, available at: https://www.theatlantic.com/magazine/archive/2017/12/the-making-of-an-american-nazi/544119/ (accessed July 28, 2018).

166 Quoted in Pete Vernon, "Reporting on Extremism, from those Who have done it Best," *Columbia Journalism Review*, November 30, 2017, available at: https://www.cjr.org/analysis/reporting-on-extremism-from-those-who-have-done-it-best.php (accessed July 28, 2018).

167 See https://twitter.com/soledadobrien/status/934576599659372544 (accessed July 28, 2018).

168 Richard Fausset, "I Interviewed a White Nationalist and Fascist. What Was I Left With?," *The New York Times*, November 25, 2017, available at: https://www.nytimes.com/2017/11/25/insider/white-nationalist-interview-questions.html (accessed July 28, 2018).

169 See https://twitter.com/JamilSmith/status/934582798077194241 (accessed July 28, 2018).

CREDITS

The author and publisher are grateful for permission to reproduce the following copyright material:

"The Pornography of Jihadism," *The Atlantic*, September 12, 2014; "Islamic State's Willing Executioners," *The Jerusalem Post*, October 6, 2014; "ISIS and the Intimate Kill," *The Atlantic*, November 17, 2014; "For ISIS and Its Ilk, Children Are Now Fair Game. What Hideous Innovation will Come Next?," *National Post*, January 20, 2015; "ISIS and the Logic of Shock," *The Atlantic*, February 6, 2015; "Why It's So Hard to Stop ISIS Propaganda," *The Atlantic*, March 2, 2015; "The Cyber Activists Who Want to Shut Down ISIS," *The Atlantic*, October 8, 2015; "Translating ISIS's Atrocity Porn," *National Post*, January 25, 2016; "The Jihad Will Be Televised," *The Atlantic*, June 28, 2016; "Why ISIS Are Using So Many Children in Their Propaganda," *Vice*, January 31, 2017; "Why Do We Want to Watch Gory Jihadist Propaganda Videos?" *The New York Times*, October 5, 2017; "Inside Europol's Online War Against ISIS," *Vice*, April 10, 2018; "Terrorism with a Human Face," *The Atlantic*, March 8, 2015; "What Exactly is the Allure of Islamic State?," *Los Angeles Times*, March 28, 2015; "What Motivates Terrorists?," *The Atlantic*, June 9, 2015; "Pilgrims to the Islamic State," *The Atlantic*, July 24, 2015; "The Challenge of Jihadi Cool," *The Atlantic*, December 24, 2015; "Reborn into Terrorism," *The Atlantic*, January 25, 2016; "Is There Any 'Logic' to Suicide Terrorism?," *The Atlantic*, March 29, 2016; "What If Some Suicide Bombers Are Just Suicidal?," *The Atlantic*, May 5, 2016; "What's the Right Way to Think About Religion and ISIS?," *The Atlantic*, July 12, 2016; "ISIS in the Caribbean," *The Atlantic*, December 8, 2016; "How a British College Student Became an ISIS Matchmaker," *Vice*, December 20, 2016; "Osama bin Laden's Secret Masturbation Fatwa," *Foreign Policy*, February 1, 2017; "ISIS Will Fail, but What About the Idea of ISIS?," *The Atlantic*, March 23, 2017; "The Islamic State's Shock-and-Bore Terrorism," *Foreign Policy*, July 27, 2017; "The 'Softer' Side of Jihadists," *The Atlantic*, November 30, 2017; "The *Zoolander* Theory of Terrorism," *The Atlantic*, May 12, 2015; "The Pre-Terrorists Among Us," *The Atlantic*, October 27, 2015; "Europe's Joint-Smoking, Gay-Club Hopping Terrorists," *Foreign Policy*, April 13, 2016; "What ISIS Women Want," *Foreign Policy*, May 17, 2016; "Anjem Choudary and the Criminalization of Dissent," *Foreign Policy*, August 19, 2016; "'The Real Housewives of ISIS' Deserves a laugh," *The Los Angeles Times*, January 10, 2017; "Trump's Travel Ban Will Not Help ISIS Recruitment," *The Atlantic*, February 1, 2017; "Terrorists Are Not Snowflakes," *Foreign Policy*, April 27, 2017; "All That We'll Never Know About Manchester Bomber Salman Ramadan Abedi," *Los Angeles Times*, May 24, 2017; "Can Ex-Militants, and Their Redemption Stories, Stop Anyone from Joining Islamic State?" *Los Angeles Times*, September 5, 2017; "The Myth of the ISIS Patsy," *The New York Daily News*, October 23, 2017; "What We Talk About When We Talk About Violent Extremism," *The New York Daily News*, January 12, 2018.

INDEX

Lightning Source UK Ltd.
Milton Keynes UK
UKHW011000051219
354770UK00001B/136/P